NEW STRATEGIES FOR
SOCIAL INNOVATION

New Strategies for Social Innovation

MARKET-BASED APPROACHES FOR
ASSISTING THE POOR

Steven G. Anderson

 COLUMBIA UNIVERSITY PRESS   NEW YORK

COLUMBIA UNIVERSITY PRESS
Publishers Since 1893
New York   Chichester, West Sussex

cup.columbia.edu

Library of Congress Cataloging-in-Publication Data

Anderson, Steven G.
 New strategies for social innovation: Market-based approaches for assisting the poor /
Steven G. Anderson.
     pages cm
 Includes bibliographical references and index.
 ISBN 978-0-231-15922-7 (cloth : alk. paper) — ISBN 978-0-231-15923-4 (pbk. : alk. paper) —
ISBN 978-0-231-53738-4 (ebook)
 1. Social entrepreneurship. 2. Social responsibility of business. 3. Sustainable development.
4. Social change. I. Title.
 HD60.A437 2014
 658.4′08—dc23

                                                                                    2014011302

Columbia University Press books are printed on permanent and durable acid-free paper.
This book is printed on paper with recycled content.
Printed in the United States of America

c 10 9 8 7 6 5 4 3 2 1
p 10 9 8 7 6 5 4 3 2 1

Cover design: Michelle Taormina

References to websites (URLs) were accurate at the time of writing.
Neither the author nor Columbia University Press is responsible for URLs
that may have expired or changed since the manuscript was prepared.

CONTENTS

ACKNOWLEDGMENTS

I SHOULD BEGIN BY EXPRESSING what a pleasure it has been to write this book. Doing so has provided the luxury of exploring ideas brought forward by many thoughtful persons from diverse fields. My rather circumspect journey in this direction began when I was a PhD student in the Department of Political Science at the University of Michigan in the 1980s. At that time, Professor John Kingdon was studying the importance of agenda setting in public policy development, and he coined the term "political entrepreneur" to convey the importance of innovative idea generators and carriers in the public policy process.

This notion resonated with me as I entered a 10-year career in politics and public service, and it influenced my thinking as I began to more broadly consider social development issues upon returning to academia. In particular, I saw a similarity between the political entrepreneurs about whom Kingdon wrote and the emergence of social entrepreneurs in the business literature. As a faculty member in the School of Social Work at the University of Illinois at Urbana–Champaign (UIUC), I became a fellow at the new Center for Entrepreneurial Leadership in the School of Business in 2005, where I focused on understanding social entrepreneurship and its possibilities in human services program development and education. I then was fortunate to serve as a Fulbright Scholar at Nankai University in Tianjin, China, in 2010, and I used that time to develop many of the ideas for this book.

I am happy to thank many fine people for their intellectual ideas, encouragement, and tangible support related to this work. I have been influenced a great deal in my thinking about social problems, governments, and markets by the work of Charles Lindblom and am continually grateful for this exposure. Anthony Mendez, then Director of the Center for Entrepreneurial Leadership at UIUC, brought together a diverse group of teachers and researchers to consider entrepreneurship more broadly than it often is, and he was very generous in the resources and support he extended to my work. Dean Wynne Korr of the UIUC School of Social Work likewise encouraged my pursuit of these ideas, as well as my Fulbright project.

I could not have asked for a better place to develop my book than Nankai University. Professor Xinping Guan was a wonderful host and also provided me with great opportunities to learn about social development in China. I also came to know Professor Feibei Zheng at Nankai University and Professors Gao Jianguo and Shenli Chen at Shandong University as I studied and taught in China, and they all exposed me to important ideas, issues, and nuances of Chinese social policy development. I likewise benefited from teaching many Chinese social work and social welfare graduate students during this period; their intelligence, hard work, and compassion about social issues were a constant source of inspiration to me. After returning from China, I became Director of the School of Social Work at Arizona State University (ASU), where I similarly benefited from a collegial and supportive work environment.

I am especially thankful for the contributions made to this book by four research assistants: Seonmi Kim and Minli Liao at UIUC and Xiang Gao and Jill Urbaeva at ASU. All provided substantial support with literature reviews on various topics, and Xiang additionally reviewed the entire manuscript. I benefited in formulating my ideas about microenterprise development from discussions with Seonmi and with Min Zhan, my long-time colleague at UIUC; Seonmi also provided excellent guidance on empirical findings related to microenterprises. Carolina Herrera and Felipe Ruiz in the College of Public Programs at ASU expertly developed all of the figures for the book. The quality of my work also was enhanced by the thoughtful comments of anonymous reviewers, at the proposal stage and in critiquing my draft manuscript, and by editing provided by Rebecca Edwards.

On a personal level, I appreciate the support and camaraderie of my family and friends, who always have encouraged my work. In addition to providing me with a happy daily life, my wife, Yali Feng, was instrumental in my completion of this book—through tangible help, constructive prodding, and by assuming increased child care responsibilities for our daughter. I am dedicating the book to Merlin Taber, who stimulated my interest in social policy when I was a student and who has been a great mentor and friend ever since.

NEW STRATEGIES FOR
SOCIAL INNOVATION

1

Introduction to Market-Oriented Social Development Approaches

THE MECHANISMS OF social provision are undergoing fundamental changes around the world. Even before the great worldwide recession of 2008, the security of social benefits provided through governmental systems was being seriously challenged. The recent financial meltdown has further attenuated such benefits, and global economic forces and demographic factors such as aging populations promise to further constrain governmental effectiveness in addressing the most fundamental needs of citizens.

Of course, governments are not the only means through which disadvantaged citizens receive social benefits. Kinship and family networks, employers, religious organizations, private market purchases, and voluntary mutual assistance organizations are all important vehicles for social benefit provision (Gilbert & Terrell, 2010), with the prominence of each varying significantly across countries. Nonetheless, governments have played unique roles in protecting the rights and basic living standards of the most challenged members of societies; thus growing limitations in their ability or willingness to do so are troubling.

Perhaps the most fundamental question arising from this state of affairs is whether governmental regimes that fail to assure basic living standards merit continued support from their citizens. I would join many social advocates in responding with an emphatic "no." This raises the difficult subsidiary question regarding whether responsive change efforts should focus on transforming regimes or on overthrowing them, and raises related questions about the most effective political tactics for achieving one or the other of these aims.

The aforementioned questions are critical in forming philosophical orientations to social change but are not the focus of this book. Rather, my intent here is to describe and assess an important set of social development approaches that have emerged largely outside of the scope of governmental provision in recent years. In particular, I will focus upon four such development models: social entrepreneurship, corporate social responsibility, fair trade, and private sustainable development.

These four change approaches often are described loosely and somewhat interchangeably in academic writing and applied change settings,[1] but I will argue that they vary considerably in their philosophical orientations and related causal logics, and therefore may be distinctly assessed. However, they also are held together conceptually in that they operate largely outside of governmental auspices and because they emphasize private market interactions and adoption of market or business principles. An interesting corollary is that these models typically consider consumer perspectives and practices as central features of program initiatives. Although there undoubtedly are other market-oriented approaches worthy of examination,[2] these four have been implemented quite broadly in practice and have enjoyed increasing research attention and support. Each therefore has been sufficiently established to allow for both particularistic and comparative assessment.

Although the models to be discussed are not all primarily philanthropic in nature, each expresses intentionality with respect to its purported social contributions and each emphasizes strategies and ideas that are intended to improve benefits for disadvantaged groups. They consequently are appropriate to consider as social development models, which I view here as program or benefit delivery strategies focused on improving the economic and social well-being of low-income or other disadvantaged groups. I should note that I define social development somewhat more broadly than some authors do. For example, in keeping with the United Nations World Summit on Social Development, Midgley (1997) defines social development as "an approach for promoting human well-being that seeks to link social programs directly to economic development efforts" (p. 75), and further contends that such programs should "contribute to economic development" (p. 76). This economic development focus is not central to all of the programs to be considered here, but it is at the heart of most of them and indirectly related to nearly all. For example, social entrepreneurship efforts to improve developing world health outcomes are not generally framed as economic development efforts, but they clearly can have important impacts on economic development. These nuances aside, I will focus largely on thinking about the market-based models to be presented in terms of their contributions to economic development and their provision of basic benefits for the poor.

The approaches to be assessed have been applied in a wide variety of settings, but my focus is on assessing their usefulness in assisting the poorest members of society in developing world contexts. These are places of pressing world concern and, in turn, where a great deal of development work is occurring. I will briefly discuss prominent developing world social problems later in this chapter, but it is worth initially mentioning the critical nature of poverty in these countries. Estimates from the World Bank (2013a) indicate that in 2010 nearly 1.2 billion people in the world were living on the equivalent of less than $1.25 per day, which is the definition the World Bank uses in defining extreme poverty. About 2.4 billion people lived on less than $2 per day, which is another common measure of severe deprivation. These figures indicate that more than one-third of the world's population lives in poverty even by very modest standards, and the vast majority of those in poverty by either measure live in three developing world regions: East Asia, South Asia, and sub-Saharan Africa.[3] Although recent reports have found striking declines in extreme poverty in the developing world (World Bank, 2013b), poverty in these countries remains unacceptably high.

ORGANIZATION OF BOOK

The four change approaches to be assessed have enjoyed their recent growth in the context of important trends regarding social provision and social change. I therefore will begin in this chapter by analyzing this broader context. In particular, I will provide a more detailed rationale for assessing market-based models and will highlight some environmental factors that have stimulated their growth. I also will provide a brief description of major developing world social problems to elaborate the primary contexts in which I will consider these models. Finally, I will conclude Chapter 1 by introducing the special role that consumers play in many of the approaches to be discussed.

As mentioned earlier, one of the difficulties in assessing market-based change models is that consistent criteria for depicting and analyzing them generally have not been well-developed in previous literature. Progress in this respect therefore requires the development and application of a comparative conceptual framework for describing and contrasting models. I will turn to this task in Chapter 2 by delineating a conceptual framework that can be used for assessing not only these but any social change approach. This framework then will be applied in assessing each change model in subsequent chapters, in order to facilitate model comparisons. My broader intent is to establish a general framework that will be useful to scholars and students in comparing other social development models as well.

Chapters 3–6 will present and critically assess each of the four development approaches. In addition to defining key conceptual components, each chapter will briefly describe the historical development of the approach, its primary applications, its primary strengths and limitations, and the environmental conditions and skill sets that appear most important to its successful application. My intent in these chapters is twofold. First, through the application of a consistent conceptual framework, I hope to set the stage for useful comparisons between approaches. Second, each of these chapters is intended to serve as a stand-alone presentation of a particular development approach, which should allow change agents to more meaningfully assess implementation and best practice implications as they consider potential model applications in specific circumstances.

Finally, Chapter 7 will serve an integration and comparative analysis function, in which I will highlight similarities and differences among the models as well as their relative strengths and limitations. In addition, I will explore the potential for collaborative relationships between governments and the practitioners of each of these approaches, as well as factors that may attenuate the development of such relationships. The roles that governments can play in supporting productive applications of market-based approaches also will be considered in this context, and reflections on the continuing importance of government social provision given the limitations of market-based approaches will be offered. I will conclude by considering the relative importance of market-based models within the broader context of social development and social change.

An overview of two features of my presentations in the following chapters may be useful to the reader. First, I will present brief case examples to illustrate various model approaches throughout the book, and I should explain my intent in this respect. Many case examples illustrating each model already have been described in the literature, so my purpose is not to develop new ones here. Rather, I primarily will rely on previously published case examples that I think best illustrate the key features of an approach, with the intent of helping the reader understand model dynamics in an ideal sense. My choice of examples therefore is not intended to be either supportive or critical of an approach but rather to be expository in nature. I will separately present my overall assessments of the strengths and weaknesses of each model, but that assessment is not reliant on case example selection.

Second, I use a good deal of terminology in describing these approaches, as well as in elaborating my general framework for assessing these approaches. I will try to be consistent in employing such terminology throughout the book in an effort to present analysis consistently across approaches. Much of this terminology is introduced in Chapter 2 (see in particular the section entitled "Some Basic Terminology").

THE RISE OF NONGOVERNMENTALLY DIRECTED MARKET-BASED CHANGE APPROACHES: RATIONALE FOR MARKET-BASED FOCUS

Some would argue that market-oriented approaches have arisen largely as reactive responses to declining governmental support, as well as from change agent frustrations in working with governmental bureaucracies (Dees, 2007). Critics sometimes add that these and related strategies collectively constitute an intentionally marginal response that deflects attention from government ineffectiveness in responding to fundamental societal problems, such as growing income and asset inequalities (Bendell, 2004; Edwards, 2010; Karnani, 2010). Others have stressed that, even if unintentional, "neoliberal" approaches such as these focus far too narrowly on instituting business practices that are insufficient to overcome more fundamental problems, and that market systems are partially responsible for causing such problems in the first place (Lindblom, 2001; Sachs, 2008; Stiglitz, 2007). A market-based social provision focus likewise may deflect attention from more promising development approaches featuring governments, nonprofit sector institution building, and inculcation of civic norms and sound community practices (Edwards, 2008).

I share some of these concerns. Nonetheless, market-oriented approaches also have featured the increasing engagement of persons with business experience and skills, which has brought new responsive techniques to the social development arena. They likewise have been encouraged by an increasing recognition among social science-trained change agents that carefully designed market mechanisms can be powerful drivers of positive social outcomes. Other societal changes, such as the increasing scope of global corporate power and the greater possibility for creative social interaction resulting from the digital revolution, have extended the reach of these approaches.

I have elected to focus on market-oriented social development approaches for several reasons. First, the approaches I will analyze all have enjoyed increasing attention in both the academic and applied worlds, and they often are depicted as improved methods for stimulating social change. Yet they typically have been promoted without accompanying conceptual or empirical assessment. An uncritical description of successful case examples has been especially prominent. Second, although specific nongovernmental market-oriented approaches have gained prominence, no comparative assessments of such change models exist. Rather, separate literatures have grown up around each approach, with little cross-fertilization of ideas. Third, although the key processes essential to change operations have been described, little attention has been given to the resources or conditions that are most essential to successful model implementation or to attendant approach limitations. For all of these reasons, a more rigorous comparative analysis can enrich thinking about the possibilities and limits of various market-oriented approaches, and that is a central intent of this book.

As one trained and working in the social sciences and in social work,[4] I also hope to promote a broader awareness of these approaches by academics and social change practitioners. This emphasis derives from the fact that these models largely emerged outside of the social sciences, so their orientations and possibilities consequently are not well understood by change agents trained in these academic disciplines and related professional fields. I believe that these market-oriented approaches are among the many possibilities that change agents should explore as they consider the best mechanisms for promoting progress in various developmental contexts, and consequently, that more rigorous analysis of their strengths and limitations is useful. In addition, many initiatives utilizing these approaches include interesting coalitions of social activists, persons with business skills, and new technology specialists, and these may offer insights about socially oriented coalition building in contemporary environments.

I therefore hope to stimulate thinking about approaches by new audiences who have not been well exposed to market-based orientations in either their academic training or practice experience, and likewise to describe business skills that can be useful in improving the delivery of services regardless of the particular service model used. I also hope that the book will appeal to more business-oriented proponents and practitioners engaged with specific market-based approaches, and that it will encourage more sober assessments and comparisons of the strengths and weaknesses of various models. In an age of great needs, constrained resources, and rapidly evolving technologies, it is essential that change agents continually renew their thinking about how best to assist disadvantaged groups. Keeping abreast of best practices in management and in innovative technology use is fundamental. The approaches to be examined here have much to offer in this respect.

In this spirit, I will consider each of these approaches from the perspective of social change agents whose primary interest is engaging in efforts with and on behalf of disadvantaged groups, sometimes in opposition to leading economic, political, and social institutions. I assume these change agents are interested in considering alternative approaches and related philosophical orientations, causal logics, required resources, and general strengths and weaknesses. My intent is to engage them as thoughtful protagonists interested in considering the developmental potential of alternative approaches. I mention this because some may assume that corporate officials, financially well-off individuals, or others in privileged positions necessarily are the primary instigators of market-based approaches. Although this is true in some cases, it is not the norm in most of the approaches considered here. For example, much of the literature on corporate social responsibility operates through the lens of corporate officials focused on either their ethical or longer-term strategic considerations. In contrast, I will assess such efforts primarily from the standpoint of consumer and investor groups utilizing pressure tactics to change corporate behaviors.

Relationships Between Market-Oriented Approaches and Governments

Although my focus is on market-oriented approaches that largely have arisen with only marginal interactions with governments, I continue to view governments as the most critical institutions for assuring benefits for disadvantaged populations. Each of the models to be elaborated in subsequent chapters has been developed primarily under voluntary auspices, and as such, they carry all of the limitations associated with voluntary provision. Among other things, these include an unevenness of coverage over time and space as well as important equity concerns with regard to which groups receive benefits. With their unique authority to tax and compel behavior, especially when accompanied by democratically controlled accountability measures, governments remain the only societal institution with sufficient power to responsibly address such issues.

One related limitation of much of the writing about market-oriented change approaches is that proponents often are dismissive of government service provision. In the more extreme cases, authors promote particular market-oriented models as replacements for inefficient or unproductive government programs (Easterly, 2006). Unfortunately, such portrayals have little balance and fail to address the more fundamental point mentioned earlier: voluntary market-based models have neither the reach nor the needed authority to replace government services.

These critiques may undercut important opportunities to blend the advantages of government social provision with those of market-based social change models. Three areas of governmental and private market or voluntary interactions are especially important in this respect. First, governmental regulations continue to be critical in areas such as establishing the rules of trade, protecting worker rights and safety, and controlling business production externalities such as pollution. Governments thus play critical roles in shaping the broader context within which many of the approaches to be analyzed here occur, and in this role, they can either stimulate or impede the effectiveness of such models. Market-based model practitioners consequently must constantly monitor government operations related to their spheres of interest and often need to advocate for related governmental changes.

Second, and more directly, government contracting for service provision has become increasingly common in many social services areas. Despite the myth that nonprofits represent a service force independent of the government, nonprofits and for-profit providers in fact rely heavily on governments for financial support through grants, purchase of service agreements, and governmentally determined rules regarding public insurance eligibility (Gilbert & Terrell, 2010). Those enmeshed in market-based provision hence often are highly dependent on governmental decision making and need to position themselves to understand and influence those with decision-making authority.

Finally, one important corollary of governmental contracting with considerable promise has largely been ignored—the potentially important interactions between governments and change agents in bringing services or products created through market-oriented models to a larger-scale (Light, 2008). That is, governments face pressures from citizens to improve service provision and typically control more resources than can be mustered toward this end in the private sector. Yet governments also increasingly have experienced staffing constraints, and bureaucratic operational procedures and public accountability demands may make internally directed service experimentation difficult. In these circumstances, government officials have incentives to contract with nonprofit and profit-making developers to test new service models. Perhaps more important, they also often control the resources needed to take successfully tested pilot innovations to a much broader scale.

For all of these reasons, there is considerable potential for change agents using the approaches assessed here to extend their opportunities and reach by more creatively collaborating with government officials. Governments can also become more innovative through the careful nurturance of such approaches. For this to occur, it is important for change agents engaged in market-oriented approaches to thoughtfully consider the governmental environment and related potential collaborations as a routine part of their planning and development processes. It likewise is useful for those in the public sector to become more aware of the possibilities of market-based change options, so that these approaches are among the options considered as governmental entities use their resources to grapple with social problems.

The Special Role of Consumers

Another important feature of market-based models is the centrality of consumers. This should not be surprising given the prominence of consumers in market transactions more generally. Nonetheless, three ways in which consumers play a role in these approaches are worth discussing briefly.

First, approaches such as social entrepreneurship and private social development often envision the ultimate beneficiaries of their efforts as customers rather than clients. This stance tends to view beneficiaries as intelligent people who can meaningfully participate in decision making related to benefit development and receipt. With respect to development, in its strongest form this sometimes equates to a participant empowerment perspective similar to those that have been prominent in the social work participatory community development literature (see, for example, Cnaan & Rothman, 2008). It often is viewed as critical to learn directly from intended beneficiaries what their needs and capabilities are, so that products or services developed as part of the change process have the best chance of succeeding.

Second, this view of clients as customers often extends to financial transactions related to benefit provision, in that many market-based development approaches require beneficiaries to pay something in return for any benefits received. This is viewed as important in generating revenues required to operate, and as such often is couched in terms of facilitating the sustainability of projects. In addition, it sometimes is argued that client or customer payment or cost sharing provides a sense of investment among participants, which may be important from a service quality standpoint. That is, those who contribute toward the cost of a service may be more likely to demand higher levels of quality than they would for free goods, much as customers in private market transactions expect some minimal quality standards in the products they purchase.

Finally, and most importantly from a social development perspective, market-based approaches such as fair trade and some variations of corporate social responsibility fundamentally depend on what have been referred to as political or ethical consumers (Freestone & McGoldrick, 2008; Micheletti, Follesdal, & Stolle, 2004). These consumers differ from more traditional ones, who focus narrowly on the value of the exchange for their own well-being. Political consumers consider broader impacts as they make purchases, such as the well-being of the workers who produce goods or the environmental impacts of the production processes involved in goods development. For example, consumers purchasing fair trade coffee generally do so with the belief that they are assisting developing world coffee growers receive fairer returns on their labor.

Social change agents thus appeal to such consumers to support particular goods or services that they believe are more ethically produced and distributed and, by doing so, drive social change in particular directions. In essence, these approaches ask consumers to "vote with their purchases." The possibilities of these strategies are especially interesting in international social development, in that developed world customers are being asked to consider how their purchases will affect the well-being of poor producers in the developing world.

Those who emphasize the growing importance of political consumerism often associate its rise with globalization and the decline of governments. They argue that government powers to regulate corporations have been attenuated through transnational economic development; the market has gained increasing sway in comparison to institutionalized political decision making. Consumers in turn may offer one of the few viable checks on corporate power. As Micheletti, Follesdal, and Stolle (2006) have argued:

> Empowered and embedded people use their purchasing choices to criticize the policies and practices of corporations in their own and other countries in situations where strong government regulation in domestic and export settings is absent. Political consumer advocates use the market to communicate their disapproval with other countries. They boycott goods from countries that violate the human rights of their own citizens and call on their states to use the market-based tools at hand to sanction these countries economically (p. xi).

THE CONTEXT FOR CHANGE: STRUGGLING GOVERNMENTS AND THE EMERGENCE OF ALTERNATIVES

Many factors have been important in stimulating the increasing use of the market-based approaches assessed in this book. Some of these are peculiar to a particular approach and therefore will be discussed when presenting that approach. However, selected forces have created a political and social environment that has ripened prospects for the development of market-based alternatives more generally, and it is to these I will turn here. Some may be thought of as demand factors, in the sense that social conditions created a perceived need for new models of service provision. Others are related to variations in the supply of change agents and pertain to new change agents being attracted into the arena of social provision. Finally, the rapid development of technology, which has so fundamentally changed the playing field of all types of production and organizational activities, likewise has powerfully affected the potential of the change models to be discussed.

Welfare State Development and Retrenchment

The twentieth century witnessed the construction of government social safety net programs across the developed world. Although the specific content differed dramatically across countries, service systems generally featured government-sponsored cash assistance and other tangible support for various population subgroups, coupled with substantial service provision by governmental employees (Esping-Anderson, 1990; Gilbert & Terrell, 2010). Measures of the extent of government social provision vary substantially and by their nature are imprecise. However, it has been estimated that welfare spending grew substantially in developed countries from 1972–1995 (Rudra, 2002). In comparison, government social provision in developing countries generally was stagnant or decreasing. For example, despite beginning from a much lower base, welfare spending in developing countries significantly decreased from 1972–1995, which was a period of rapid globalization (Rudra, 2002). These differential spending patterns increased the gulf in welfare spending as a percentage of gross domestic product (GDP) between developed and developing countries.

There are many reasons for stagnant developing country governmental welfare spending, most of which are beyond the scope of this book. However, it is worth noting that these patterns are not all strictly tied to economic development. Midgley (1997), for example, uses the term "distorted development" in referring to the frequent disconnect between economic development and the flow of public resources to disadvantaged citizens. Furthermore, the limited governmental assistance provided in developing countries often was stimulated by assistance agreements with developed countries or international agencies, which commonly were conditioned on factors of importance to donor nations and agencies as opposed to indigenous disadvantaged populations. In the worst cases, these included austerity measures that cut existing benefits to poor persons and communities in return for macroeconomic assistance (Midgley 1997; Sachs, 2005; Stiglitz, 2007).

Beginning around the 1970s, more advanced welfare state social programs also came under increasing attack, and an era commonly referred to as welfare state "retrenchment" began (Clayton & Pontusson, 1998). The contours of this new era varied across countries in their timing, reach of programs affected, and specific nature. However, welfare state expenditures began contracting or at least stabilizing in many countries. Program expenditure patterns within welfare state systems also began shifting, as did the mechanisms through which benefits were delivered (Gilbert & Terrell, 2010; Pierson, 1996).

The principal reasons for welfare state retrenchment are complex, with the relative importance of various factors widely debated. Although it is beyond my scope to weigh in on this debate, selected factors deserve mentioning. First, dissatisfaction with the performance of governments grew in many countries (Kumlin, 2007; Newton & Norris, 2000). Perhaps this was an inevitable consequence of the growth of government programs and increasing public attention to them; as the scope of these programs expanded, there was an accompanying focus on government performance, and failures in this respect generated increasing public and media scrutiny. The burgeoning of new mass media and other information outlets likewise made it much easier to publicize shortcomings in governmental operations, and higher profile performance failures often played prominent roles in political campaigns.

Second, aggregate economic factors likewise placed new pressures on many governments and, in turn, increased attention to the size and nature of government-sponsored social programs. Both theory and empirical evidence have long suggested that economic development and growth are positively associated with welfare state development, because positive economic performance stimulates population demands and provides resources that can be invested in the public social sector (Korpi, 1985 Lenski, 1966; Wilensky, 1974). Yet during a period that many have traced to the Arab oil embargo in the early 1970s, aggregate economic performance in many countries lagged (Darby, 1982). This resulted not only in declining tax revenues but in higher service demands as larger segments of societies turned to governments for support. Income inequality also increased substantially during this period in many countries, again fueling both demand for services and simultaneous scrutiny of tax proposals (Beer & Boswell, 2002; Organization for Economic Co-operation and Development [OECD], 2011).

Third, economic globalization also has stimulated increasing debate about the role of governments in social provision, as well as academic attention to how welfare state performance may be affected. Among other things, economic globalization has made it much easier for businesses to shift production and other operations from country to country, based on their assessments of costs and economic climate. Although empirical evidence is equivocal, many scholars have argued that this climate has produced "a race to the bottom" in terms of governmental social provision (Castles, 2004). That is, governmental officials understand that tax levels are one factor that businesses assess when making location decisions, and relatively generous public social provisions can contribute to higher tax levels. Although less often noted, more generous welfare state provisions also may attract increasing numbers of persons viewed as "unproductive" to a jurisdiction or may subsidize behaviors that companies view as constraining labor supply or otherwise inhibiting their efforts to operate in the least costly manner (Berry, Fording, & Hanson, 2003).

Finally, demographic and other factors worked to challenge overall program sustainability and to change the relative composition of publicly supported provision. In particular, the rapid aging of populations in most developed countries placed increasing demands on old age income support programs as well as on government-sponsored health care programs (Disney, 2007; Peterson, 1999; Razin, Sadka, & Swagel, 2002). Health expenditures were further exacerbated by the growing sophistication and costs of medical technology and longer life spans (Moran, 2000). Public retirement and other benefits for government employees likewise rose dramatically in many countries, fueled by the growth of welfare state programs (Anderson, 2009). New forms of family composition, such as the growing number of single parent families, similarly strained state welfare systems (Hacker, 2004) and fueled critiques that welfare benefits actually stimulated unproductive family forms (Mead, 1986; Murray, 1984).

As the aforementioned pressures to control the size of government increased, these demographic patterns thus tended to reinforce or even increase service demands. A compromise that emerged in this complex environment was for governments to contract with both nonprofit and for profit agents to provide services, while limiting the number of governmental employees in the social sector (Carey, 2008; Pavolini & Ranci, 2008; Gilbert & Terrell, 2010). The trend gave rise to the often used term "privatization" of social services (Gilbert, 2002). Rising demands in the context of constrained aggregate resources also tended to squeeze out discretionary spending for other social purposes. This stimulated interest in alternative approaches to social development, especially with respect to issues unlikely to receive adequate governmental attention.

As this period of welfare state retrenchment proceeded in developed countries, awareness of and demand for social provision grew in many developing countries. The reasons for this again are complex and widely debated, but a few observations merit attention. Consistent with previous theory on the emergence of welfare states, economic development moved forward in much of the developing world, providing increasing governmental resources and associated public demands for social provision. Unlike the previous establishment of welfare states in developed countries, however, internal social demands in the developing world were much more likely to be accompanied by external assistance from developed countries. Such external efforts represented a combination of self-interest and altruism, and their broad directions again are vigorously contested. Nonetheless, international aid by developed country governments, international agencies such as the United Nations and the World Bank, and international nongovernmental organizations (INGOs) was influential not only in the direct assistance rendered but in the models employed in service delivery (Kang, Anderson, & Finnegan, 2012).

Further, this prominent external advisory presence in developing countries occurred during a period when governmental social provision was being transformed in the countries from which these foreign change agents came. This often fostered conditions ripe for experimentation with new social service models, and this climate was reinforced by very different "on the ground" environments in developing countries. For example, the physical and institutional infrastructures often taken for granted in developed countries generally existed at best in rudimentary form in the developing world. Although these limitations offered many challenges for the delivery of social services, change agents also learned that the application of innovative service models often allowed them to provide important new benefits for disadvantaged populations at much lower costs than would be possible in developed countries (Bornstein, 2007).

The Rise of the Corporate and Nonprofit Sectors

As the cycles of welfare state retrenchment and rising economies proceeded in tandem in developed and developing countries, other important societal institutions were undergoing transformations that had widespread implications for social benefits provision to the disadvantaged. As will be described in more detail in Chapter 3, the size and scope of corporations in the developed and developing world rose dramatically during the twentieth century (Bakan, 2004), and this rise provided both social benefits and costs. Of particular importance from a social development perspective was the growing power of large multinational corporations. On the one hand, these corporations provided new jobs and important social benefits in many developed countries. However, their growth also raised important questions regarding employee wages and benefits, pollution and safety standards, and many other socially related issues. In response, government officials and social change agents pressured corporations to meet selected standards of social responsibility, and in turn, many corporations developed liaison offices and grant programs to deal with such demands and to put forward a more socially acceptable identity.

A second powerful trend involved the rapid emergence of the nonprofit sector as a provider of public goods and as a force for advocacy. Although the extent of such growth varied among countries and in terms of the substantive areas encompassed, it was dramatic in both the developed and developing worlds (Salamon, 1994). For example, according to several estimates, there are between 30,000–50,000 INGOs worldwide (Ruiz, 2009), and approximately two million nonprofit organizations in the United States alone (Holland & Ritvo, 2008). A great deal of this nonprofit sector growth has occurred in the social service, educational, and health fields, which now are estimated to encompass nearly three-fifths of the nonprofit paid and volunteer work force cross-nationally (Salamon, Sokolowski, & List, 2003).

The qualitative merits of nonprofit service provision have been widely debated, with their argued advantages over more bureaucratically driven government service models generally more romanticized than empirically supported (Clarke, 2001; Dimaggio, Weiss, & Clotfelter, 2002; Kramer, 1994). Nonetheless, the rather amorphous development of nonprofit agencies results in substantial service variations; nonprofits, therefore, often are fertile grounds for experimentation with new target groups, service types, and service delivery models. The growth of nonprofit provision thus has created a context that has allowed increasingly easy entry for the expression of new ideas and approaches, as well as the possibility for extensive and rich linkages with similarly situated organizational forms.

An important subset of nonprofit growth occurred in the developing world, especially with the establishment of new and increasingly sophisticated INGOs. Emerging as part of the rebuilding movement after World War II, these INGOs established operations in many developing countries and brought new service delivery expertise (Brown & Moore, 2001). Their officials often became influential in developing country policy debates, and their presence likewise stimulated indigenous change agents to initiate their own services (Kang, Anderson, & Finnegan, 2012). To illustrate the rapidity of this growth, Keohane and Nye (2000) estimate that the number of INGOs grew from only 6,000 to more than 26,000 during the 1990s.

Although the explosive expansion of nonprofits often has been portrayed as an alternative to government service development, the important role that governments played in nonprofit development should not be overlooked. As previously mentioned, developed country government officials increasingly turned to nonprofits for service provision as the earlier noted pressure to constrain the growth of government employment grew. This was accomplished through the extensive establishment of contracting and purchase of service agreements, which not only stimulated nonprofit growth but led to increasing nonprofit dependence on government assistance (Gilbert & Terrell, 2010; Guo, 2007). For example, in one recent study of 34 countries, 36% of all nonprofit agency revenues were obtained from government sources (Salamon, Sokolowski, & Associates, 2010).

Developed country governments likewise played important stimulative roles in supporting nonprofit social service expansion in the developing world. This generally occurred in the form of financial aid provided to INGOs through governmental international assistance agencies. The U.S. Aid for International Development Agency (USAID) provides a prominent example in this respect. In 2002, USAID provided approximately

41% of U.S. overseas development funds to INGOs (McCleary & Barro, 2008). More broadly, Reimann (2006) estimates that external funding for INGOs totaled $6–8 billion annually by the late 1990s; prominent sources of this external funding included the United Nations, the European Union, bilateral aid agencies such as USAID, and various foundations.

Beyond the infusion of social service investments that foreign assistance brought to many developing countries, two other aspects of government supported INGOs are noteworthy. First, such agencies typically were subject to government required accountability demands, which helped stimulate a culture geared toward improving planning and business practices in developing country nonprofits (Kang, Anderson, & Finnegan, 2012). Second, in some cases, these INGOs and the service models that accompanied governmental assistance served as examples for indigenous development, because local people received training from or observed INGO operations and then branched out to establish their own nonprofits (Kang, Anderson, & Finnegan, 2012).

Revolutions in Information and Other Technologies

Revolutions in information, health, and other technologies likewise had powerful effects on international social development strategies. New technologies not only provided opportunities for improving the manner in which services were delivered, but more fundamentally offered the possibility of innovative new products for improving the well-being of the disadvantaged. Although a large number of technological applications played prominent roles in these respects, the advent of the personal computer, the Internet, and the cell phone and mobile communication technology probably had the most widespread influence.

The impressive span of new technology impacts easy categorization, but three aspects seem particularly noteworthy in terms of innovative service provision. First, information technology innovations allowed agencies to provide existing services more efficiently and effectively. For example, the personal computer and related software applications allowed impressive gains in small agency capabilities to process and track clients, advertise services, carry out basic business service functions, and to meet external accountability demands (Cortés & Rafter, 2007). In addition, direct service workers could use such devices to better monitor and document the services they provided to clients. Cell phones likewise allowed important advances in the communications between workers and clients, as well as among workers. This was especially important for the many service workers who traveled across communities and rural areas to serve clients.

Second, in addition to improving such basic operational functioning within social service agencies, new technologies increased the innovative possibilities of individual change agents. That is, by substantially increasing the productivity and creative potential of individuals, technology fostered ever expanding opportunities for small groups or even individuals to engage in meaningful change initiatives. For example, with access to a personal computer and good knowledge of Internet capabilities, a very small group could engage in research, marketing, recruitment, reporting, and other critical functions related to delivering social services.

This innovative potential was manifested in many ways and was especially influential in international social development initiatives. Not only did the new technologies provide increasing productivity possibilities for generally cash-strapped change agents working in difficult social environments, but perhaps more importantly narrowed geographic gulfs that traditionally have compromised service efforts in developing countries. Within countries, this provided much improved possibilities for establishing linkages between those in better off areas and those they sought to serve in poorer areas. Perhaps nowhere is this better illustrated than in the world's most populous countries—China and India—where a growing focus on the development of poor rural areas and of services for urban immigrants was greatly enhanced by technology assisted communication and service delivery improvements.

In addition, information technologies allowed greatly expanded interchanges across countries, which were particularly important in bringing technical assistance and expertise from developed countries and in linking diverse and geographically spread change agents (Shirky, 2010). These technologies likewise were influential in connecting change agents involved in advocacy related initiatives across geographic spaces, as was evidenced in the launching of social issue driven demonstrations, boycotts, and "buycotts" that increasingly crossed international boundaries(Keck & Sikkink, 1998). The organization of the 1999 Seattle protest against the World Trade Organization by NGOs around the world is but one of many increasingly sophisticated advocacy efforts made possible with the new technology, and the Arab Spring uprisings provide another more recent example (Eagleton-Pierce, 2001; Keohane & Nye, 2000; Papic & Noonan, 2011).

Third, and most fundamentally, technology advances allowed many critical product and service innovations. The new capabilities that information technologies brought to disadvantaged groups were especially important in this respect. In fact, they often were considered so potentially transformative that many scholars and change agents focused on information products as a primary form of service provision, and advocates for the poor argued that access to such technologies was critical to the development of capabilities needed to succeed in society. Perhaps best known in this sense have been intellectual and advocacy efforts related to the "digital divide" between rich and poor (Eamon, 2004; Mossberger, Tolbert, & Stansbury, 2003; Servon, 2008; Warschauer, 2003), and the growing intellectual importance of the "capabilities" approach developed by Amartya Sen (1999).

The advent of community centers to train the disadvantaged on computer use, as well as the emergence of many initiatives to provide the poor with personal computers, serves as just one prominent example of how social change agents have focused on providing access to new technology (see, for example, Welch, 2008). The importance of the cell phone as a product to help the disadvantaged in the developing world likewise cannot be overestimated. For example, cell phones allowed poor farmers in rural areas to test market prices for their crops in distant cities, thus enhancing their ability to plan their sales and obtain better profits (Yunus, 2007). In addition, the Internet provided the means for those with limited access to services to learn about services and products and to develop new skills.

In addition to these three forms of capabilities that technology advancements encouraged, information technology in particular provided dramatic new platforms for demonstrating the extent and importance of social problems. At the same time that gated communities, segregated schools, and other exclusionary devices were allowing the well-off to divorce themselves from broader societies, information technology provided a lens for more easily connecting those with social consciences to the problems facing diverse populations not only within their home countries but around the world.

The impact of a greater populace developing better understanding of social problems is variable and difficult to predict but nonetheless in many circumstances can be profound. For example, as early as the late 1960s, the nightly television coverage of the Vietnam War had been argued to help turn the American public against this conflict (Mandelbaum, 1982). More recently, widespread coverage of natural disasters such as the Asian tsunamis and Haitian earthquake, as well as coverage of wars and human rights abuses in remote parts of the world, have brought international attention to social problems that would not have been possible before the advent of the Internet and various forms of satellite assisted communications (see, for example, Bennett, 2003; van de Donk, Loader, Nixon, & Rucht, 2004). An interesting subscript has been the emergence of relatively inexpensive but sophisticated audio and visual technologies, which has allowed individuals to document social issues and provide perspectives on them that often serve to broaden the breadth of public debates on social issues (Nisbet & Aufderheide, 2009).

The New Philanthropists

Increasing income inequality also has been prominent in many societies in recent years, fueled largely by changing market conditions and the contraction of progressive government taxation and regulatory policies. For example, between 1985 and 2008, income inequality as measured by the Gini coefficient increased in 17 of the 22 OECD economies (OECD, 2011). Measures in many countries similarly indicated that those in the top 1%, 5%, and 10% of the income distribution received increasing portions of total income in many countries. In the United States, for example, the percentage of income received by the highest quintile increased from 46.8% to 50.3% between 1989 and 2009 (U.S. Census Bureau, 2010).

This rising income inequality across societies has very troubling implications and demands ongoing empirical scrutiny, publicity, and political debate that transcend the scope of this book. However, it has had one side effect that is important in terms of the social development models to be examined here. That is, the growing incomes accruing to those at the top of the income distribution resulted in the emergence of many fabulously wealthy individuals with very large amounts of disposable income (Bishop & Green, 2009). For example, the number of billionaires in the world increased from 140 to 798 between 1986 and 2009 (Bishop & Green, 2009), and the number of millionaires in the United States alone increased from 7.7 million to 10.5 million between 2000 and 2010 (Deloitte Center for Financial Services, 2011).

Societies of course have long had individuals and families with vast fortunes, and many of these have been involved in philanthropic endeavors. However, the rise in wealthy individuals during this period differed in a few important respects. For one thing, the increasing returns to education coupled with relatively open market conditions contributed to the creation of many large fortunes among relatively young people. Perhaps nowhere was this truer than in the information technology sector, where entrepreneurs such as Bill Gates, Google founders Sergey Brin and Larry Page, and many others became extremely wealthy at young ages.

This new wealth generation occurred in a context of increasing attention to social problems, growing awareness of economic and social inequalities, and changing expectations about the roles of the rich in society. Important subsets of the well-off felt compelled to contribute some of their resources and talents to work on social issues, and governments in the United States and some other countries reinforced these inclinations through tax incentives for charitable giving. Whether contributions by the newly rich were based on altruism or by a desire to promote their own and related corporate images is debatable, and this point likewise is not meant to undercut more fundamental questions concerning the extent to which such wealth accumulation should be allowed. Nonetheless, it is unquestionable that many wealthy individuals became increasingly identified with efforts to alleviate social distresses, and that their efforts often transcended national borders. For example, the contributions of Bill Gates and Warren Buffett on world health issues are well-known. Furthermore, such efforts increasing extended to wealthy individuals in developing countries, where individual fortunes have multiplied rapidly. For example, China's richest person, Li Ka-shing, was named one of the world's ten most generous philanthropists after promising to donate one-third of his multibillion dollar fortune to charity (*China Daily*, 2009).

Within-group challenges to extend charitable giving by the rich also became more prominent. Perhaps best known of these was Cable News Network (CNN) founder Ted Turner's advocacy for the well-off to donate substantial portions of their wealth to philanthropic causes (Wulfson, 2001). Taken together, these trends toward growing social awareness, philanthropic role modeling by some wealthy individuals, and advocacy by the rich to make greater social contributions created a climate in which social contributions by the well-off were more valued.

The increasing fascination with celebrities in a media-driven world similarly provided broadening platforms for well-off and well-known musicians, actors, and other artists. Many of these artists strongly identified with selected social issues, and they were able to use their skills and images to contribute to work on such causes (Bishop & Green, 2009). For example, the work of the musician Bono in the area of debt relief, hunger, and other issues in developing countries is legendary, and the creation of large country-crossing benefit concerts and other artistic events on behalf of social causes similarly is well-known.

Such well-off individuals did not just bring new sources of funding to the social arena; they often contributed unique skills and new perspectives concerning how best to respond to social problems. Several related points are noteworthy in this respect. First, many of the newly rich who became engaged in social missions had gained their fortunes through developing innovative products or services, and they frequently brought a receptiveness to or demand for innovation in framing their socially oriented efforts. They likewise often exhibited distain for bureaucratic organizations and, in turn, actively considered alternative service delivery mechanisms for whatever services or products they developed. Second, many had gained their wealth through information related technology or at least had made prominent use of it in the development of their commercial enterprises. They hence often brought very sophisticated and cutting-edge knowledge about potential information technology applications to the social sector. Finally, their commercial success had required very result-oriented perspectives and associated expectations with respect to accounting for results and evaluating processes and outcomes. This orientation again often was translated to their social endeavors.

Some may question whether the aforementioned points constituted something sufficiently "new" in philanthropic service provision because many talented and well-off people historically have contributed to social development efforts. However, Dees, Emerson, & Economy (2001) have argued that philanthropists in recent years increasingly have come to view themselves more as investors than as donors. That is, these authors contend that philanthropists traditionally found a cause in which they were interested, donated their money, and then left the development and management of that endeavor to others. In contrast, "investor" philanthropists tend to become more engaged in shaping responses to the causes to which they give money and to demand better accounting for results.

The extent to which a trend toward more investor-oriented philanthropy has occurred is debatable, but it certainly is the case that many new philanthropists have brought investment-oriented thinking and strong technology and business skills to social missions. It likewise is evident that foundations and nonprofit organizations increasingly have adopted similar perspectives, so that practices such as strategic planning, performance measurement, and more sophisticated communications with various stakeholders have become more commonplace. When coupled with increasing governmental attention to performance measurement and related accountability measures in contracting with nonprofits, performance expectations in the social sector generally have risen and have required more careful attention to practices commonly employed in business enterprises.

THE CONTEXT OF DEVELOPING WORLD POVERTY AND RELATED SOCIAL PROBLEMS

As previously mentioned, I am particularly interested in the potential of market-based models to improve the economic and basic well-being of poor persons in developing countries. A developing world focus presents many unique challenges, but three are notable from an overview perspective. First, the approaches to be considered usually involve interactions among actors from both developing world and developed countries and hence often present challenges associated with these radically different lived experiences. Second, and related, the international reach of many projects requires change agents to develop a special sensitivity to cultural differences as they engage in projects because such differences can be critical in determining the receptivity to and effectiveness of projects. Finally, change initiatives typically are carried out in material circumstances far different from those from which change agents come, which requires not only re-orientation but re-education regarding the tangible aspects of what is possible. These circumstances often present very difficult logistical problems for carrying out projects, such as limited infrastructure and technology and diverse problems associated with poor living conditions.

The context of developing world poverty and other social issues is not a new one, but it has been shaped by some of the forces discussed earlier. It also has been more fully recognized because economic globalization and communications improvements have underscored the interconnectivity of countries and people around the world. Many spectacular developmental successes have occurred in this context, such as unprecedented economic growth and attendant poverty reduction in China over a 30-year period as well as the economic revitalization of many smaller societies (Sachs, 2005). But many failures and seemingly intractable challenges likewise have been brought into sharper focus, such as the widespread devastation facing much of Africa and continuing difficult circumstances in rural areas throughout the developing world (Sachs, 2005).

Developmental economists, political scientists, and others have extensively debated the best means for addressing social problems in developing countries, with no clear consensus emerging regarding best development practices (see, for example, Sachs, 2005, 2008; Easterly, 2006). However, there is much greater agreement with respect to the nature and scope of problems that are inhibiting the well-being of many developing populations. Further, improvements in data collection and research have allowed increasing clarification of problem incidence levels and the monitoring of developmental progress indicators. This has provided researchers, policy analysts, and program developers alike with dramatically better tools for comparing progress among countries in different substantive areas, as well as changes in societies over time.

The emerging consensus on social development issues perhaps is best reflected by the articulation of the Millennium Development Goals and the related development of problem and performance indicators through the United Nations. The goals were established at a United Nations meeting in 2000, through unanimous adoption of the Millennium Declaration by the 191 member governments (Sachs, 2005). The goals articulated the most pressing world developmental challenges and included specific targets to be achieved within particular time frames. The eight Millennium Development Goals include: eradicate extreme poverty and hunger; achieve universal primary education; promote gender equality and empower women; reduce child mortality; improve maternal health; combat HIV/AIDS, malaria, and other diseases; ensure environmental sustainability; and develop a global partnership for development. An example of the quantitative and time-oriented targets attached to these goals pertains to the eradication of extreme poverty and hunger goal, which is to reduce by half the number of people worldwide who suffer from extreme poverty and from hunger by the year 2015. It is important to note that progress on most of these goals has been rather anemic, especially in the face of worldwide global recessions. However, the goals remain as important reminders of world challenges and related useful foci for developmental efforts.

Although analysis of progress in these problem areas is not the focus of this book, briefly highlighting some of these most pressing issues is useful in establishing the context in which the change models to be discussed in subsequent chapters operate. The aforementioned issue of high poverty levels probably is the most overarching of these problems because severe economic disadvantage is associated with a broad range of other social maladies. These include diverse individual and family well-being issues—such as limited educational prospects, a variety of health and nutrition problems, inadequate housing, and substandard consumption possibilities. Important gender differences in these issues likewise more seriously disadvantage women in many developing countries.

Rising income and asset inequality within developing and developed countries also have generated increasing concern and are creating new social cleavages that, among other things, increase the risk of political instability. For example, within China's "development miracle," new class distinctions are redefining the more egalitarian aspects of that society and are fueling debates regarding acceptable levels of income equality (Wan & Zhang (2012).

Many aspects of public health infrastructural components such as clean drinking water and health related environmental concerns likewise are especially prominent in developmental initiatives. Progress again has been made in terms of many health indicators, including longevity, infant mortality, and prevention and treatment of many diseases (Sachs, 2005). However, life spans continue to be much shorter in many developing countries, and infant mortality and childhood diseases remain very high. In addition, diseases such as AIDS and tuberculosis have ravaged Africa and many developing countries in other regions, and continuing substandard public health conditions and poorly planned industrial development have created the conditions for new outbreaks of many diseases (Corbett, Marston, Churchyard, & De Cock, 2006; Sachs, 2005).

Educational and related human capital deficiencies in developing countries also are of continuing concern. Progress in this respect has become increasingly important as the world economy has placed greater emphasis on knowledge production and as technological developments have radically altered the skill sets required to be productive workers and citizens. Yet striking deficiencies in literacy rates and other educational indicators remain in many developing countries, and these typically encompass important gender biases as well. For example, it is estimated that more than 770 million persons, or 16% of the world's population, remain illiterate; more than 98% of these individuals live in developing countries. Nearly two-thirds are girls and women (UNESCO Institute for Statistics, 2013).

Availability of nutritious foods likewise remains a significant problem in many parts of the world, only partially due to limited incomes. Conflicts and environmental degradation have taken large quantities of land out of production, and many countries continue to operate agricultural systems with limited water, irrigation systems, and modern equipment (Pretty, et. al, 2006). The Food and Agricultural Organizational of the United Nations has estimated that more than 870 million people worldwide were chronically undernourished during 2010–2012; nearly all lived in developing world countries, where they represented approximately 15% of the population (World Hunger Education Service, 2013).

Most scholars and practitioners engaged in developmental undertakings emphasize the importance of stable and sustainable employment in moving individuals and their families forward. Considerable progress has been made in many countries in this respect, with important contributions from diverse actors such as governments, multinational corporations, and microenterprises. However, these newer forms of employment have generated important issues of their own, especially related to the conditions under which people are employed. These include concerns about employee compensation, working conditions, product safety, and environmental effects of production on communities (Brown, Deardorff, & Stern, 2004).

Finally, all of these problems often occur in a context of limited political and social rights, and poor persons are usually ill-prepared to exercise any rights that do exist (Farmer, 2005; Hafner-Burton & Tsutsui 2005). Thus, internal pressures for social change and reforms often are poorly articulated or easily suppressed. This has led some change advocates to focus not on the more tangible circumstances discussed earlier but rather on creating the political conditions under which capacity building can occur through the extension and exercise of rights or related improvements in citizen involved decision making.

There are of course many other challenges facing developing world citizens besides those briefly described here. Nonetheless, I hope the foregoing provides a rough sketch of the difficult circumstances faced by change agents who work to improve conditions for the disadvantaged in these countries. It is in this terrain that the market-based approaches to be discussed have been tested and in which many of their greatest claims of success have been made.

A FERTILE MIX FOR SOCIAL DEVELOPMENT INNOVATION

The factors discussed in this chapter collectively have produced a fertile mix for social innovation. Social problems of devastating consequences continue at significant levels throughout the world, while fantastic improvements in communications technologies provide the capability to better observe and understand them—and the accompanying responsibility to act. At the same time, rising affluence among selected segments of societies has provided new sources of ideas and resources for social change, and new technologies have come forth as important allies in this respect. These problems and capabilities have arisen at a time when governments have faced increasing obstacles for acting, and when citizens in many countries doubt the capabilities or willingness of governments to provide social benefits.

It is in this context that nongovernmentally oriented market-based social change approaches have emerged and grown. I will turn to an assessment of the most important of these in succeeding chapters. However, I first will present an overarching framework for guiding the presentation of these approaches, and for thinking about social development approaches more generally, in the next chapter.

2

Developing Social Change Models

ONE OF THE GREATEST DIFFICULTIES in comparatively assessing the social development approaches considered in this book is that model proponents often use varying terminology and emphasize different components or processes essential to model operation.[1] In addition, authors commonly leave selected aspects or assumptions about a model unstated, either through carelessness or due to the belief that such features are obvious or relatively unimportant. A further complication is that, even in describing the broad parameters of an approach, authors disagree on key processes or terminology.

This differential focusing is partially a natural consequence of attending to those aspects of change that authors consider most fundamental to a particular approach and, in this sense, may be useful in understanding the principal intent of an approach. However, to the extent that such focusing is accompanied by inattention to other essential change considerations, practitioners and analysts are left to fill in the blanks regarding intended model operation. At the practitioner level, this can lead to lack of fidelity to an approach; at the research level, it results in limited ability to clearly depict and compare models.

These of course are challenges common to most comparative endeavors, and the strategies for meeting them are critical to the quality of analysis. In this chapter, I therefore will present a basic conceptual framework that will be applied in considering the social development models in succeeding chapters. My intent is to provide a cohesive approach for presenting and comparing these models. In addition, given the previous limited attention to the more general dynamics of social change models, my framework is useful in analyzing any approach intended to stimulate social change.

I will argue that rigorously applying the framework to a particular social change approach allows for more systematic assessment of the capabilities and resources needed to implement it and, in turn, sets the stage for defining contexts in which the probability of success is enhanced. In this sense, I will introduce general concepts of resource and capability assessment, and indicate how they will be applied in the analysis of each change approach.

BROAD ISSUES IN CONSTRUCTING AND ASSESSING SOCIAL CHANGE APPROACHES

There are two distinct aspects critical in assessing how various models are intended to create social change. First, change approaches usually predict that the delivery of a particular benefit package will lead to specific changes in targeted individuals and communities. This change focus either explicitly or implicitly puts forward a behavioral theory of change, or at least reflects an underlying philosophical orientation about how specific activities or outputs will change those who receive them. For example, human capital theory has occupied a prominent role in debates about the most effective means of social development. It basically postulates that *if* we can provide selected groups with additional human capital, *then* they are likely to enjoy higher incomes or some other positive outcomes. Theories of this type also often put forward in considerable detail the behavioral mechanics through which these changes are expected to occur. In more applied settings, such as international and governmental organizations, this elaboration of behavioral mechanics and related program development strategies frequently is referred to as defining "logic models" (Frechtling, 2007; W. K. Kellogg Foundation, 2001).

Second, change explications sometimes focus less on particular outputs or outcomes, but rather on steps or processes that are most critical to generate any desired changes. I will refer to these aspects of change approaches broadly as implementation processes. I use the term implementation processes here more broadly than some because implementation often is applied narrowly to the processes necessary to bring an idea to fruition *after* it has been generated. Such definitions essentially take the generation of an idea as a given starting point, and also may assume that the political exchanges critical to mobilizing support around an idea already have occurred. This narrower implementation focus centers on designing the most effective processes for taking an idea and maximizing the chances that it will be successfully operationalized.

I instead view implementation more broadly as consisting of all of the processes central to creating a change model and bringing it to fruition, aside from the particular behavioral logic conceptions noted earlier. In particular, there are three fairly discrete implementation processes that are important in assessing change orientations. I will refer to these as idea generation, political logic, and business logic. The first process, idea generation, is concerned with the processes associated with generating and selecting ideas on which to focus change efforts, as well as at times reaching initial decisions regarding who should be involved in overarching decision making to guide model development. The second process, political logic, refers to the identification of key stakeholders and the interactions among them that are considered most integral to change development; it may be seen roughly as the "who needs to be involved in what ways" aspect of model development and thus is broadly strategic in its orientation. Finally, business logic refers to the more traditional implementation focus on operational steps that must be accomplished to turn conceptually oriented behavioral and political ideas into actual benefits for defined populations. The term "business logic" obviously is very much in keeping with the focus on market-based models in this book. However, it also is a useful term in thinking about change models more broadly, because nearly all intentional change efforts are highly affected by the manner in which mundane operational activities are carried out, and these practices have close kinship to those that must be accomplished in operating businesses.

Unfortunately, the distinction between behavioral and implementation aspects of change rarely is made in the explication of change approaches, which sometimes confuses analysts and leads to inapt comparisons. That is, the behavioral orientation focuses more on the substance of a change delivery approach and on questions related to what benefits are delivered to which particular target groups with what intended effects. In contrast, the implementation orientation centers on how the processes of benefit creation development and delivery should be structured and conducted, regardless of the types of benefits to be delivered. Attempts to compare particular exemplars within these two broad orientations thus are likely to be muddled and may result in inappropriate conclusions.

Social entrepreneurship (SE), which will be explored more fully in Chapter 4, provides a good example of why a careful consideration of model intent in these respects can be important. SE emphasizes a particular orientation to change that can be applied regardless of the specific benefits to be delivered, and it has relatively little to say about the manner in which benefit delivery is intended to affect beneficiaries. Models such as this that focus on change implementation processes implicitly assume that, regardless of the behavioral mechanics through which delivery of products or services is intended to affect beneficiaries, there are more generalized developmental and delivery processes that can contribute to better change outcomes. Contrast this approach with the aforementioned human capital orientation, which focuses on the behavioral substance of change but generally is less attuned to the best means of bringing this substance to fruition.

Fully analyzing and comparing social change approaches requires an understanding of the central tenets of approaches with respect to both the substance of the change proposed (behavioral theory) and the processes through which changes will be selected and brought to reality (implementation theory). It is rare for specific change approaches to be well-articulated across each of these domains, and as mentioned earlier, many approaches focus on either specific intended behavioral changes on the one hand or the process of implementation on the other.

It is not my intent to argue that each of these facets requires equal attention in model development and explication, but rather that the approach emphasis should be clearly articulated and should define not only what is included but what is not. It likewise is critical for the analyst examining approaches to clearly understand which change aspects various models are proposing to elaborate, so that critical analysis is appropriately focused. For example, it makes little sense to analyze social entrepreneurship primarily in terms of the substance of what it may provide, because it is intended more as an approach to implementing a wide variety of substantive changes.

In the following sections, I will present a generalized framework intended to integrate behavioral and implementation considerations in the construction and analysis of social development approaches. I also will develop categorizations of change intended to capture most of the change approaches used to promote social development. As a first step, I present some basic terminology that will be employed.

Some Basic Terminology

I begin with the assumption that any change approach includes identifiable actors who consciously engage in a series of actions designed to stimulate a desired set of changes for specified target groups. The subset of change actions in which I am interested, which I will refer to as social change processes, further is distinguished by the fact that it generally involves one set of actors engaged in activities designed primarily to benefit another set of actors. Although beneficiary groups may be active participants in the change process, the models to be considered here rarely are purely indigenous in nature. They rather assume that exogenous change agents play important roles in instigating and bringing change ideas to fruition.[2]

Direct practice social work offers among the simplest examples of this type of process; a mental health counselor engages in a series of counseling sessions that are intended to improve the well-being of persons experiencing mental health problems. However, the social change approaches to be considered here rarely are as straightforward as the direct practice social work example. In particular, most change efforts require instigators to alter the behaviors of intermediary actors in a manner that results in benefits accruing to selected groups. For example, the instigators of the fair trade initiatives considered in Chapter 6 ultimately may be interested in raising the wages of poor farm laborers. However, in order to achieve success, they must influence consumers to change their purchasing decisions.

Some other basic terminology also requires definition. First, I will refer to the instigators or organizers of change initiatives as "change agents" or "social change agents." In a broad sense, all who work on an initiative with intentional designs of instigating social change are change agents, but in my usage throughout the book I am referring mainly to those engaged in instigating and fulfilling leadership roles on particular projects. I will refer to the particular projects in which they are engaged as "change initiatives" or "change efforts."[3]

Second, I will use the term "benefits" to refer to the particular outputs that the change activities are intended to provide. These outputs may include a wide mix of basic products, various types of services, or the creation of broader social and economic conditions considered important in allowing selected disadvantaged groups to progress. I distinguish benefits from services, in that I see services as a subset of benefits. In addition to services such as education or counseling, benefits can include tangible items such as cash. They also may include a wide range of products such as those produced by "bottom of the pyramid" (BOP) developers in Chapter 5, or less tangible but important conveyances such as voting rights or legal rights to education. Finally, change approaches at times focus on broader economic, political, or other infrastructure development, and such broad structural developmental features likewise are viewed as benefits for those in the affected jurisdictions in which they are targeted.

Third, those for whom such benefits are intended will be referred to as "beneficiaries" or "target groups."[4] Occasionally, I will further distinguish between primary and secondary beneficiaries, to better reflect the possibility that some change efforts provide important side benefits extending beyond the primary beneficiary groups to which efforts are targeted. For example, poor women may be the targeted beneficiaries of a literacy program, but their children in turn may experience improved health outcomes as mothers become better equipped to learn about childhood nutrition and other developmental issues. The children also may be more likely to learn to read because of their mothers' literacy, resulting in an intergenerational effect from the program.

Fourth, the individuals or groups that are not intended beneficiaries, but who are the focus of change efforts directed to helping beneficiaries, will be referred to as "intermediaries." For example, corporate social responsibility (CSR) approaches described in Chapter 3 often are directed at providing benefits for corporate employees or for corporate subcontractors. However, in order for this to happen, consumers and corporate officials must be convinced to change selected behaviors, and these groups will be referred to as intermediaries. Government officials likewise would be intermediaries in this case if they are lobbied by change agents to alter laws or regulations affecting corporate practices.

Finally, social development strategies typically involve a series of steps or actions designed to result in the desired change. These discrete steps will be referred to interchangeably as "actions" or "activities." It should be noted that such steps are important to articulate whether we are describing the mechanics central to stimulating behavioral changes, or alternatively, the processes associated with change implementation.

Describing the activities in which actors engage to create change is at the heart of understanding different social development approaches. Because I am focusing only upon approaches that are intentional in nature, understanding the essence of change approaches requires determining the underlying philosophy of their promoters. In some instances, change agents rigorously articulate their philosophies, in which case an approach may offer a fairly well-defined theory of change. In others cases, it is necessary to make assumptions of philosophical orientations based on less specifically stated goals or objectives. When discussing behavioral and implementation theories of change, I therefore will use the term "underlying philosophy" or "philosophical orientation" as a general descriptor to capture the intent of change agents in developing a particular approach.

Bringing this terminology together, I view social development change efforts as intentional processes in which change agents design and implement strategies to deliver benefits to targeted groups. They generally are driven by underlying philosophies about how change best occurs, and so they construct action steps or activities to bring their ideas to fruition. It is relatively uncommon for such change agents to be able to implement these ideas with their own resources, power, and talents, and so the engagement of intermediaries usually is central to the successful development of change efforts.

A General Framework for Analyzing Social Change Approaches

Employing this perspective, I next present a generalized framework for developing and analyzing social change models. I will begin by briefly sketching out the central features of this framework, with the goal of providing a broad orientation to my thinking on change models. I then will delve more deeply into the behavioral and implementation aspects that are central to applying the framework.

The framework is depicted in its most elementary form in Figure 2.1. There are four core sets of activities that are most pertinent in thinking about change models. Three of these pertain to implementation processes mentioned earlier that transcend a particular substantive approach; the other focuses directly on the more substantive behavioral aspects of

Developmental Activities

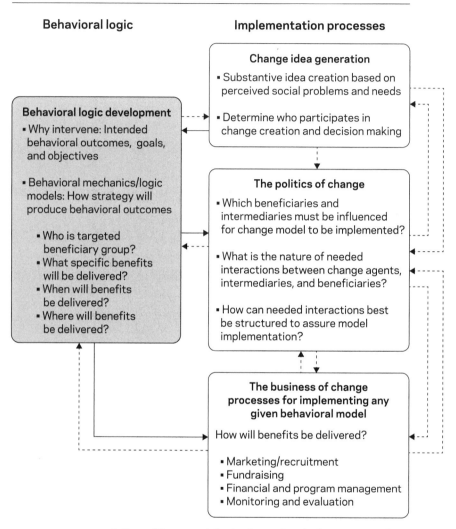

FIGURE 2.1 A General Framework for Analyzing Social Change Approaches

change approaches. The four sets of activities are sequential in nature as one moves from the top to the bottom of the figure and will be described here as such. However, I should note that precise sequencing rarely is systematically employed in change model development, and the distinctions between activities in each set generally are not as clean as depicted here for expository and analytic purposes. In addition, practitioners also commonly refine different model components over time based on experience, so that one may think of these activities as being refined over the life course of any initiative.

The first set of activities summarized in Figure 2.1 pertains to the processes associated with creating central change ideas. The selection of the main substantive change focus is probably most important in this respect. For example, do change initiative instigators plan to focus on human capital development by improving educational services for poor children or will they instead deliver immunizations and other basic health-care services? Regardless of the answer to such questions, change agents must first work through a process of selecting a developmental focus. I will refer to this process broadly as idea generation—thinking through big picture issues of change activity as opposed to focusing on more refined issues associated with fleshing out behavioral logic.

Ideas for change are driven by preconceived notions that a societal problem merits intervention; this is what motivates change agents to consider social change ideas in the first place. Both substantive and methodological considerations have received attention in this respect. From a substantive perspective, scholars have considered different types of problems that merit social attention, and these vary greatly depending on philosophies and values. Taber (1987), for example, has categorized social problems according to those affecting individuals and the broader society. In terms of methodology, a fundamental issue has been how governments or individual change agents determine the existence of a problem, and how priorities are selected among competing problems. This issue often is considered under the rubric of needs assessment, especially among proponents of rational decision making. However, it is important to note that change perceptions and ideas often originate through individual or practice experiences and, in turn, may lead to new interventions quite apart from the conduct of more formal needs assessment.

My framework assumes that these variable considerations of need are ongoing, and they collectively contribute to a deep pool of issues regarded as social problems. It is from this pool that new ideas for responses emerge, in terms of broad change approaches as well as more specific program initiatives. A closely related issue regarding big picture idea generation concerns consideration of who will participate in decision making related to the change effort. Social change initiatives largely are driven by the ideas of their instigators and the colleagues with whom they work, and their related intellectual capital has much to do with change initiative success. The relative participation of beneficiaries is especially important in this respect; involving beneficiary groups in decision making about initiatives intended to affect their lives increasingly has been viewed as vital (Cnaan & Rothman, 2008; Zosa-Feranil, Green, & Cucuzza, 2009). Making initial determinations about who will participate in decision making therefore is not only important to later stage operational development but, more fundamentally, may be central to the creation of the change idea itself.

The second set of change activities depicted in Figure 2.1 pertains to more clearly developing a substantively oriented model that predicts how targeted individuals or groups are expected to alter their behaviors based on the change initiative. My assumption here is that an initial process of thinking through needs and possible responses has been conducted through some type of idea generation process, and that a general approach and target groups have been tentatively determined.

Attention to behavioral model considerations then focuses in more detail on how a particular approach will operate to change targeted beneficiaries and intermediaries. This involves clarification of goals and objectives, particularly with respect to the specific initiative outputs and ultimate outcomes that are expected. Change agents in turn ideally work through the logic of how the activities undertaken will result in the outcomes envisioned. The intent at this stage is not to develop fine-grained detail concerning how the model should operate, but rather to create a fairly broad-brushed conceptual road map that allows stakeholders and analysts to understand what is expected to happen if the model is well implemented.

Readers may assume that my use of terminology such as behavioral change and behavioral logic implies a narrow focus on individual level changes by individuals or on the delivery of concrete benefits to them. But that is not my intent in thinking about either change processes generally or with respect to the particular market-based models discussed in this book. It certainly is true that considerable social development work focuses on individual level change by intended beneficiaries, but approaches such as external corporate social responsibility presented in Chapter 4 are geared more toward changing the behavior of consumers and corporate officials so that benefits accrue to targeted groups.[5] I therefore view behavioral change very broadly; it can range from changes in individuals due to particularistic benefit receipt to more collective or communal changes resulting from altering the behavior of corporate or political elites through political mobilization or other forms of organized action.

A third set of change activities centers on what I refer to as "the politics of change." It involves defining the stakeholders who are essential to bringing about any desired substantive change, and articulating the nature of interactions among these stakeholders that needs to occur. As in defining the behavioral mechanics of change models, the intent here is conceptual in nature. It involves the process of thinking through the strategic interactions that are most important, so that operational resource allocation (see following) can be structured in a manner that furthers these interactions.

I have found that both student and change practitioners at times blend this second and third set of activities together and so confuse their nature. I like to use the analogy of being king or queen for a day in making this distinction. If one is queen for a day, she has the power to do anything she wants, and so change construction basically involves thinking through the logic of what one thinks is the best set of benefits and related delivery system for moving a targeted group forward. It is assumed that once these decisions are made, the queen has the power and resources to make the desired strategy happen. However, in reality, few of us find ourselves in this powerful position; once we construct ideas and related behavioral change models, we must immerse ourselves in the more political world of convincing others to help us bring our ideas to fruition.

Finally, even if behavioral and political change aspects have been well-constructed, many critical operational steps are required to move a model from a conceptual level to street level reality. I refer to these later operational steps as "the business of change," and I assume that this set of activities is critical in implementing the behavioral model and the political development strategies associated with it. Although generally more mundane than the idea generation and conceptual model development stages, this later stage implementation process is critical to the ultimate success of any approach. Activities in this stage focus on aspects such as marketing and recruitment of beneficiaries, communication strategies, fundraising and financial development, recruitment and training of staff, technology development and use, data collection, and evaluation.

I again should emphasize that there is considerable crossover between these sets of activities, and I thus have included feedback loops in Figure 2.1 between each set. Highlighting those that appear most prominent merits mention. First, there is likely to be considerable overlap between the idea generation and behavioral model development stages. In particular, as change agents assess needs and think through potentially responsive approaches, they are likely to consider associated behavioral logic models in at least rudimentary form; doing so in turn may lead to refinement of broader ideas as well. Change agents in practice often may generate a limited set of potentially promising change approaches and then work through the behavioral logic of each in reaching a decision regarding which one to pursue.

Second, selected "business of change" activities are an ongoing source of information about how well the behavioral mechanics of a selected model operate in practice, and more broadly may generate new ideas for revising initial approaches or even selecting new ones. This is most often discussed in terms of monitoring and evaluation functions within organizations. However, it also can be thought of more broadly in terms of the various ways in which program operational experience informs thinking about change approaches.

In summary, it is my belief that nearly all change models can usefully be framed by carefully considering these four broad sets of activities. I will refer back to these continually as I assess the four market-based models in Chapters 3–6. Those readers most interested in these particular models, and less so in general change approach perspectives, may wish to proceed directly to those chapters. In the remainder of this chapter, I turn to more detailed explanations of each of the sets of activities included in the general framework.

Idea Generation, Participation, and Change

All change approaches focus on developing strategies for improving the life circumstances of targeted beneficiaries, whether through the direct provision of a benefit or through engagement in actions or activities thought to eventually improve well being.[6] There are of course countless possibilities in this respect, so an initial question in change model construction concerns how ideas are generated. In some cases, change agents simply are drawn to an approach that they find appealing and so perhaps do not consider a broad range of alternative approaches. However, if one thinks about this issue from a grounds-up developmental perspective through which change agents consider possible responses to perceived need, the idea generation process becomes particularly important. In fact, figuring out ways of shaking up the idea generation process is critical to many attempts to create decision-making environments conducive to innovation. Among the approaches to be considered in this book, this focus on alternative idea generation is most central to social entrepreneurship (SE), in that SE proponents typically emphasize how to establish the conditions for thinking about problems in new and diverse ways.

It is noteworthy that, although the idea generation process often is not the principal focus of social change models, it has received increasing recognition. This has partially been driven by criticism regarding the lack of success of traditional development models, which has stimulated attention to strategies for developing new ideas. Part of the criticism has been that traditional solutions to developmental issues usually are based on narrow problem conceptions, and hence have responded to too few aspects of what are often multidimensional problems (Kessel, Rosenfield, & Anderson, 2008; Selsky & Parker, 2005).[7]

A second important consideration at this early stage concerns who will participate in the change process. At times this is relatively straightforward, such as when a single change agent has an idea she wants to test and begins a small project on her own or with a few friends. However, there generally are strategic aspects to the participation question that are fundamental during initial stages, as opposed to determining who might participate later in various operational aspects. In particular, the question revolves around who will participate in decision making about the change approach itself. As mentioned earlier, this has become an increasing concern to change agents who believe that change approaches in developing communities must include some level of indigenous participation in early decision-making stages about the most central aspects of developmental strategies (Cnaan & Rothman, 2008; Zosa-Feranil, Green, & Cucuzza, 2009).

The importance of community participation in this sense tends to center on at least one of three related issues. First, there is the basic issue of whether change approaches will be accepted by leaders or others in a community if there has not been engagement by community members in the most basic discussions pertaining to community needs and how responsive approaches can best be shaped. Second, there is the issue of whether selected changes will be effective if members of targeted audiences are not engaged in approach construction. That is, even if a community accepts the basic tenet that an intervention is needed and potentially worthwhile, that intervention may be ineffective if community members are not intimately involved in program design (Polak, 2009). This is related to the importance of beneficiary culture and capabilities when thinking about effective intervention strategies. The former can tell the change agent a lot about program features that may or may not work well given a community's unique belief systems, customs, and norms; the latter is concerned with how differing resources, skills, and other beneficiary or community attributes affect the development of intervention strategies. Although this issue is important in many approaches discussed in this book, it perhaps best has been captured in discussions by private sustainable development (PSD) proponents (see Chapter 5) regarding how best to design products and employment strategies for poor consumers and workers.

Third, the ultimate goal of many development strategies is not merely improved goods or services provision. Rather, the intent is to develop new capabilities in beneficiary populations that will become self-sustaining and in turn evolutionary. Development strategies thus often are considered at least partially in terms of expected community or beneficiary empowerment. To the extent that such empowerment is central to particular models of development, the meaningful engagement of beneficiaries and community leaders in decision making about initiatives is especially important.

The more specific processes through which ideas are generated are complex and multifaceted, in general, are beyond the scope of my purposes here. However, it is worth mentioning that the ideas that constitute the reasons to engage in change come from many sources. Academics who focus on rational social planning typically emphasize a process of systematic problem analysis and needs assessment, with an associated focus on quantitative data collection and analysis. However, change efforts often evolve more informally based on field observations or from the personal experiences that a change agent has had in interacting with particular individuals or systems.

As mentioned, approaches such as social entrepreneurship strive to shake up the idea generation process. Although SE proponents sometimes rely on traditional problem identification techniques such as formal needs assessments to set the stage for idea generation, they consciously try to stimulate responses that move beyond existing routines. This may include the use of strategies such as brainstorming, consideration of novel approaches or contexts, and more generally encouraging participants to stretch their normal response patterns.

Behavioral Change

Social change models typically focus on how delivery of specific benefits to target groups will result in identifiable changes for members of that group. Articulating the manner in which such behavioral changes are intended to occur constitutes a behavioral theory or orientation to change, which generally involves two distinct realms of development. First, change agents need to specify the particular outcomes they hope will be achieved through development of the change approach. Second, they must develop a logic model that articulates how provision of specific benefits to target groups at particular times and in particular contexts will lead to the desired outcomes. These conceptual considerations ultimately should determine the primary substantive orientation of a change approach, and I will turn next to a more detailed discussion of the most important aspects of each.[8]

Outcome Goals or Desirable States of Affairs

Most fundamentally, change approaches generally begin with an explication of a desirable end point or state of affairs, which corresponds closely to what often are referred to as "goals," "outcome goals," or "outcomes" in the planning literature (Kettner, Maroney, & Martin, 2013). These desired states provide the primary rationale for engaging in a change effort, in that they constitute a vision of the positive results of collective engagement. They generally are framed as a response to a designated type of social ill or social need. In simple terms, intended goals or outcomes should provide an answer to the question of why we should invest in a social change approach. They typically articulate how a particular target group is expected to be different as the result of engaging in the approach, and sometimes how this difference is expected to affect broader functioning as well.

In addition to defining a desirable end state, underlying philosophies of change at times emphasize specific aspects of a change process that are considered fundamental beyond any immediately tangible benefits they convey. For example, as mentioned earlier, many change advocates believe that participation of beneficiaries in decision making is critical because it conveys benefits such as empowerment, consciousness raising, or confidence in dealing with authorities that extend beyond whatever more tangible outcomes are envisioned (Freire, 2000; Lister, 2002). Such participatory benefits often are embedded in the explication of logic models described in the next section; however, they are mentioned here as well because they also may constitute one of the basic outcomes of an intervention.

Logic Models and Theories of the Dynamics of Change

Underlying behavioral change philosophies also encompass causal theories or perspectives concerning the processes through which change is intended to occur if a given approach is successfully implemented. As previously mentioned, this aspect of change approaches often is referred to as developing "logic models" or "causal models," and I will follow this convention and will use these terms interchangeably. Logic models basically hypothesize that if a selected set of activities occurs with potential beneficiaries and/or intermediaries, then positive benefits will result for specified groups. Oftentimes, logic models further explicate how such benefits will lead to additional positive outcomes beyond the initial benefit provision. For example, change agents may determine that child hunger is problematic in a particular geographic area, and they in turn develop a program that provides food coupons to poor families. The intended alleviation of hunger may be considered a sufficient outcome to justify intervention. However, the change agent may further hypothesize that hunger reduction will lead to lower childhood health problems or to better performance in school.

More specifically, a well-defined logic model should clearly address four "W" questions beyond the "why intervene" question discussed earlier. Who will receive the intervention? What will be delivered to the designated target groups? When will the intervention occur? And where will the intervention occur? Providing clear descriptions and expectations with respect to each of these questions collectively should flesh out a behavioral theory about how the benefits provided (what?) to selected target groups (who?) in specific places or contexts (where?) at certain times (when?) should result in desired outcomes. Each of these four questions merits further elaboration because decision making related to each is critical in understanding conceptual intent and in creating an actual change initiative.[9]

THE TARGETS OF CHANGE: WHO SHOULD RECEIVE BENEFITS?

The question of who should receive benefits generally revolves around considerations of need and/or merit. Clearly describing the need for benefits is the more fundamental of these, because the belief that particular people require a benefit in order to rectify an identified need is the underlying rationale for most social interventions. The process of assessing and answering this "who" question more technically is referred to as defining target groups or target populations.

Two broad types of factors usually are influential in defining who needs a benefit. First, financial need often is a determining factor. The logic of targeting based on financial need is that those with limited financial resources will be unable to purchase the designated benefits through private markets or else will be particularly disadvantaged by any costs they may incur in doing so.

Second, demographic, social, or functional characteristics may be considered if they are viewed as being predictive of whether one is likely to benefit from an intervention. In some cases, these are applied to broad population groups, such as selecting the elderly as a group on which to target home-delivered meals. The logic in these circumstances generally centers on the fact that selected population groups are more at risk of encountering the problem the intervention is intended to address, and so that resources can be targeted more efficiently on such groups (Gilbert & Terrell, 2010). In other cases, specific diagnostic criteria are developed to determine if individuals or families should receive benefits. For example, children only receive special education services if they first take tests that indicate their cognitive functioning falls below a level suggesting that such services are beneficial.

Determining who should receive benefits also often involves assessments of merit. By merit, I mean a consideration of whether one deserves a benefit based on some particular effort or contribution that they have made. There are many different respects in which merit is considered. First, many benefit programs are constructed based on providing benefits to persons who have provided their own financial resources or labor in anticipation of receiving benefits. These contributions are at the heart of most social insurance programs, such as old age pensions. For example, in the United States, the Social Security system is based on contributions provided by employees through taxes on their earnings as well as on the requirement that persons engage in labor over designated periods of time (i.e., working for 40 quarters or 10 years). The essence of this type of insurance system is that people are entitled to benefits because they meet certain predetermined standards.

Second, benefits often are constructed to reward merit for certain types of performance that societies have determined are important to the collective. For example, many countries offer special benefits for those who have served in the military. In the United States, for example, these include financial support for higher education as well as special health-care benefits. This type of merit is similar to the insurance category in that it is based on contributions; it differs in that the benefits are based on fulfillment of specified functions thought to be especially important, as opposed to the more general requirements of insurance programs.

Third, in some cases groups are seen as meritorious because they are perceived to be victims of previous mistreatment. Examples would be special benefits provided to freed slaves or to the victims of war. This category rightly may be seen as overlapping with general considerations based on financial need. However, it differentiates among groups of similarly needy individuals based on the meritorious criterion. That is, two groups of people may have similar current needs for income, food, and shelter, but one may be given priority for benefits due to perceptions that its members are more worthy based on previous poor treatment. This category likewise may have considerable variation within the group receiving benefits, such as when rich and poor victims of previous mistreatment receive comparable benefits.

Finally, merit sometimes is considered in terms of exemplary performance or is based on the prospects of such performance. This category is well known in educational programs, in which students who perform especially well may receive awards or in which scholarships are granted based on students' unusual potential. Merit considerations in this respect may be seen as investments in promising assets or as mechanisms for rewarding positive behaviors and thus stimulating increases in such behaviors.

A closely related issue of increasing prominence in modern social policy discussions concerns whether selected behavioral expectations should be a condition for receiving benefits. That is, some programs require beneficiaries to engage in specified actions in order to receive benefits. This issue overlaps substantially with the broader target group criteria outlined earlier, but differs in that it generally is a second order criterion applied after a broader target group has been selected. One of the more prominent examples has been the growing expectation in many countries that those in need of cash financial assistance must either work or be engaged in a job search in order to receive benefits. The Fair Trade models to be considered in Chapter 6 provide another example, in that those who become Fair Trade producers must agree to engage in selected production practices and also, in some cases, to be open to audits or inspections to ascertain that agreed-upon practices are being followed. Similarly, many educational programs mandate that students meet a certain level of performance in order to continue receiving benefits.

Behavioral expectations of a different nature also are sometimes pertinent on the financial side. These are most often operationalized in terms of co-payments that those otherwise eligible must provide in order to receive benefits. As we will see in later chapters, such financial contributions are prominent in terms of many market-based approaches and generally are promoted on one of two grounds. First, they may be considered important to the financial sustainability of an initiative, in that they provide a needed revenue source. Second, financial contributions often are viewed as signaling a higher level of commitment or need by those who receive benefits;

they are viewed as demonstrating that beneficiaries significantly value the benefits to be received.

In addition to merit and need, the capabilities of potential beneficiaries also often are taken into account in ascertaining who should receive benefits. That is, even if one meets basic needs and merit targeting criteria for a program, many interventions require that beneficiaries have selected capabilities in order to benefit. For example, a program to train poor persons to fill selected employment roles may require potential beneficiaries to have at least minimal beginning literacy levels, or an apprentice program for young inner city artists may require at least a modicum of artistic talent.[10]

Finally, determining who the primary target group is may differ substantially in terms of the complexity of causal chains involved. This consideration often is very straightforward, such as when food pantries distribute food to the hungry or when health programs give immunization shots to poor children. In other cases, change efforts may be intended to benefit multiple groups or may have more complex causal streams that must play out if they are to have their intended impacts. For example, recent research has found that important health-care indicators for children improve as women in developing world countries receive additional education (Gakidou, Cowling, Lozano, & Murray, 2010). It may be that a program to provide basic education to women in such circumstances is perceived by its developers primarily as serving women, but the children of these women likewise may be viewed as secondary target groups or even the primary one in some cases.

In practice, deciding who should receive benefits typically involves combinations of many of the diverse considerations discussed here. For example, a program developer may choose to limit beneficiaries in an early childhood learning program to a certain age group, based on the belief that early learning best occurs during a particular developmental stage. The developer may further limit participation based on income criteria, due to the perception that those with limited incomes are less likely to receive other learning resources or as much stimulation within the family. Some such programs also require parental volunteer involvement in the program as a condition of benefit receipt. The main point is that, regardless of the particular criteria selected, carefully thinking through and providing a rationale for who is to receive benefits is a critical component of developing a well-articulated logic model.

THE TIMING OF CHANGE: WHEN SHOULD BENEFITS BE DELIVERED?

Determining the point in time at which it is most advantageous to provide benefits to designated populations is another key issue in defining logic models. The "when" question generally centers on deliberations concerning the stage in the possible development of a problem that intervention is most appropriate. These possible intervention points can be seen as occupying a continuum ranging from benefit provision before a problem even has manifested itself to points when a problem has reached an acute or critical stage. The first of these points corresponds to prevention programs; the latter focuses more narrowly on those with severe problems and thus is viewed as remedial in nature. In practice, there are many possible times in which interventions can be structured along this continuum.[11]

An example from the health-care field illustrates the wide range of intervention points that program developers may consider in response to an identified social problem. It is well known that lung cancer is a leading cause of death around the world, and research further has established that smoking is a major factor in causing lung cancer. Social change agents interested in this problem have many options regarding the points at which they want to intervene in response. Some may choose to stress assisting those who are most immediately and directly affected by the problem, such as through improved health treatment or related services for those already suffering from cancer. Others may focus on those exhibiting behaviors most likely to cause cancer, in the hopes of preventing people with high risks from getting the disease. These change agents consequently initiate programs intended to help smokers quit smoking, for example. Others concerned with broader prevention may create prevention programs to convince people not to begin smoking in the first place. It can be seen that the three intervention points in the example here constitute what may be referred to as late-stage intervention, early intervention or prevention, and primary prevention, respectively. In practice, there are many other points on the continuum regarding when to intervene as well as various strategies that can be developed for interventions at any particular point.

Decisions regarding when to intervene should be closely related to underlying program philosophies and also are likely to vary somewhat with change agent assessments regarding the etiology of the problem.

Nonetheless, two general considerations are pertinent in decision making concerning when to intervene. First, the further one moves toward later stage intervention, the easier it is to identify those who are affected by a problem and who may benefit from the proposed intervention. This issue is referred to as "targeting efficiency" and generally is related to targeting resources on those in most immediate need (Gilbert, 2001; Mkandawire, 2005).

However, a second issue or trade-off for increased targeting efficiency in later stage interventions is the likelihood that problems are more advanced and hence may require greater levels of resources to correct. In fact, in some cases, the problem that the intervention seeks to correct may be so advanced that the intervention is ineffective. The earlier cancer example readily illustrates this possibility; late stage cancer interventions may prolong life a bit or reduce suffering but may rarely keep the affected person from dying.

Positions on these issues provide fodder for interesting debates between change agents wishing to focus on prevention programs versus those who are later stage oriented. Prevention advocates rightly argue that their interventions generally are less expensive per person served than later stage interventions, but they often overlook the fact that their overall programming costs may be higher due to targeting inefficiencies. That is, prevention interventions are likely to serve many persons who would not end up with the problem even if the benefit was not provided; this expansion of benefits to larger audiences sometimes is called "net-widening."

A related issue concerns demonstrating results of benefit receipt. It generally is easier to assess the results of late stage interventions. Because greater targeting efficiency allows late stage beneficiaries to be more clearly identified as having the indicated problem, it is easier to measure the effects of interventions compared to similarly situated others not receiving the benefit. Although it is possible to make such comparisons in prevention programs, doing so generally requires more advanced research methodologies and assessments of aggregate impacts on larger populations. Finally, there is an interesting political dynamic that sometimes arises in debates regarding whether programs should be late stage or prevention focused. Prevention advocates argue that late stage benefits are offered so late that they are ineffectual and thus waste precious resources on persons who really cannot be helped. Although this appeal may be powerful, it typically flies in the face of human nature. That is, we tend to be most inclined to deal with a problem when it reaches an acute stage, such as dealing with health issues only when we are sick or being responsive to issues related to crime only after we have been victimized.

THE VENUES OF CHANGE: WHERE SHOULD BENEFITS BE DELIVERED?

There are two key questions that change agents must answer in contemplating where benefits can most usefully be delivered, which I think of in terms of geographic space and family and community context. The first of these pertains to the geographic area in which benefit delivery is to be targeted. This spatial determination generally involves a combination of need and pragmatic considerations as well as the personal inclinations of change agents. For example, a change agent may select a particular neighborhood or city in which to initiate a program because it is viewed as having high levels of need for the benefit to be delivered, such as large numbers of at-risk girls for a program intended to deliver sex education. More pragmatically, change agents may have to modify such needs-based criteria due to considerations such as neighborhood receptivity to programming, building or other resource availability, and safety issues. Many change ideas also originate from affiliations that change agents have within communities, such as the places in which they live or work. Change agents also may have high personal regard for selected areas due to previous personal experiences or other reasons.

There are two other aspects of spatial decision making that have become especially important in modern social program development and that are prominent in many of the development models to be elaborated in later chapters. First, an issue facing programs that have initial success is whether or not to expand, and if so, where such expansion can best occur. The same considerations noted earlier in initial location decisions are pertinent in expansion decisions, but other factors related to the proximity of initial program sites also may be important (i.e., closeness of staff expertise or supplies from initial site). The expansion issue has received increasing attention because many social program advocates and developers have argued that it is important to bring successful program ideas "to scale," so that they can provide benefits to the largest numbers of people in need.

Second, decisions about where to locate services historically have been fairly narrowly constrained by practical limitations related to organizing program delivery inputs. Factors such as the travel distances required for benefit delivery, limited communication systems in some geographic areas, and other resource barriers tended to force the initial development of change efforts into well-defined and relatively narrow boundaries. Although such constraints remain important, the rise of computer technology and related communications systems, improved transportation, and the globalization of many trading rules and regulations have opened new opportunities to deliver benefits in previously inaccessible geographic spaces. The organization Kiva, which will be discussed further in Chapter 4, provides a good example. Although its headquarters are in the United States, it has used computer technology in an innovative way to solicit funding and arrange microloans in developing areas around the world.

A related development is the emergence of remote or virtual benefit delivery systems through which benefits can be delivered to vast and diverse geographic areas with little if any attention to geographic targeting. The advent of online shopping, through businesses such as Amazon or eBay, provides a well-known example of virtual delivery systems for broader audiences. These same capabilities are being used by some organizations for delivering benefits to low-income individuals, such as through mail order pharmacies utilizing Internet ordering schemes and through online educational programs. Although it is true that these examples require some transportation and delivery capabilities, they significantly expand the possibilities of persons receiving benefits without having to travel to a particular location. In some instances, such as when the benefit to be delivered is informational in nature, such as in an online training program, even transportation and related personal delivery systems are not needed.

The second key question with respect to where benefits should be delivered pertains to the family, community, and institutional context in which change actions most meaningfully can occur. It is well-established that potential beneficiaries are embedded in a complex web of social environments, and philosophies about which of these is of greatest importance in various situations are important in determining which contexts to emphasize in benefit delivery (Bronfenbrenner, 1979). This includes considerations of the family and social structures in which beneficiaries are embedded, such as whether change activities are best targeted to individuals, families, or other groups. For example, marital counseling may be delivered to either couples together or separately depending on circumstances and philosophies, and change agents in counseling programs often must consider whether interventions are best delivered individually or in groups. This consideration of social context likewise should take into account institutional arrangements in which potential beneficiaries are involved, such as when an after-school recreation or learning intervention takes place at a school because of the aggregated presence of beneficiaries and service provision resources.

Some may consider this family and community context issue more of a second order implementation concern, but it often is fundamentally connected to change philosophies and related logic models. For example, decisions to provide health care in the home for selected populations are fundamentally related to conceptions concerning the most effective location of delivery. The same may be said for providing many services for domestic violence victims in "safe," identity protected locations or providing services for some ethnic minorities in trusted community settings rather than in public buildings. In each of these examples, the selection of the general community or institutional locale for service provision is a basic overarching design feature requiring a consistent focus in development. In comparison, the selection of a specific location for service provision once a model has been designed constitutes a business-oriented implementation decision.

THE SUBSTANCE OF CHANGE: WHAT BENEFITS
SHOULD BE DELIVERED?

The type of benefits to be delivered says much about the underlying philosophies of change agents because benefit choices typically convey what is considered important in moving target groups forward. Many social service texts and scholarly works on social development have classified social program benefits with the intent of aiding description or analysis. Some classification schemes focus largely on the subject matter of benefits provided, such as health, education, and income. Another approach is to categorize benefits according to the functional outcomes they are intended to instigate, regardless of the specific subject area in which they may fall. That is, benefits are classified more directly in terms of the logic through which they are seen as moving individuals forward. For example, basic food, housing, and health provisions obviously are substantively different types of benefits, but they have a similar orientation of providing at least a foundational level of functioning required to survive and grow.

I favor this latter approach, largely because it generally allows for the clearer linkage of benefits to the logic of change models. Yet I have not found existing classifications that capture this functional orientation particularly well, and so I will briefly put forth a classification scheme here. This classification, which is summarized in Table 2.1, considers the major benefit categories that encompass most change efforts on behalf of disadvantaged groups. I refer to the first of these as crisis remediation, which probably remains the focus of most social change activities. By this, I mean to convey the very diverse range of services that are provided in response to day-to-day crises or disturbances that people face. Defining how crisis remediation is intended to affect functioning is challenging in its own right. However, the intent generally is to allow individuals to meet immediate survival needs, such as sustaining basic levels of food, shelter, and health, without much if any consideration of future growth and development. These benefits are meant to allow affected individuals to return to a preexisting state or at least to minimize the negative consequences of a disturbance. Relief assistance to refugees or those affected by natural disasters is a good example of this type of benefit, as is health care for those affected by acute illnesses or injuries.

The second category, which I refer to as "enhanced security," is similar to crisis remediation in its focus on basic well-being for targeted groups. However, change efforts in this vein are less oriented to rectifying an immediate acute presenting crisis and are intended rather as ongoing interventions meant to help sustain those who otherwise would have high probabilities of falling below minimally acceptable functioning levels. An example of this form of assistance is the well-known welfare state income assistance benefits provided to individuals who are unable to sustain their incomes in market economies. Social insurance programs to provide ongoing income and health care for retirees or others also would fall within this category, as would efforts to secure higher wages or benefits for workers.

It may be obvious that there is a significant gray area between these first two categories. For example, those receiving benefits through cash

TABLE 2.1. Categorizing the Intended Outcomes of Social Change Initiatives

APPROACH	BASIC BEHAVIOR MODEL	EXAMPLES
Crisis remediation	Meet immediate survival needs, or return to preexisting state	Relief assistance during natural disasters or conflicts
Enhanced security	Sustain groups with high likelihood of falling below socially defined minimum levels	Income and health insurance for retirees
Financial capital	Provide money or other tangible benefits designed to develop productive capacity	Microenterprise loans; low-income savings and asset development programs
Human capital	Increase knowledge, information access, or skills designed to enhance productive capacity	Education and training programs
Social capital	Improve social networks to enhance linkages to jobs and other socially meaningful benefits	Social mentoring programs; cultural enrichment programs
Political capital	Improve capacity to affect decision-making by governments or other institutional systems	Voting registration projects; policy advocacy programs
Infrastructure development	Create broader economic and political institutions and structures in which individuals and groups develop capacities	Government job creation and public transportation systems

welfare assistance programs typically have a precipitating event that requires them to apply for assistance and so initially may be seen as needing crisis remediation. The primary difference is that enhanced security benefits are viewed as more ongoing and longer term, as opposed to temporary solutions to acute problems. Both share an underlying philosophy that benefits will allow recipients to either return to (crisis remediation) or sustain (enhanced security) at least a basic level of functioning—however that may be defined.

Nonetheless, neither of these broad approaches suggests any particular philosophy regarding how beneficiaries may move forward, beyond perhaps a general belief that those able to return to or sustain basic functioning will be in a position to move forward according to their own proclivities and talents. My view on this issue is similar to that of Sachs (2005), who has argued that the purpose of many basic developing world interventions is simply to get beneficiaries on the first rung of a ladder through provision of benefits that improve basic functioning.

Unlike the first two benefit categories, many types of social change efforts attempt to do more than simply reinstitute or sustain basic functioning. Rather, they intend to provide the tools through which disadvantaged individuals can attain higher levels of functioning. Partially because they have been well-explicated theoretically, I believe that different forms of capital building are very useful in representing this third broad type of change approach. I have included four of these in my classification scheme: physical or financial capital, human capital, social capital, and political capital, and I will describe each briefly.

Of these, physical or financial capital building may most closely resemble the previously described approaches because it focuses on providing individuals with cash or other tangible benefits such as equipment for production. However, it differs in that the intent is not to provide such benefits simply to restore or stabilize well-being. Physical capital approaches instead are intended to provide individuals with the means of promoting further growth, generally of an economic nature. For example, microenterprises have become popular in much of the developing world; these programs provide loans to individuals to be used to start a small business, as is discussed in Chapter 5. In addition, Michael Sherraden (1991) has popularized the consideration of asset building approaches in the United States and elsewhere through which individuals are provided with funding for explicit savings and investment purposes. The underlying principle behind these approaches is that low-income people tend to be institutionally disadvantaged in market economies, and that provision of physical capital can help overcome these shortcomings and propel individuals to higher levels of economic functioning (Yunus, 2007).

Human capital has much the same intent but focuses more directly on skill development. Popularized from a theoretical perspective by economist Gary Becker (1994), it emphasizes the importance of what people know in forwarding their economic interests. Human capital development strategies have received increasing attention as the returns to education and intellectual development have grown with the ascendancy of knowledge-driven economic activities (Psacharopoulos & Patrinos, 2004).

Although there are countless forms of human capital interventions, most fall within two primary domains. First, many deliver or encourage general forms of education, such as basic literacy or the enhancement of college opportunities through financial aid and recruiting. The logic behind these approaches is that even the most general types of human capital are positive for most people, and that individuals who acquire such capital will be able to further their interests in a wide variety of ways. Second, some human capital approaches are more specific in nature, and I will refer to these broadly as training approaches. They typically target one or more very specific economic niches and provide training designed to prepare individuals for them. In this sense, they are intended to be more immediate and narrowly applied than general education approaches, but in turn they may be less likely to be transferrable to other realms of economic activity. Training for specific types of jobs, such as through a program that trains apprentices to work in hospitals, serves as an example of this approach.

The growing importance of information technology may suggest that it be separately distinguished as a substantive category of capital building. I instead choose to consider it as a specialized form of human capital because for the most part it is a tool for increasing human skills and capabilities. Regardless, two forms of information technology development are prominent in thinking about potential developmental benefits. First, many interventions have focused on delivering computer hardware and related software applications to those who otherwise would be unable to access them, such as school-aged children in poor neighborhoods. Second, other change initiatives have focused more on specialized computer application training that is seen as having a high probability of paying off for selected disadvantaged groups. For example, teaching rural farmers how to use existing Internet sites to better monitor the prices being paid in nearby markets for their crops is an approach for improving human capital through computerized training.

Social capital theory, which was developed by Bourdieu (1986) and Coleman (1988), focuses on the role that social connections play in determining life outcomes. It postulates that those with social connectedness are likely to obtain important information and other benefits that will allow them to prosper. For example, people who have social networks that include employers may learn about job opportunities about which others are unfamiliar. From a practice perspective, the lack of such connections in poor communities and neighborhoods has been viewed as an important impediment to social development (Brisson & Usher, 2005; Fox & Gershman, 2000). Programs such as cross-class mentoring and exposing poor individuals directly to prominent individuals and institutions are examples of approaches intended to improve social capital formation. More broadly, Robert Putnam (2000) and others have argued that the lack of social capital in communities leads to lower aggregate economic well-being, suggesting the importance of developing richer social connections as a tool for economic development.

A final form of capital is more congruent with ideas about human rights or political power. By political capital, I mean the ability that individuals have to affect government or other institutional systems to further their own interests. In the crudest sense, the right to vote is considered fundamental in democratic societies as a tool for furthering individual interests through pressing demands on elected officials. More broadly, the abilities that individuals have to advocate for various benefits from governments and institutions constitute their stock of political capital. Programs geared toward obtaining political rights for individuals, such as voter registration drives, are examples of political capital building, as are programs that train individuals about how to advocate for their interests in governmental and institutional systems. The development of employee unions and other mechanisms for democratizing workplaces likewise can be seen as political capital building strategies.

It should be noted that in practice these forms of capital development often overlap, and it is likely that possession of high levels of one form of capital will position one to accumulate other forms (Zhang, Anderson, & Zhan, 2011). Most prominently, high levels of physical capital may be easily transferrable to other forms, for example, by allowing individuals to purchase additional education or memberships in prominent social institutions. Relatively high human capital stocks likewise may facilitate the acquisition and use of political capital, because human capital skills typically allow one to more easily articulate demands in institutional systems. Despite these overlaps, the four types of capital described here remain distinguishable. Each incorporates a differing underlying philosophy concerning how acquisition of the capital form promotes well-being, and each suggests unique programming possibilities for promoting capital accumulation.

Although the strategies for moving people forward have varying causal logics and related programmatic emphases, the basic remediation, enhanced security, and capital building approaches described here all generally aim to provide a specified benefit to a targeted group of people. However, not all development assistance is so directly oriented, and one other important strategy for assisting the disadvantaged merits attention. That is, a diverse range of development activities are oriented more toward creating broader infrastructures intended to improve the opportunities for disadvantaged groups. For example, human capital building programs may be relatively ineffective in a context in which the market is not providing an adequate number of jobs, and government job creation programs may be one vehicle for attempting to rectify such an imbalance. Investments in transportation and environmental safeguards likewise often are critical in creating conditions that allow individuals to fully use any benefits they may receive. Careful attention to such issues therefore is crucial to social development and generally requires thoughtful governmental collaboration.

Even after a broad substantive focus is selected, change agents face additional questions regarding how best to develop benefits. This consideration sometimes is framed in program and policy discussions according to whether interventions should occur at the micro, mezzo, or macro level, or by some similar schema that designates the personal or institutional focus of interventions. The emphasis selected generally says a great deal about change agent perspectives regarding the etiology of a problem and philosophies about how change best occurs. Micro level change approaches generally focus on interventions with individuals, families, or other small groups. Mezzo level interventions instead target mid-level institutions such as schools or community organizations, with the belief that strengthening these will in turn lead to improvements on behalf of designated target groups. Macro level interventions focus more broadly on policies and institutional constructions that provide "the rules of the game" and the opportunity structures for various forms of advancement. For example, change agents who work to establish voting rights laws are engaged in macro level efforts to enhance political capital, with the belief that voting will lead to collective involvement of more diverse groups and ultimately result in more equitable benefit distribution.

In summary, the preceding sections hopefully have illustrated the range of possibilities available to change agents as they contemplate approaches, as well as the complexity of thinking needed to fully develop a change strategy and related behavioral logic. Creating initiatives first involves a careful consideration of why a problem needs to be addressed and what outcomes are intended as a result of any change approach. It then requires a carefully constructed behavioral logic that specifies how the approach to be employed will result in the intended outcome.

THE POLITICS OF CHANGE

As mentioned at the beginning of this chapter, another important perspective in initiative development centers on the specific processes and activities in which change agents engage in order to make desired changes happen. This focus involves moving beyond a desired program vision and related behavioral model, and instead requires strategically determining how to make that vision become a reality. Two aspects of this implementation focus are critical. One is the more narrow consideration of business operations that I will turn to in the next section. The second is more broadly strategic and requires determining how a structured set of interactions involving various stakeholders can lead to sufficient support for an envisioned program idea to come to fruition. It involves creating strategies and related action plans aimed at generating sufficient support for a change idea to be tested in the field.

I will use the terms political development or strategic development interchangeably to refer to this aspect of change. Although there obviously are many strategic possibilities, most change attempts can be usefully categorized according to a few types that capture the most important political development activities related to implementing change ideas. I turn next to presenting a classification for thinking about such strategies.

Political Development Approaches

Political development requires change agents to think through the series of interactions considered most important in allowing their ideas to move from an abstract to a tangible state. Change agents in turn work to structure interactions among various actors toward the objectives of producing benefits for selected groups, and are guided in doing so by their beliefs and values about how change best occurs. Successful change agents often subsequently reevaluate such strategies, based on their initial experiences in implementation and on changing environmental conditions.

Political development generally requires change agents to engage multiple audiences or stakeholders in diverse ways on behalf of the development of their cause or initiative. Central to most strategies is the need to raise resources to promote various aspects of change initiative development. Resources in this sense are broadly conceived to include not only money but volunteer effort, media support, approval by community leaders and authoritative stakeholders, support of consumers, and actions by any other group pertinent to moving an initiative forward.

Some change approaches explicitly articulate the specific steps or processes that those involved in an initiative must carry out, and these processes often are implied even when not fully described. In the discussion that follows, I will present four political development approaches that capture the most essential variations in this respect. These model types vary primarily in terms of the scope and nature of interactions among change agents, beneficiaries, and intermediaries. I will return to these general model types throughout the book in discussing the dynamics of particular market-based approaches. I should note that these "pure" model types rarely exist in practice exactly as described here due to the nuances that accompany particular change initiatives. Nonetheless, defining idealized political approaches can be useful in explicating the range of change efforts that may be undertaken as well as in thinking about the principal strengths and limitations of various approaches.

A brief reorientation and refreshing of terminology introduced earlier may be useful to clarify the presentation that follows. I use the term change agents to refer to the instigators of the political development strategies to be discussed; they are the protagonists or primary strategists in each of the approaches. Initial development generally involves a single change agent or small group, but as change initiatives grow they may evolve into more complex organizational patterns complete with voting rights over developmental decisions. Beneficiaries are those who ultimately are targeted to receive benefits if the model is successfully carried out, and intermediaries are those whose resources or efforts must be induced if the change action is to occur. I do not focus upon paid staff, contractors, or other interactions that are primarily purchased by the change agent to support model development or implementation. Rather, these are seen as transactions under the control of agents that result from their ability to raise resources either from their own means or by inducing intermediaries.[12]

DIRECT MODELS

The simplest form of social change effort involves interactions primarily between change agents and intended beneficiaries—there is little if any need to involve intermediaries in order to achieve the aims of the model. Rather, change agents are able to conceptualize or plan the program initiative largely by themselves or else solely with the assistance of intended beneficiaries. Then, they likewise are able to carry out the initiative solely in conjunction with beneficiaries, with assistance through others such as paid staff or market-based vendors from whom selected work or needed products are purchased. I will refer to such change strategies as "direct models."

Change strategies of this nature tend to be simple structurally and also to require fairly straightforward production processes. From a financial standpoint, they require either an existing pool of funding or else the capability of provision through market exchanges between change agents and beneficiaries. That is, in the direct model, the assumption is that there is little if any need to raise money from anyone other than the change agents themselves or the beneficiaries they seek to serve. Similarly, there is little need to obtain intellectual or other nonfunded technical assistance or the support of government officials or others in the communities of operation. The model may be depicted as follows:

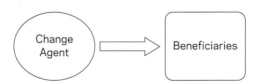

The above constraints may suggest that change efforts of this nature are relatively uncommon, and in fact they probably are the most infrequently employed. However, they merit discussion because they do occur in many communities around the world, and they are particularly important in the early stages of some development projects. In terms of the change approaches to be considered in this book, direct change models are most common in the early stages of social entrepreneurship or private sustainable development.

There appear to be three primary variations in direct change approaches. First, and probably most rarely, individuals with large amounts of money become interested in a social problem and believe in a particular approach for its remediation. In this instance, the change process largely involves wealthy change agents purchasing staff and other resources to implement their vision on behalf of a selected disadvantaged group. This philanthropic approach has been important historically, for example, in the development and operation of many private foundations, through which donors create an overarching vision of the cause to be supported and then provide funding to agents who will support its implementation (see, for example Bishop & Green, 2009).

Second, persons with an idealistic bent may become interested in the problems facing a particular group and in turn develop a responsive small-scale social intervention with limited if any external funding. Change efforts of this nature are the fodder of much of the literature on social entrepreneurship, and they are akin in many ways to the creation of small businesses by those without substantial initial capital. Constrained by the lack of capital and external support, these efforts typically are very cost conscious and must employ creative strategies to survive and grow.

Finally, some direct change initiatives are self-help oriented. They typically evolve from dissatisfaction experienced by persons directly affected by a social problem, which creates the impetus for an innovative response not available through existing channels. The unique aspect of this variation is that those engaged in planning and implementing the intervention also initially may be the beneficiaries; they then typically work to extend the benefits they create to other similarly situated individuals or groups. The case of Erzsebet Szekeres portrayed in Bornstein's (2007) book on social entrepreneurship exemplifies this type of initiative. The mother of a disabled son, Szekeres was frustrated by the inadequate care available for the disabled in her native Hungary. She consequently worked for many years to establish assisted-living facilities and sheltered workshops, primarily to help her son and other similarly situated families she knew. However, as she achieved initial success, her interest and that of others grew, and she eventually established 21 centers across Hungary.

From both a developmental and an operational perspective, the striking feature of direct model social change efforts is that change agents can more tightly control them compared to other types of interventions. Because they do not rely on external funding support, change agents can more narrowly focus their attention on the service aspect of the particular initiative, including their interactions with beneficiaries. The limitation of this approach, except for the rare cases of relatively wealthy change agents, is that the reach of even successful efforts may be limited by funding constraints. Similarly, to the extent that direct model interventions are isolated to change agents and beneficiaries, broader community support that often is vital to enriching programs may be absent. In practice, interventions that begin with the direct model approach typically evolve into the community engagement model described next as they grow, because change agents either learn of the need for broader support or are approached by intermediaries who have observed their positive impact on communities.

COMMUNITY ENGAGEMENT

A second type of change model, which I will refer to as community engagement, relies heavily on the cultivation of intermediaries on behalf of desired social change missions.[13] Further, the nature of interactions with such intermediaries is framed in a positive manner in which the change agent tries to engage intermediaries largely based on altruistic or service-oriented motives. In the simplest form of the community engagement model, change agents may interact with a small number of intermediaries who they consider critical for the successful development of a project. In other initiatives, the number of intermediaries involved may be large and functionally variegated. For example, large nonprofit organizations often are successful in generating substantial financial resources through multifaceted fundraising drives, and in these instances, they may have the need to interact intensely with a subset of their largest donors. At the same time, they may cultivate a large cadre of volunteers to perform service functions related to the change effort, which in turn may be differentiated by functions such as direct service provision, financial advice, technology expertise, and other aspects of program development.

Regardless of the number of intermediaries involved, the distinguishing feature in this model is that intermediaries are conceived primarily as being friendly or supportive, as opposed to being more adversarial intermediaries such as will be discussed in the following section. The following diagram depicts this model in a simple form; a more developed community engagement model simply would include more intermediary boxes that distinguish the different types of intermediaries involved and the relationships between them. It is important to note that these supportive intermediaries vary substantially in their intensity, so that some may be essential to political development while others may be of relatively minor importance. In some cases, the more active intermediaries become so involved that they become part of the change agent group; what distinguishes them is that as intermediaries they largely are working at the direction or urging of the change agent, as opposed to being more actively involved in decision making.

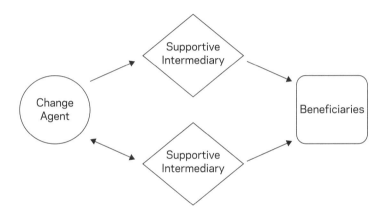

The primary advantage of a community engagement approach, especially when contrasted with the direct model approach, is that it encourages a broader range of sympathetic actors to become involved in change efforts. Doing so often is critical in bringing sufficient financial and other resources to bear on a problem. This is especially important in the common situation in which intended beneficiaries have insufficient resources to allow a change initiative to function strictly on a market exchange basis. In addition to the immediate and tangible provision of needed resources, such positive relationship building can be crucial over time in establishing social capital that is useful in sustaining, refining, and growing change initiatives.

There are two primary limitations of approaches that emphasize community engagement. First, the advantages that extensive relationships can bring in terms of resource development and other support can be offset by the difficulty of managing these same relationships. In particular, contributors may have differing expectations regarding the primary goals or operational features of the change initiative and may demand adherence to these in return for contributions. This problem is well-known in the world of many nonprofits, in that funding agents often require specific performance stipulations in return for providing grants or other financial assistance. In some cases, the demands of different community stakeholders may even lead change agents to drift away from their primary objectives, which is referred to as mission creep (Babb & Buira, 2004).

Second, it is possible that exclusive reliance on positive community building obscures more fundamental conflictual relationships between selected stakeholders and the broader community, which must be addressed if beneficiaries are to move forward in meaningful and healthy ways. In particular, the argument is made that community stakeholders who gain from the exploitation of selected groups may deflect criticism by contributing in trivial or cosmetic ways to change efforts intended to benefit the same groups (Bendell, 2004). For example, a corporation may systematically pollute the air or groundwater in a community or engage in the exploitation of its workers. At the same time, it may curry community favor through support for local social services, recreation, or arts programs.

CONFLICT MODELS

A third political development approach begins with the assumption that benefit improvements primarily require changes controlled by actors with some aspect of market or other control over the well-being of targeted beneficiaries. Further, it is assumed that such changes require conflict because those in control of resources will be disinclined to initiate or agree to needed actions without being compelled to do so, or else will only agree to cosmetic efforts that change agents consider inadequate. I will refer to these actors upon whom conflictual change efforts are targeted as adversarial intermediaries.

Conflict models thus first require identifying sets of interactions in which targeted beneficiaries need assistance if they are to force adversarial intermediaries with power over them to make changes. Strategies then are developed, usually with the help of supportive intermediaries, to engage those with power. The strategies for doing so are diverse, but are also similar in that they attempt to stimulate change through presenting adversarial intermediaries with disincentives to continue status quo relationships. Common tactics of conflict-oriented change agents include boycotts, demonstrations and other protests, and in the most extreme cases, armed interventions. A simple example of this approach is an employee strike, in which employees as potential beneficiaries provide often powerful incentives to employers to improve benefits or working conditions. The following diagram depicts the basic form of this approach.

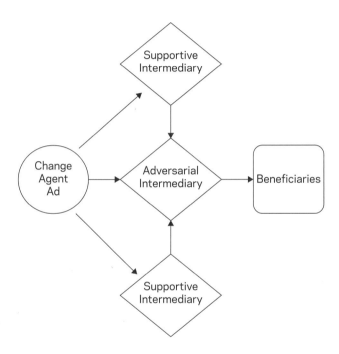

Although any group with power over intended beneficiaries can be the adversarial focus for conflict change efforts, two groups generally are prominent. First, corporations and other businesses often are targeted because of their influence over employees and communities, and increasingly because of their broader environmental impacts. Second, many conflictual change efforts target governments, with the intent of either changing governmental policies or changing regimes. The most common form of organized conflict in democratic societies involves electoral processes. However, when the fairness of these processes itself is questioned, or when government performance suggests that problems are not amenable to more conciliatory interactions, conflict often moves outside of the electoral process.

Change agents who engage in conflict typically are faced with significant power disadvantages in relation to the adversarial intermediaries they are trying to influence. A key to the success of conflict initiatives therefore almost always revolves around the capability of change agents to recruit large numbers of friendly intermediaries to help them bring pressure upon the identified adversary. For example, in the pressure-based corporate social responsibility approach to be presented in Chapter 3, beneficiaries may be corporate employees in developing countries who are receiving very low wages or benefits. It would be highly unusual for change agents to be able to significantly alter corporate behavior simply through their own direct pressure efforts, because they generally are not particularly influential with corporate officials. Instead, a common tactic is to try to entice as many friendly intermediaries to the change initiative as possible, such as consumers, media, and perhaps some governmental officials. With the strategic prodding and organizational skills of change agents, these friendly intermediaries then are central to affecting adversarial intermediaries in ways required to bring about desired changes on behalf of beneficiaries.

MIXED APPROACHES

The aforementioned presents a community engagement approach to change that focuses on consensus building around mutual interests, as well as a conflict approach that centers on working with or on behalf of intended beneficiaries to pressure more powerful adversaries. In reality, many change models mix these approaches, and it probably is fair to say that this mixing is more common as the complexity of action increases. Mixed approaches also are more likely to be observed if one considers change initiatives over a longer horizon, as opposed to at a single point in time.

More specifically, two sets of circumstances involving mixed approaches are notable. First, change agents sometimes initiate community engagement approaches with one set of actors while simultaneously being involved in conflicts with another. For example, those interested in corporate social responsibility may target one corporation to boycott due to perceived poor practices, while simultaneously building a "buycott" campaign to support different corporations that are more positively regarded.[14] The fair trade initiatives examined in Chapter 6 provide another example. I think of fair trade largely as a community engagement political change model, in that it has tried to convince intermediaries to consider alternative purchasing options largely based on altruistic motives. However, some fair trade initiatives simultaneously publicize negative production and distribution strategies by mainstream businesses, and so may be seen as engaging in conflict designed to encourage corporate change.

Second, more complex change processes generally involve multiple iterations over time between change agents and other actors. The nature of these interactions often changes based on the satisfaction with previous engagements, and as a result can either become more consensual or more conflict oriented. For example, a change agent may initially attempt community engagement strategies designed to bring benefits to targeted groups. However, if powerful agents are viewed as impeding the provision of such benefits, change agents may alter their strategies to become more adversarial. It should be pointed out that the reverse sometimes holds true. That is, change agents may engage in conflictual actions with adversaries but then subsequently find more common ground on which to work consensually. This may occur, for example, if the adversary determines that the conflicts are too costly, or if learning occurs in which the two parties determine that less conflictual possibilities may be beneficial.

Evolution of Political Strategies

I would argue that any social change initiative can be analyzed and meaningfully classified according to the relatively simple political development orientations discussed earlier. However, as previously noted, successful change efforts normally evolve over many years, and during that time, tactics or even basic change approaches may shift dramatically. In principle, such shifts may involve the changing of any of the political development orientations to a new type depending on circumstances. However, there generally is an inextricable trend in practice toward increasing levels of complexity regardless of the model type that is employed.

This increasing complexity naturally occurs as small projects grow and as larger numbers of more diverse actors become familiar with an initiative and their interests in relation to it. Change agents often stimulate this process through marketing and publicity efforts, because they see the benefits that can accrue from wider financial and other supports. At any rate, as change efforts become more complex, the strategic tasks facing change agents generally become more challenging and require increasing levels of political and management skills.

The Organizational Venue of Change: Who Provides Benefits?

A final important consideration in developing change models concerns selecting the organizational auspices or venues under which an initiative will be operated. Change agents ideally want to choose the type of organizational entity that offers the best chance for program success. This choice generally represents a combination of philosophical orientations and pragmatic considerations. Many may consider this more of a "business of change" decision, and in fact, it may be partially predicated by considerations of which organizational form may be the most efficient service delivery mechanism. However, this choice often is a more basic one involving political considerations of what is possible and what is desirable in terms of engaging the most stakeholder support.

In particular, choosing a venue generally involves deciding whether to operate initiatives within governments, nonprofit agencies, corporations, or other public or private organizations. The pragmatics of this determination often are driven by where the change agent currently resides occupationally, such as when a corporate official naturally chooses the corporation where she works to target change attempts. Similarly, those without internal access to a powerful entity are likely to choose a nonprofit or even an ad hoc structure from which to develop initiatives aimed at changing more established institutions such as governments or corporations.

From a more philosophical perspective, change agents also take into account issues concerning the organizational form in which they think change initiatives can best be operated. For example, if a particular project is being implemented in an environment featuring considerable distrust in government, a change agent may shy away from government operation and instead choose a nonprofit entity as an organizational choice. Conversely, in more positive governmental climates, change agents may prefer governmental auspices because of the greater authority and resources they may offer.

The Business of Change

Even if political development strategies are very well conceived and employed, the narrower and more traditional aspect of implementation related to how one operationalizes any agreed upon benefit delivery system remains critical to the success of a change initiative. This final aspect of change model construction is depicted in Figure 2.1, and I refer to it as "the business of change." It focuses on management and administration, and it includes issues such as development of staffing and financial management systems, marketing, technology use, and the like. The skill with which such activities are carried out is critical to the relative success of change efforts, regardless of the particular behavioral change focus or political strategy employed. The business of change is the subject of countless public administration and business texts, and so I will comment on it here only to highlight a few of its more prominent features in relation to the market-based models discussed in this book.[5]

I like to think of the business of change activities as the "how" of benefit delivery. In the initial stages of program delivery, they are largely planning and design oriented. They focus on questions such as how we will recruit beneficiaries and market the program to other stakeholders; how we will staff the program and provide relevant training; how we will generate sufficient revenues to finance the program; how we will evaluate program results and use these results to refine the program model; how we will develop relevant information systems for basic service delivery, monitoring, and evaluation purposes; and increasingly, how we will employ technology to improve performance in all of these functions. In the business-oriented lexicon that is commonly used in market-based model descriptions, these functions collectively encompass what may be referred to as a business plan or an operational plan that ideally is designed comprehensively to guide the development of a program. Once a program is designed and initiated, these functions obviously are ongoing and need to be continuously adjusted over time as experience is gained and as circumstances change.

Several of these business-oriented features are emphasized in market-based change models, and I would argue that each of these is receiving increasingly attention in the program development and administration fields more generally. The four I will briefly describe here are marketing, financing, evaluation, and technology use, because I view these as especially critical to program success. However, as suggested by the "how" questions posed here, many other program operational aspects are important and are well considered in public administration and planning texts.

Marketing is a term that at times is shunned in the nonprofit social development world, because it smacks too much of business and implies the selling of something based more on image than on actual value. Yet, marketing does capture the idea that social agencies need to make the benefits they provide known to potential clients and to supportive intermediaries, and it is well known that many agencies do not perform particularly well in this respect. In my opinion, such performance difficulties often are partially rooted in the depth of commitment change agents have to their idea—they believe in it so fundamentally that they initially think that if they open their doors beneficiaries and supporters simply will come.

There are many reasons why this assumption generally is false, and so developing effective multifaceted marketing strategies is essential to the business of change. There are at least three critical audiences for such strategies, all of which demand distinctive attention. First, beneficiaries need to be recruited. This requires not only making the benefit known, but convincing potential beneficiaries of its value and assuring them that transaction costs for obtaining it are reasonable. Transaction costs include not only tangible aspects such as the accessibility of benefit sites, but more psychic ones such as the way that beneficiaries are made to feel as they obtain benefits. Second, fundraising from donors is an important part of the financing strategies of many agencies, and developing marketing appeals that articulate the value of investing in the initiative are central to attracting and reinforcing donations. Finally, most human service operations are staff intensive, and so attracting skilled and committed staff is particularly important. Differentiated marketing for paid staff and volunteers therefore is needed, which not only must establish the unique value of the benefits to be provided but also the more tangible returns associated with working in the particular initiative.

Financing is the lifeblood of most change initiatives, and those without sound strategies in this respect often enjoy an initial surge of energy and even accomplishment that ultimately is very difficult to maintain. As mentioned earlier, the marketing of donors is an important component of financing strategies, but it generally is only that. Other aspects include strategically developing grants, contracts, and third-party payment opportunities; establishing client or customer payment mechanisms; investing of cash and assets; and creating earned income strategies.

Most agencies require some mix of these financing mechanisms, and it should be evident that the skills required for various financing strategies vary considerably. For example, soliciting funds from donors is fundamentally different from grant writing or from creating investment portfolios. Strategies for enhancing client payment and earned revenue perhaps are most characteristic of market-based models, because these often are viewed in the context of financial sustainability and are seen as philosophically compatible with market orientations. Developing earned income ventures in particular requires still another skill set, and again speaks to the need for a fairly high level of business skills. Collectively, the variegated skills required to effectively implement diverse financing strategies suggest the need for a range of skills not commonly held by internal personnel in most change initiatives. The ability of change agents to recruit outside talent to provide assistance in this respect, either through contracting or volunteerism, therefore often is critical to the construction and implementation of sound financing strategies.

Evaluation is another facet of change initiatives that has grown in prominence. Attention to evaluation has been driven by improved academic training and technology availability and by increasing demands from external stakeholders to demonstrate program results. Effective evaluation strategies in turn can contribute to organizational learning and related change model refinement, as well as to program sustainability by providing evidence that initiatives are delivering intended benefits and outcomes.

As is thoroughly described in many program evaluation texts, well-designed evaluation strategies ideally involve both process and outcome components. The former are especially important in early stages of program implementation, in that they determine whether change models are being delivered in the field as intended and, in particular, discern any significant implementation difficulties. Process evaluation activities can remain prominent even as initiatives become well-developed, and they can serve as an ongoing test of issues such as program implementation fidelity, changing internal and external environmental circumstances, and changes in client referral patterns or needs. Ongoing process evaluation activities likewise can serve as a routine source of troubleshooting for all types of operational issues likely to affect program performance.

Outcome-oriented evaluations center on testing whether the outcomes and related behavioral assumptions put forth in change models are borne out once benefits are delivered. At their most basic level, these evaluation strategies may focus on whether or not the initiative was successful in delivering benefits to targeted audiences. In some cases, if resulting behavioral logic simply assumes that those receiving benefits will improve functioning in some important way, evaluations focus solely on documenting the extent of benefits actually delivered. However, it increasingly is expected that evaluations move beyond such output measures to demonstrate that those who received benefits are better off in some important ways. For example, a basic literacy program may measure the number of poor women who completed literacy classes as an initial measure of performance. Yet the ultimate concern is that those who complete classes in fact are more literate and, in turn, somehow improve their life circumstances, such as through obtaining better jobs. In addition, some programs move beyond attention to ascertaining individual outcomes tied to program involvement, and attempt further to measure whether such outcomes collectively impact communities more broadly.

As should be obvious from this description, sound evaluation activities require thoughtful planning and construction and typically require specialized expertise. From a change initiative or program design standpoint, it is useful to think through evaluation strategies early in the development process. This allows for the more careful establishment of needed data collection systems, training, and other operational steps that are essential to the ultimate quality of evaluation results.

Finally, technology always has played an important role in the business of change, but its importance has grown rapidly with the technological transformations described in Chapter 1. Change initiatives have much to gain from the effective use of technology, and correspondingly may miss out on important opportunities if they do not effectively employ it. Technological advancements increasingly have been incorporated as central components of the basic change idea, such as when the Internet serves as the vehicle through which beneficiaries connect with or receive benefits. When speaking of the business of change, however, I instead am referring to the more traditional sense in which technology improves the functioning of key operational functions.

For example, the quality of computer hardware, software, and networking applications is central to the operation of all of the other business functions described here. Information systems have a long history of importance in areas such as internal finance operations, client tracking, and program monitoring and evaluation, and modern technology has provided new opportunities for improving performance in these areas. In addition, Internet technology increasingly is being used in client and other stakeholder recruitment as well as in program fundraising.

As technological importance has grown, change agents have increasingly recruited technology specialists to their teams. For smaller change initiatives, a single technology person may be employed to perform or oversee a wide range of technology functions. As initiatives grow, the need for technological sophistication and specialization likewise commonly increases, and groups of technology staff often are needed. In order for different aspects of technology in an organization to be tied together for cross-functional use, the development of overarching technology plans sometimes becomes critical to facilitate systems compatibility and efficiency.

CONDITIONS RECEPTIVE TO CHANGE APPROACHES

By clearly understanding the philosophical intentions of social change models, their expected behavioral logic, and the nature of intended political interactions among important actors, analysts become better positioned to assess the conditions under which a particular change approach is most likely to succeed. Of course, "conditions" is a very broad term that encompasses many distinct and often poorly understood dimensions. Nonetheless, it is possible to make some useful distinctions regarding factors likely to influence the success of various change approaches generally, as well as of particular political development strategies employed to bring about change.

Factors both internal and external to the change effort are likely to be important in this respect. By "internal factors," I mean those that are most directly related to the actual implementation of the change approach. These include needed financial and technology resources, as well as the specific skills required to carry out activities central to initiating the approach. Such factors may be seen as the most essential capabilities that are required to allow a change approach to operate effectively, regardless of the particular environment in which it is engaged.

Two broad sets of external environmental factors beyond the direct control of change agents also are noteworthy. First, as with the operation of private markets, social change approaches may be susceptible to what economists refer to as barriers to entry. Such barriers include obstacles such as governmental licensing requirements or other operational rules, taxation levels, zoning issues, or any other specific requirements that may make establishing an initiative difficult. Some of these barriers may seem similar to the financial resource needs mentioned earlier as internal factors. Although that is the case, the distinguishing point is that entry barriers are considered as variable here, in that they differ as one moves from one locality to the next. In contrast, the financial resources considered as internal factors refer more to basic operational components that would be needed to make an approach work in any environment.

The second set of external factors is less concrete and more difficult to measure, and yet can be very important. I will refer to it broadly as environmental receptiveness, by which I mean the general receptiveness of various actors in the environment to the social change approach in question. For example, the success of CSR approaches may be critically conditioned by the views of the public about corporations, and the success of fair trade initiatives is likely to depend heavily on the general perceptions consumers have about the adequacy of wages paid to laborers. External environmental factors of this nature are of course subject to change, and in fact, fostering receptiveness for new or alternative perspectives is a central task of many change agents. Nonetheless, the point here is that regardless of the structural nature of barriers facing change agents, population receptivity to ideas is an important consideration in social change efforts.[16]

SUMMING UP: THE COMPLEXITY OF SOCIAL CHANGE DEVELOPMENT

The preceding discussion hopefully reflects the complexity of creating and implementing a social change initiative and provides a coherent framework for thinking about key aspects of change approaches. My framework breaks down change development into four principal components: idea generation, behavioral logic, politics, and business. In practice, these functions overlap substantially, but I nonetheless believe that it is very useful for change agents and academics to think through each of these features systematically. It also is true that conceptualizations of particular change approaches rarely emphasize all of these developmental components, and instead typically focus on aspects of change development considered most unique or important.

In the next four chapters, I will turn to a description and analysis of leading market-based change models. In doing so, I will try to frame each of these models in terms of the more general model components put forth here, or alternatively to note where particular features are not well-articulated in a particular approach. This is intended to facilitate more structured comparisons of the strengths and limitations of these approaches, which I will explore in the final chapter.

3

Corporate Social Responsibility

AS DISCUSSED IN CHAPTER 1, corporations are omnipresent in the modern world, and their power in most societies has increased dramatically over time. Corporate ascendancy has been magnified with the rise of the globalized economy and the related growth of large and often poorly regulated transnational corporations with business operations spanning many countries (Bakan, 2004; Stiglitz, 2007). Corporate power also is being manifested in the context of heavily constrained governments competing to attract corporate investments to bolster economic growth, which often has left disadvantaged populations vulnerable to negative impacts associated with unrestrained corporate practices. The 1984 chemical leak in the Union Carbide plant in Bhopal, India, is among the most notable examples of the disastrous effects that can accompany poorly regulated corporate practices. Thousands of people were killed or seriously injured in this incident, and criminal court cases and litigation continue 30 years later (Fortun, 2009).

The total scope of corporate involvement in the world economy is difficult to capture, because laws of incorporation vary across societies. However, the number of corporations worldwide has risen dramatically, and the growth of transnational corporations has been especially important from a development perspective. According to a United Nations Conference on Trade and Development report (2007), there are more than 78,000 transnational corporations, and these in turn have many more foreign affiliates. The size of the largest of these transnational corporations is striking. For example, it has been estimated that 51 of the 100 largest economies in the world are corporations, and that the largest 500 multinational corporations account for nearly 70% of worldwide trade (World Trade Organization, 2013). Some analysts have gone so far as to suggest that corporations are replacing governments as the most powerful institutions in society, and that this has far-reaching and largely negative ramifications for the provision of social benefits (Bakan, 2004; McMillian, 2007).

Given this extensive corporate reach, as well as limitations in governmental effectiveness in regulating corporate excesses, it should not be surprising that many persons interested in social development focus on strategies designed to influence corporate behavior. Although approaches and orientations differ, the basic idea is that affecting corporate practices can result in substantial benefits to disadvantaged populations. This chapter describes and assesses the principal approaches that have been promoted in this respect, which I will collectively refer to as corporate social responsibility (CSR).

OVERARCHING CORPORATE SOCIAL RESPONSIBILITY CHANGE IDEAS

Although there has been an explosion of interest in CSR in academia and in the broader public in the past 30 to 40 years, there is no widely accepted definition of what CSR should encompass. In fact, the scope and nature of CSR is widely contested, with varying viewpoints regarding what the responsibilities of corporations should be beyond producing products and making profits for shareholders (Dahlsrud, 2008; Lindgreen, Swaen, & Johnston, 2009). CSR proponents likewise vary in their perspectives about how best to influence corporate behavior. They also focus upon many different beneficiary groups and specific benefits expected to be conveyed through influencing corporate behavior. Nonetheless, they share recognition that corporate activities have major social impacts and that identifying and responding to these is important to social development.

Regardless of the particular approach that is emphasized, CSR basically is an intermediary model in which corporations and their decision-making officials are the primary targets of change activities, with the belief that changing the behavior of these targeted intermediaries in turn will result in benefits accruing to selected groups. This conceptual idea has been developed in rich and diverse ways, with respect to the particular benefits argued to accrue to targeted groups and in terms of the political strategies used to influence corporate behavior. In particular, CSR approaches vary substantially in terms of whether they are internally or externally directed. In the former case, officials working within corporations serve as change agents and try to move the corporations for which they work in more socially responsible directions. In the latter case, change agents are external to the corporation and attempt to pressure corporations to change through organized appeals to consumers and investors. I will turn to these differing approaches to CSR and related considerations after a brief historical review of the evolution of CSR as a social development approach.

CORPORATE SOCIAL RESPONSIBILITY
IN HISTORICAL PERSPECTIVE

Efforts to promote responsible behavior by corporations are not new. In fact, they extend to the Industrial Revolution, when concerns about unabated corporate power and exploitation of workers led to public pressures for restrictions on corporate practices (Welford, 2002). Although there were relatively few publicly traded corporations by the end of the nineteenth century, corporate ascendancy then progressed rapidly (Bakan, 2004). In fact, by the end of World War I, large and powerful corporations not only had emerged but were actively engaged in public relations attempts to portray themselves as socially responsible agents (Bakan, 2004).

The concept of CSR was articulated more explicitly by Bowen (1953) during the period of corporate growth after World War II. Early writings often used the term "social responsibility" in writing about desirable corporate actions. Bowen's definition is reflective of perspectives on CSR during this period: "It refers to the obligations of businessmen to pursue those policies, to make those decisions, or to follow those lines of action which are desirable in terms of the objectives and values of our society" (p. 6). Socially oriented behavior was seen as a civic responsibility of business, as opposed to deriving primarily from self-interest.

Since that time, there have been ebbs and flows in attention to CSR, which scholars have suggested stem from factors such as the aggregate state of the economy or the relative prominence of corporate scandals (Cheney, Roper, & May, 2007). Most analysts agree, however, that there has been a new wave of attention to CSR since the early 1990s (Jenkins, 2005). This is partly due to the now well-understood reach of corporate power throughout the world and its corresponding widespread influence on most societies. It consequently is reasonable to assume that prominent attention to CSR issues will continue.

The rise of global economic development likewise has been widely viewed as a critical contributor to the recent interest in CSR (Cheney, Roper, & May, 2007; Jenkins, 2005). Globalization has been especially important for two reasons. First, it has rendered governments less powerful in controlling corporate impacts, and hence, it has created increasing interest in establishing alternative forms of control (Welford, 2002). Second, with the advent of modern communications technology that has made the world "smaller," diverse publics have growing access to information on corporate impacts around the world (Stiglitz, 2007). At the same time, interest in social issues related to corporate production impacts, such as environmental degradation or the exploitation of corporate workers, has steadily risen (Cheney, Roper, & May, 2007; Welford, 2002). Working together, these forces have helped fuel major increases in the level of activists and voluntary groups interested in changing corporate practices (Bendell, 2004).

In addition to rising overall interest in CSR, the prominent models of CSR also have changed. Especially in the 1980s and 1990s, academic and corporate attention increasingly turned to models of CSR that focused on corporations engaging in socially responsible behavior due to perceptions that it could be beneficial to the corporation in the longer term (Wood, 2010). These more self-interested conceptions formed the basis for what became known as "double bottom line" and "triple bottom line" CSR (Elkington, 1998) or the "business case" for CSR (Carroll & Shabana, 2010). The triple bottom line involves systematic consideration of economic, social, and environmental factors in corporate decision making.

The growing interest in CSR is recognizable in many ways, some of which will be elaborated in later sections. For example, before 1970, university business programs rarely focused on business ethics, but in the United States and many other countries nearly all strong business programs now include such courses (Christensen, et al., 2007; Shaw, 1996). Further, some programs include entire courses or even entire programs related to corporate social responsibility.[1] Corporations have responded to the internal interests of some officials and to rising external pressures by establishing more sophisticated corporate strategies for considering and demonstrating social impacts, and increasingly have created units tasked with implementing such strategies and interacting with stakeholders around them (Weaver, Trev-iño, & Cochran, 1999). These corporate efforts have been at least partially driven by a perceived need to protect and improve corporate imaging with the public. Further, media interest in corporate practices and impacts has grown steadily in the last 20 to 30 years, and has included many investigative reports that have resulted in external pressures being generated for corporate change (McWilliams & Siegel, 2001).

External advocates, many of whom are located in nonprofit organizations or very loosely affiliated groups, likewise have emerged in increasing numbers to challenge corporate practices along many dimensions (Kendall, Gill, & Cheney, 2007). These advocates often have engaged in large-scale and widely publicized demonstrations and boycotts directed either at broad corporate practices or at those of specific corporations. For example, the Royal Dutch Shell oil company suffered significant sales losses in 1995 in the face of protests by Greenpeace and other activists related to Shell created environmental damages and the hanging of Nigerian activists associated with this struggle (Schwartz & Gibb, 1999). The boycott of the Nike Corporation in the late 1990s due to its heavy use of sweatshop labor practices in Southeast Asia is another prominent example (Knight, 2007). These and other boycotts of or demonstrations against corporations have received considerable media attention, which has been an important factor in the success of these efforts (Greenberg & Knight, 2004).

Collectively, these diverse stakeholders have created rich possibilities for promoting changes related to the social impacts of corporate production. At the same time, the previously alluded to weakening governmental regulation of many corporate activities has led change advocates to consider mechanisms for controlling corporate behavior outside of the governmental realm (Cheney, Roper, & May, 2007). I turn next to a more detailed examination of the behavioral logic and related political development of CSR approaches, including some of their principal variations.

CHANGING CORPORATE PRACTICES: THE BEHAVIORAL DIMENSIONS OF CORPORATE SOCIAL RESPONSIBILITY

Thinking through the behavioral dynamics of CSR models can be complicated. This stems from the fact that CSR approaches not only focus upon diverse benefits and beneficiary groups, but also differ with respect to how various stakeholders are perceived to influence corporate behavior. Thus, the specific outcomes sought and the associated behavioral logic through which changes are hypothesized to occur vary in different CSR characterizations.

Intellectual debates concerning the appropriate reach of corporate responsibility to society have been central to considerations of the nature and scope of CSR initiatives (Werhane, 2007). The Nobel-prize winning economist Milton Friedman is famous for his article, "The Social Responsibility of Business is to Increase its Profits" (Friedman, 1970), and for related statements arguing that business officials should not be oriented to social concerns in their professional roles. Although many view such "greed is good" statements with cynicism, serious thinkers like Friedman believe that such a unitary focus creates otherwise unobtainable efficiencies that enlarge the collective benefits ultimately possible in a society. The most benign form of this argument is that corporations should focus on what they do best, which is to produce goods and services that result in profits for their shareholders. It is argued that other more socially or environmentally oriented behaviors serve as distractions from this primary purpose, and are unlikely to be done well at any rate; it is best to leave such tasks to governmental or voluntary sectors that focus on such collective values and benefits.

Many corporate scholars have balked at this narrow view of corporate behavior. They argue that corporations are products of societies and therefore incur important societal obligations. As Lindblom (2001) and others aptly describe, governments create the broad rules of the game by establishing and enforcing general market structures, private property rights, and the more specific operating environments in which corporations function. It is reasonable to assume that such favorable treatment should only be granted with the expectation that resulting societal benefits will result, and additionally, that externalities that seriously diminish the quality of life for affected groups will be avoided or paid for (Blomström & Kokko, 1998). Free market enthusiasts counter that the jobs and products that corporations produce represent sufficient social returns.

These arguments are complex. But as Werhane (2007) has argued, corporations cannot be expected to solve all of society's problems, and the breadth of their responsibilities may be very extensive if broadly construed. For example, should CSR extend mainly to corporate consumers, workers, and the communities in which corporations operate? Are corporations responsible for the dealings of corrupt governments where they have an operating presence? Should they be responsible for the business practices of their suppliers as well as their own employees? These are just a few of the thorny questions raised in the literature that illustrate the difficulty in defining the scope and limitations of CSR.

Although definitional issues remain largely contested, there does appear to be a broadening of the concept of CSR over time. For example, Stohl, Stohl, and Townsley (2007) argue that CSR has evolved in three stages, much akin to broadening conceptions of human rights. In the first stage, CSR advocates focused on assuring that corporations did not deny access to certain corporate benefits. Then, a second stage concentrated more proactively on what it is the corporation should provide to various groups, such as the right to a living wage, health benefits, or free assembly. Finally, attention recently has extended to the impacts of corporate operations beyond their own operations and markets, and to their attendant broader societal responsibilities. This more collective orientation considers longer-term sustainability issues, such as environmental impacts that extend well beyond corporate locations.

Debates about the specific actions that corporations should or should not take occur in this broader context of disagreements about the scope of corporate responsibilities. The list of potential social impacts resulting from corporate actions is long, and discussions concerning those social domains with which corporations should be most concerned are complex. I am unaware of any work in the literature that attempts to prioritize or rank which corporate behaviors should be or are the most common targets for those promoting CSR. A useful first step therefore may be to define and classify the range of behaviors that CSR advocates have focused upon. It then is the task of empirical research to measure whether CSR initiatives appear to meaningfully impact any of these corporate behaviors and, in turn, to determine if some behaviors may be more affected by these approaches than others.

Some analysts have attempted to at least crudely classify the domains in which corporations are influential, and so to stake the broad terrain in which corporate responsibilities can be characterized. For example, Dahlsrud (2008) assessed existing CSR definitions and identified five dimensions of CSR that were most prevalent: environmental, social, economic, stakeholder, and voluntariness. Carroll (1979) defined four CSR categories: economic, legal, ethical, and philanthropic. For the purpose of thinking

TABLE 3.1. Potential Beneficiaries of Corporate Social Responsibility Initiatives

BENEFICIARY GROUP	BENEFITS OF GREATEST INTEREST
Corporate employees and subcontractors	Wages, fringe benefits, working conditions, hiring practices, gender and racial equity
Consumers	Product safety and quality, psychic values related to production practices
Community members in corporate locations	Environmental effects on local communities—air, traffic, congestion, water, noise, and other quality of life indicators; effects on local businesses
Broader community members	Nonlocal environmental effects, such as global warming, depletion of nonrenewable resources or other production activities with far-reaching externalities

through the dynamics of CSR change models, it is preferable to think of corporate impacts on different beneficiary or stakeholder groups and, in turn, to consider how corporate behaviors are most likely to influence these groups. Table 3.1 consequently summarizes the range of social concerns that CSR advocates have focused upon in attempting to affect corporate behaviors in relation to different beneficiary groups. Four broad groups are seen as being impacted by corporate actions: employees and contractors, consumers, corporate location community members, and broader communities. I will describe here how corporate social actions most often are argued to affect each of these groups.

Many CSR initiatives have focused narrowly upon those who work for the corporation, either as direct employees or as subcontractors; I will refer to such individuals collectively as employees. A wide range of employee concerns have been the subject of CSR initiatives, with wages and related compensation perhaps the most prominent. This issue has been most dramatically portrayed in CSR campaigns that pressure corporations to improve wages to subcontractors who either produce goods or serve as suppliers. The aforementioned boycott of Nike in 1996 due to the low wages paid to subcontractors in Southeast Asia is a good example of this type of CSR initiative (Wang, 2005). More recently, CSR advocates have focused on wages and working conditions in Bangladesh garment factories; a fatal 2012 fire at a factory making clothes for global retailers including Walmart and Sears served as an important galvanizing event in this area (*New York Times*, 2012).

Employee-related CSR efforts also have focused on a variety of corporate working conditions. In some cases, these include considerations such as the number of hours that employees work, safety of working facilities, and other measures affecting the quality of the work environment for individual employees. In others, CSR initiatives emphasize broader compositional issues in the workforce, such as workforce diversity or employment of specific disadvantaged groups. Some CSR initiatives also have focused on discouraging corporations from hiring workers considered at risk of being exploited, especially children.

Despite responding to a wide range of corporate practices, these employee-related CSR activities share a focus on improving benefits for employee and contractor groups. The ultimate intended outcome of such CSR initiatives is to improve income or related material circumstances for these groups, usually with the general idea that these improvements will allow groups to better move forward in whatever manner they choose.

The behavioral dynamics of consumer participation in CSR is more complex and may involve a mix of tangible and psychological benefits. Initiatives targeted at consumers most directly result in tangible benefits for specific consumer groups based on the resulting production of safer, more effective, or longer lasting products. For example, encouraging or pressuring corporations to assure that children's toys are safe is one example of a strategy to promote consumer-related CSR, as are attempts to stimulate corporations to provide product quality and safety related information about the products they sell.

However, consumers also may be more idealistically interested in CSR if they believe they carry responsibilities to consume products that are made in responsible ways. In this sense, consumers may be seen as attaching psychic value to selected corporate production practices, and they may derive either positive or negative value from consuming various products. These psychic benefits may be related to the wages and working conditions of corporate employees or to issues such as the environmental imprint of corporate production practices. As will be discussed in the following section, psychic benefits extend beyond improving life satisfaction for individual participants; they are the driving force in aggregating interests to improve benefits for corporate employees or broader communities.

In addition to employees and consumers, other community members may be affected by corporate actions. Such effects often are viewed by economists and corporate officials alike as externalities, in that persons outside of the immediate realm of market exchange nonetheless bear some costs due to corporate activities. Most obvious in this sense are persons living in communities in which corporate production or distribution activities are common. For example, corporate presence in a community may result in increased traffic or noise or other inconveniences that may diminish quality of life. More dramatically, corporate production practices may result in high levels of air or water pollution, and the impacts are likely to be concentrated most heavily in the immediate vicinity of corporate production. In addition, corporations such as Walmart often have been argued to have unfair competitive advantages over locally owned small businesses, and to ruthlessly exploit such advantages in attempts to run local competition out of business (Dukes, Zhu, & Singh, 2005). This also has been contended to have related effects such as the removal of profits from communities, the loss of local business role models, and the diminishment of community spirit and voluntary participation (Goetz & Rupasingha, 2006; Haltiwanger, Jarmin, & Krizan, 2010).

Although typically less concerned than employee-driven CSR initiatives with providing money or immediately tangible benefits to a well-defined group, CSR initiatives aimed at influencing corporate effects on communities generally focus on providing benefits in a specifically defined location. For example, an initiative that seeks to reduce the noise emitted by a local factory during production processes would have the primary intent of improving the quality of life for nearby community residents. Similarly, efforts to convince a corporation to change its building plans in a manner that is friendlier to local traffic patterns are intended to have a targeted effect on local residents.

Finally, corporate activities commonly extend well beyond the communities in which production is located. In the simplest case, production often results in externalities that transcend narrow spatial boundaries, such as when industrial pollutants get into the air or water and carry their damage to distant localities. More recent concerns with worldwide environmental degradation have made the definitions of such extended communities broader and more difficult to demarcate. In particular, CSR advocates have increasingly focused on examining the sustainability of corporate production practices, and on advocating for changes in sustainability related practices that are national or international in scope (Marrewijk, 2003; McIntosh, 2007). Examples in this respect are initiatives to encourage corporations to more sustainably manage global fishing resources, or to decrease practices that may contribute to global warming such as depletions of rain forests and inadequate industrial pollution controls (Cummins, 2004; Stohl, Stohl, & Townsley, 2007). This emphasis may increase the potential for CSR change agents to more extensively aggregate interests regarding corporate behavior, and at the same time makes geographic foci on bringing together such interests somewhat less important.

The benefits thought to result from CSR efforts targeted on such non-place-specific environmental or social outcomes often are more difficult to identify precisely. In this sense, they are more likely to be largely ideologically driven and to have the intent of affecting broader patterns of practice as opposed to conveying narrowly defined benefits. For example, if a corporation makes a decision to use only wood harvested using sustainable forestry techniques, the short-term effects on consumers or local communities may be negligible or even result in additional costs. However, CSR advocates in this case are likely to be driven by the belief that such practices will result in more diffuse benefits that will be shared across society over time. A similar argument can be made with respect to most initiatives directed at stimulating corporations to engage in sustainable production practices; in essence, corporations are being asked to forsake some level of immediate profit to enhance or preserve longer-term benefits. The difficulty of such actions is that the immediate costs are fairly easy to define and measure, while the longer-term benefits are more diffuse and uncertain.

Regardless of whether the benefits of CSR actions are narrowly targeted on particular employee groups or are broader and more diffuse, one other aspect of many CSR initiatives is notable. That is, CSR advocates often view the corporate practices targeted for action to be pattern setting in that if one corporation acts, others may follow. I will return to this issue momentarily when discussing political strategy, but the point with respect to behavioral logic is that CSR change agents often are hoping to bring about changes in corporate practices that extend beyond the confines of the particular corporate interaction in which they are engaged.

THE POLITICAL DEVELOPMENT OF CORPORATE SOCIAL RESPONSIBILITY APPROACHES

CSR approaches share an emphasis on influencing corporations to focus on selected social issues in addition to profit-making. However, CSR advocates follow very different strategies in pursuing their objectives. In particular, three strategic variations emerge most clearly in previous literature, with the differences in approaches mainly related to who the primary instigators are and how they view the driving motivations for corporate change. I will turn next to an elaboration of these issues.

The first two of these, which I will refer to as internally driven CSR approaches, emanate largely from within the business and corporate world. One emphasizes attempting to improve corporate ethics through inculcating corporate leaders with broader perspectives on social values, while the other involves the more strategic consideration of social values as a part of corporate planning. Both of these internal approaches to improving corporate social practices have received extensive treatment in the business literature, and are exemplified by growing attention to social responsibility plans, corporate philanthropy offices, or to comparable vehicles for promoting community or service endeavors within corporations.

The third approach instead emphasizes the potential of external agents to affect corporate behavior, largely by influencing consumption and investment decisions of those on whom corporations depend for support. This approach, which will be referred to as externally directed or pressure-driven CSR, involves strategies such as boycotts, buycotts, and socially conscious investing designed to either economically punish or reward selected corporations for particular practices. Many case examples of externally driven CSR strategies have been presented in the literature, but more generalized conceptualizations regarding the mechanics of such approaches have been limited. I therefore will develop a general model of externally driven CSR in conjunction with describing that approach.

Internally Driven Corporate Social Responsibility Approaches

Many corporate scholars have balked at a narrow view of short-term profit maximizing behavior, and instead have developed approaches intended to broaden corporate decision-making perspectives to include attention to social impacts. Although the rationales for such thinking vary, they generally follow two lines. First, some business scholars and leaders view the role of corporations and people within them as extending beyond corporate shareholders, and they are desirous of including broader social impacts in corporate decision making for altruistic reasons. Second, even among those who believe that a focus on shareholder value should be exclusive or at least predominant, some view socially responsible actions as resulting in longer-term corporate benefits. I will describe these two variants of internally driven approaches in this section.

The Ethical Leader

The most idealistic of the CSR approaches focuses on the importance of leadership in corporations, which for simplicity I will call the ethical leader approach. It begins with a central operating premise that one of the major problems with corporations is that people who lead them or play important decision-making roles lack ethical values and are overly consumed with profit maximization (Giacalone & Thompson, 2006). This notion has been continually reinforced in public consciousness in recent years by widely publicized corporate scandals, which fueled discourse on how to improve the ethical fiber of business leaders (Baker & Comer, 2012; Ritter, 2006).

Although the ethical leader approach has not been rigorously formulated in the literature, it can be roughly derived based on interpretations of various writings in this vein. Ethical leader proponents recognize the centrality of profit making in corporations but argue that there is room for consideration of social impacts even in corporate environments. They accept the perspective that corporations have broader responsibilities to the societies in which they are enmeshed, and believe that better inculcating corporate leaders with knowledge about social issues and responsibilities can lead to more socially responsible corporate behavior (Ritter, 2006). In this sense, they view CSR largely as an altruistic activity driven by more enlightened corporate leaders, or as necessary in a general sense to enhance public confidence and support. As shown in Figure 3.1, corporate leaders with enlightened ethical attitudes are the change agents in this model, and they engage in socially responsible actions as they carry out their corporate decision-making roles. The model is mainly internal to the corporation, in that these officials only need to convince other corporate officials and

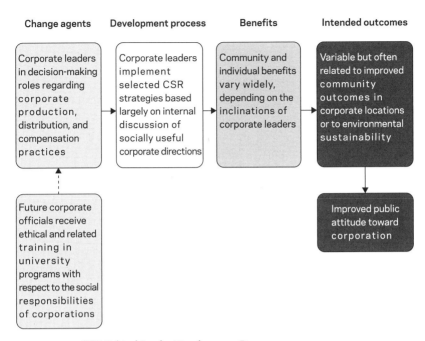

FIGURE 3.1   CSR Ethical Leader Development Process

perhaps shareholders of the usefulness of selected socially oriented actions. The resulting benefits are highly variable, depending on the proclivities of corporate leaders.

There are several arguments with respect to why corporate leaders fall short in this respect. Some scholars point to the lack of training that corporate leaders receive pertaining to ethics, corporate social responsibility, and sustainability in undergraduate and graduate business programs (Christensen, et al., 2007). As a result, corporate leaders often are viewed as being unaware of social concerns. As business schools have responded with increasing ethics training, a variation of this theme has been that ethical training is insufficiently infused across the curriculum, or that it only is taught in a disembodied way as a single course. As such, it is not seen as being powerful enough to compete with the more fundamental attention to profit making well-embedded across business curricula.

Another line of argument pertains to the situations in which even ethically trained corporate officials find themselves. That is, they typically enter extremely competitive work environments focused on profit making, and so may be dubious about their ability to convince shareholders or corporate employees of the value of social investments (Giacalone & Thompson, 2006). They likewise may be caught up in their own desire to advance, and so disregard whatever ethical training they may have had.

From the ethical leader perspective, improvements in corporate behavior can be made if corporate officials are better exposed to social and environmental issues and, in turn, ingrained with a broader set of social values that guide or at least influence business decision making. Corporate officials are seen as being potentially open to broader perspectives on social issues and to the corresponding roles of corporations. Responsive strategies therefore need to focus on training future or current corporate officials about societal corporate impacts, as well as the related responsibilities of corporate officials, so that they are more responsive to these perspectives when they enter corporate practice (Baker & Comer, 2012; Christensen, et al., 2007; Ritter, 2006). For future corporate leaders, such training may be best provided during undergraduate and graduate university business study. For example, courses on business or corporate ethics can be offered or even required of all students, and interdisciplinary coursework can be designed to include more serious social components (Baker & Comer, 2012; Christensen, et al., 2007).

Another possibility is that more ethical corporate cultures can be developed internally and then propagated, so that new corporate officials receive training intended to ethically guide the parameters of their behavior. Most narrowly, such training may be directed toward cementing the dimensions of allowable behavior within corporate practice, which is likely to be seen as important to protecting corporate functioning and reputations and so is largely defensive in nature. However, this concept may be extended to demonstrate broader corporate impacts and responsibilities to corporate employees, as well as possibilities regarding corporate public service opportunities or other vehicles through which to express socially oriented behavior as representatives of the corporation. Given that training in this respect is based on the assumption of openness to CSR within corporations, its success hinges on corporations adopting more humanistic organizational cultures as starting points (Giacalone & Thompson, 2006).

The extent to which these strategies are being implemented in either academia or in corporate training environments is an under-studied empirical question, but in a general sense, they appear to be growing at least within academia. For example, Christensen et al. (2007) found that 84% of the top 50 Masters of Business Administration (MBA) programs included an ethics or CSR course, and these authors note that coverage of such issues in leading programs has increased substantially over time.

The impact of improved ethical training on corporate behavior has been questioned, however. There are two primary difficulties in this respect. First, the effectiveness of any type of education and training approach in influencing behavior varies depending on factors such as the quality of content, its intensity, its applicability in particular settings, and the receptivity of trainees. In addition, business and corporate officials receive many forms of training, and permeating this broader information pool with knowledge concerning ethical values is challenging, especially if ethical training comprises a relatively minor portion of the overall education and training received. In terms of university training, the applicability to setting issue seems especially vexing because the corporate cultural contexts that university graduates enter are likely to differ markedly from idealized academic presentations received as students. This suggests that university training may need to be bolstered with subsequent in-house corporate training if it is to be effective. Further, developing corporate cultures that clearly express value for service and socially responsible actions most likely will be needed if corporate employees are to believe that CSR is taken seriously within the corporation (Giacalone & Thompson, 2006).

Second, and perhaps more difficult, regardless of the values they may hold, corporate officials function not as unbounded individuals but as constrained representatives operating in a context that may not be supportive of ethical behavior. As long as profit maximization remains the central concern of corporate board members and shareholders and, in turn, affects corporate compensation and job security, it is very difficult for even well-intentioned corporate officials to behave along the lines of their ethical intentions. Although some corporate leaders likewise may decry what they see as unscrupulous business practices or a single-minded focus on profits, they know that failing to extract every competitive advantage can lead to dissatisfaction from corporate supervisors and shareholders if profits and in turn investment decisions are in any way compromised. This is a point I will return to momentarily in considering more strategic CSR orientations.

Some empirical work on the effectiveness of ethical training provides support for these concerns. For example, in a recent meta-analysis of 25 programs, Waples et al. (2009) found that overall "business ethics instructional programs have a minimal impact on increasing outcomes related to ethical perceptions, behavior, or awareness" (p. 133). In addition, in a survey of accredited North American undergraduate business programs, Nicholson and DeMoss (2009) found that curriculum coordinators consistently viewed ethical and CSR curriculum content as inadequate. Cornelius, Wallace, & Tassabehji (2007) have argued that curriculum shortcomings are partially due to the great proliferation of business schools in recent years, and to the marginal attention given to such issues in financially constrained curricula.

These difficulties place serious limits on the efficacy of the ethical leader approach, especially if it is viewed as the primary vehicle for enhancing CSR. Nonetheless, inculcating future corporate officials with socially sensitive values, as well as working to create corporate cultures that foster consideration of values beyond profit maximization, may be important for setting the stage for more socially responsible actions. Even if the focus of the corporation must remain on profit maximization, awareness of ethical values may at least partially constrain especially egregious actions and also may foster limited improvements in instances in which corporate officials believe they have discretion on the margins of profit-driven decision making.

Despite the limitations with the ethical leader approach highlighted here, in practice many corporations continue to direct whatever socially oriented support they provide along these lines. In particular, there are countless examples of corporations engaging in social actions with the goal of "giving back to the community" or being good corporate citizens, which generally exemplify the ethical leader model in practice. At times, such exemplars are difficult to differentiate from strategic CSR examples, and I think in fact there is considerable overlap as corporations have increasingly recognized the value of CSR branding. I distinguish these primarily by their stated intent, while recognizing the imprecision of the type of identification.

Some examples of the ethical leader have been quite longstanding, and were established before strategic CSR became fashionable. The delivery giant UPS is one such case. UPS was started in 1907, and company President Jim Casey established a related foundation in 1951 to coordinate UPS charitable efforts. The company today focuses on giving to the United Way as well as on four specific substantive areas that intersect with UPS business culture or goals (UPS, 2012). These include diversity, the environment, community safety, and volunteerism. Despite these intersections, giving does not appear to be clearly related to any strategic plan that assumes that company profit-making will increase due to the action. UPS also has long engaged in a practice that increasingly is being used by other corporations–encouraging its employees to volunteer to social missions of their choice. For example, UPS estimates that employees typically volunteer about 80 hours per year.

The Double and Triple Bottom Lines—Strategic Corporate Social Responsibility

A second stream of internally directed CSR thought is markedly different from the ethical leader approach. Sometimes referred to as the "double bottom line" or the "triple bottom line" (Elkington, 1998), or more broadly as the "business case" for CSR (Carroll & Shabana, 2010; Wood, 2010), this approach does not rely on altruism or on improving the ethical fiber of corporate leaders. Rather, it posits that, if well considered and crafted, socially responsible behaviors may be in the best economic interests of corporations. The task for corporations is to think through economic, social, and environmental considerations together in developing corporate strategies, and to strike a balance in decision making that recognizes the importance of each. One key to this proposition is for corporate officials to take a broader time horizon as they consider profit-maximizing strategies, because economic benefits resulting from socially responsible corporate behavior are most likely to accrue over time. For simplicity, I will refer to this type of approach as strategic CSR, and I have depicted its basic strategic orientation in Figure 3.2. Like the ethical leader approach, change agents in strategic CSR are corporate officials with decision-making authority. These officials similarly must convince corporate officials and shareholders to engage in selected practices, and the particular benefits are variable and subject to corporate determination. However, unlike the ethical leader approach, the impetus for engagement is not philanthropy, but rather a determination of how socially responsive actions can improve the profitability of the corporation.

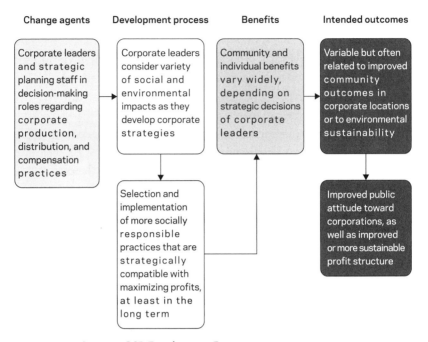

FIGURE 3.2 Strategic CSR Development Process

Broadly speaking, the benefits of this more strategic internal orientation to CSR derive from predicted differences in profits associated with
socially responsible behavior as corporations move from a decision-making
framework focused on a limited number of interactions to one considering
repeated interactions over time. The basic idea is that even though ignoring
social considerations may lead to higher profits in the short run, such inattention may lower revenues or increase costs over time. To put it another
way, the costs of socially irresponsible behavior are seen in some sense as
being unsustainable, or alternatively that the net benefits of socially responsible behavior materialize over time.

Arguments about why this may be the case tend to fall into two categories. First, some strategic CSR proponents point to the importance of
employee and customer loyalty, and argue that more positive social behaviors can improve loyalty among each of these groups (Du, Bhattacharya, &
Sen, 2007; Pivato, Misani, & Tencati, 2008). For example, with respect to
employees, those who receive higher pay or who experience better workplace

treatment may be more likely to remain with the corporation longer and increase corporate human capital and reduce worker replacement costs. Some research suggests that workers may also identify more broadly with corporate efforts to be good citizens, and thus may view such stances as a benefit that encourages loyalty to the corporation (Devinney, 2009; Lindgreen, Swaen, & Johnston, 2009).

Attention to social issues may likewise translate into improved customer loyalty if customers identify with selected corporate behaviors and then factor these behaviors into their purchasing decisions. Ben and Jerry's ice cream, for example, has a well-known history of contributing to various social causes, and the argument would be that some consumers understand this and consequently tilt purchasing decisions toward Ben and Jerry's (Siegel & Vitaliano, 2007). More broadly, research has shown that subgroups of consumers are interested in whether the corporations from which they purchase products behave in socially responsible ways, and hence may be influenced in purchasing decisions based on such criteria (Devinney, 2009). Corporations involved in strategic CSR recognize and respond to these consumer tendencies, and work to incorporate related socially responsible themes into their corporate branding efforts (Hess & Warren, 2008).

Notice that the causal logic concerning worker versus customer loyalty is different. That is, predicted gains from improved worker loyalty are expected to result in higher worker productivity or lower employee turnover costs, and workers are seen as responding more to corporate behaviors that directly affect their personal well-being. In contrast, corporate benefits derived from customer loyalty result if customers are willing to consider social issues related to product production in their purchasing decisions; the same logic applies to socially conscious investing. In this sense, consumers and investors typically are being asked to weigh benefits for others as they make decisions (Kendall, Gill, & Cheney, 2007; Micheletti, 2003).

Despite these differences, there is a common unifying force among workers, consumers, and investors as they engage in socially responsive decision making. Each is making a conscious choice to weigh social considerations as they contemplate options, rather than focusing narrowly on expected economic returns.

The consumer and investment logic implied by such a formulation is quite revolutionary. It implies that consumers and investors are willing to consider not only tangible factors such as product quality, stylistic design features, overall costs, or investment returns as they make decisions. In many cases, they are expressing willingness to pay a premium, either in higher product costs or lower investment returns, if they can be convinced that social benefits are associated with such decision making. This of course suggests the importance of sophisticated education and advertising efforts to convey how social benefits will result from selected corporate production practices, and to subsequently demonstrate that these benefits have occurred.

A second way in which inattention to social concerns may be unsustainable pertains to nonlabor effects on the production process, especially with respect to the raw materials required for product production. For example, suppose that a corporation that supplies fish products to market has access to fish supplies that are viewed as being depletable over time if overfishing occurs. A short-run model may suggest very high levels of fish production to maximize profits as long as demand exists, but total profits in the long run may be lower if fish supplies ultimately are depleted. In this sense, corporate officials taking a longer-term perspective may have similar interests with persons who are more altruistically oriented toward environmental sustainability. If corporations are able to coordinate these common interests, they may receive the dual longer-term benefits of sustaining potentially depletable supplies while generating increased customer loyalty from environmentally interested customers. This thinking has been central to the emergence of the sustainable fishing movement and related fish certification efforts, and large corporations increasingly have committed to using certified fish (Ward & Phillips, 2009).

One may wonder if the strategic CSR principles described here simply constitute a longer range and more sophisticated economic planning model, and that in fact is the case. The task for strategic CSR proponents therefore is to convincingly bring both immediate and longer-term social concerns into corporate decision-making processes, so that corporate practices better reflect social factors in meaningful ways. Corporations increasingly have incorporated social and environmental considerations into their strategic planning for this purpose. To the extent that social impacts are viewed as financially profitable, they not only can be adopted but vigorously marketed. That is, although some of the economic incentives for pursuing socially responsible actions may be directly demonstrable in analysis of comparative production functions, more often economic impacts are thought to derive from improved customer or worker loyalty. Capturing these potential benefits in turn requires very strong marketing of the socially desirable attributes of products, much as corporations market more tangible product features. In marketing lexicon, the task is to "brand" the corporation, and particular product lines within it, as sensitive to social concerns.

Walmart provides an interesting example of the more recent thrust toward strategically oriented CSR. It may seem surprising to some readers to consider Walmart under this or any other CSR category, as the company has been among the most widely criticized corporations in terms of its social responsibility record. In fact, such criticisms have taken root with many consumers, and may be a reflection of the efficacy of pressure-based CSR approaches to be considered later in this chapter. For example, a study in 2005 reported that significant numbers of consumers had turned away from Walmart due to concerns with its corporate practices (Gogoi, 2006).

Perhaps partially in response to such criticisms, CEO H. Lee Scott launched an aggressive new initiative in 2005 that was clearly couched in the language of strategic CSR (Plambeck & Denend, 2008). The goals of the initiative included "To be supplied 100% by renewable energy; to create zero waste; and to sell products that sustain our resources and the environment" (Plambeck & Denend, 2008, p. 53). The company also established 14 networks to establish more sustainable practices related to these three goals.

Among the substantive areas in which work is proceeding are the rapidly increasing use of certified seafood that is sustainably harvested, and the growing use of organically grown cotton in the apparel Walmart sells (Plambeck & Denend, 2008). The overarching emphasis of all of these new practices is to enhance sustainability, which is seen as providing longer-term competitive advantages. Some may view this broad new initiative as little more than an attempt to deflect criticism regarding Walmart's often maligned employment policies, cutthroat competitive practices, and negative community impacts. Be that as it may, the initiative is among the broadest designed in terms of environmental sustainability by a major corporation.

To summarize, the ethical leader and strategic CSR approaches largely are directed and controlled from within the corporation, but they differ dramatically in their motivations and developmental strategies. The former relies primarily on the altruistic motivations of corporate leaders, which are viewed as being inculcated through training and education and

are consistent with broader views about corporate responsibilities beyond profit-making. In contrast, strategic CSR is completely consistent with narrower profit maximization perspectives and is not dependent on altruistic motivations; in a popularly coined slogan associated with this approach, the corporation is seen as "doing well by doing good." It logically follows that the primary task for CSR change agents using this approach is to demonstrate within strategically oriented corporate settings that net positive corporate economic benefits will result if selected socially responsible practices are followed.

External or Pressure-Driven Corporate Social Responsibility

Some CSR proponents have little confidence in the willingness of corporations to voluntarily engage in socially responsible behaviors such as those described in the two internal CSR models mentioned here. Rather, they believe that corporations almost always will be primarily motivated by shorter-term profit-maximizing considerations, and that such motives will seriously limit their voluntary engagement in socially responsible behaviors (Bakan, 2004; Edwards, 2010). Change agents holding such views instead favor an approach through which outside advocates put pressure on corporations to engage in selected behaviors. The underlying assumption is that corporate officials will be responsive only if they can be convinced that failure to do so will result in decreasing profits, or alternatively, that their positive social actions will result in increasing profits. In this sense, the logic overlaps somewhat with the strategic CSR perspective described in the previous section. However, it differs in that strategic CSR is postulated as a rational corporate planning process in which corporate officials prospectively attempt to incorporate longer range social considerations into planning. In contrast, the primary impetus for pressure-driven CSR resides outside of the corporation, and it generally is instigated by change agents who are dissatisfied with corporate efforts in selected domains.

There are many case examples of pressure-driven CSR presented in the literature, as well as some conceptual representations of related strategies and tactics (Kendall, Gill, & Cheney, 2007; Friedman, 2006). These are highlighted by well-known examples of consumer boycotts, as well as more positively oriented consumer initiatives such as socially responsible investing. However, none of this work appears to have created an overarching

framework encompassing these various forms of externally driven CSR. I consequently will attempt to do so in the following section, as a means for setting the stage for examining this approach.

THE PRESSURE-DRIVEN DEVELOPMENT PROCESS

Pressure-driven CSR initiatives can be complex, but in general they involve interactions among three primary groups of actors: organizers or advocates, consumers or investors, and corporate officials. Media representatives and governmental officials also often play important roles in pressure-based initiatives. I will refer to organizers and advocates as the change agents in this model, and should note that they often create and implement CSR initiatives under nonprofit agency auspices, such as through an agency with a social advocacy mission. I will begin by focusing on consumers as an intermediary group for simplicity reasons, and for illustrative purposes also will use negative actions against target corporations as the primary tactic employed. However, some CSR initiatives focus upon investors rather than consumers, and on more positive incentives for corporations to change selected behaviors. I will return to these variations later in the chapter, but the basic logic of this approach is similar in either case.

In thinking about the CSR actors in terms of the framework presented in Chapter 2, the change agents attempting to influence corporate behavior can be seen as the instigators or drivers of action, with consumers serving as a supportive intermediary group that change agents seek to influence in order to affect corporate practices. The beneficiaries are selected groups seen to be adversely affected by some aspect of corporate behavior, or at least as those who could benefit from changes in corporate behavior. In some cases, the beneficiaries may significantly overlap with the consumer intermediary groups, such as when a change initiative focuses on product safety issues directly pertinent to consumers. However, more often, consumers are purely an intermediary group that the change agent is attempting to engage to improve benefits for other groups. Change agents therefore have two primary groups of actors that they must influence if external CSR initiatives are to be successful—corporate officials directly and the consumers to which corporations are seen to respond. In this sense, consumers may be viewed as friendly or supportive intermediaries, while corporate officials may be seen as adversarial intermediaries. The basic developmental logic of this approach is depicted in Figure 3.3.

Change agents   Development process   Benefits   Intended outcome

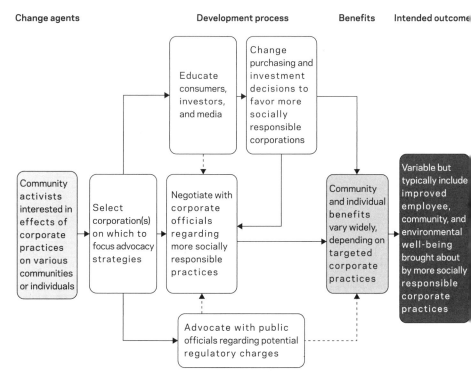

FIGURE 3.3   Pressure-Based CSR Development Process

The process generally begins with change agents identifying particular corporate behaviors that they want to influence, such as those discussed earlier in this chapter. They may focus actions upon either a single corporation or on multiple corporations. In practice, choices on corporate targets rarely follow a process of rational calculation. Rather, an analysis of pressure-based CSR case examples suggests a more opportunistic and evolutionary approach to CSR (Balabanis, 2012; Friedman, 2006; Kendall, Gill, & Cheney, 2007). That is, initiatives often begin with perceptions of corporate wrongdoing at a specific location or else through a galvanizing event or from negative publicity about the behavior of a particular corporation. This arouses the awareness of change agents and/or those in immediate publics affected by the practices, and CSR initiatives emerge in response. The action in turn may spread to a wider geographic area or set of corporations.

In initiating CSR efforts of this nature, change agents first generally must gather data and information that document the specific behaviors in which the corporation is engaging, with a focus upon identifying the social harms that these behaviors are causing for selected groups. Change agents then may directly complain to corporate officials about the alleged socially offending behaviors and request that the corporation take corrective actions. This form of initial engagement may have become easier in recent years, because corporate officials have more actively monitored social impacts and have increasingly established corporate public relations or community engagement units. Depending on how difficult or costly the advocated change would be for the corporation to implement, in some cases corporate officials may agree to changes as a preemptive strategy to avoid larger conflicts.

However, this type of initial engagement generally is unlikely to have a powerful influence on corporate behavior, because corporate stakeholders are diffuse and there may be little reason for corporate officials to believe that change agent actions will be effective. Instead, initial engagement typically serves three distinct purposes. First, it may be seen as providing an educational function for the corporation, in the event that corporate officials do not fully recognize the social costs of behaviors in which they are engaging. Second, it can be seen as a necessary step before more aggressive calls for action can justifiably be made, in the sense of change agents being able to demonstrate to potential supporters that they first tried to convince corporate officials to change the behaviors in question. Finally, and perhaps most importantly, such exchanges are designed to convince corporate officials that more aggressive and potentially damaging actions from the corporate perspective will follow unless responsive corporate changes are made. In this respect, the advocates essentially must convince corporate officials that they pose a viable threat, especially in terms of their ability to aggregate and organize consumers or other intermediaries on behalf of the issue in question.

Consumers are the third critical group in pressure-driven CSR initiatives. They generally hold the key to the potential effectiveness of CSR initiatives; it is their purchasing behaviors about which corporations are concerned. Change agents consequently must be able to convince consumers that a particular corporation is engaging in socially irresponsible behavior, and that the behavior is sufficiently egregious that consumers should consider altering their purchasing behaviors.

Engaging consumers for this purpose may be a difficult challenge for several reasons. First, change agents must be able to identify a significant number of consumers or potential consumers of corporate products, so that communications regarding the particular corporation and its practices can be made. Second, these consumers must be convinced that taking action against the corporation is a worthwhile endeavor in which to invest time or money, which may require not only effective demonstration of harms but providing an alternative product that meets consumer needs. Third, change agents must have the skills and resources to organize consumers to engage in selected actions against the corporation, such as product boycotts, demonstrations, or other publicity-seeking efforts.

There also is a useful distinction to be made between two types of consumers in these change efforts, which I will refer to as private consumers and institutional consumers. Private consumers are individuals involved in the markets, who daily consider a variety of personal purchasing options. These private consumers are the stock and trade of many pressure-driven CSR initiatives, especially in the early stages of development.

However, institutional consumers may be even more important in many change efforts, and consequently may become prominent targets of change agents. These institutional consumers are large organizations that constantly are involved in making purchasing decisions. For example, staff in a university purchasing unit routinely must choose among corporations in selecting the food and drinks that will go into their vending machines, the companies from which they will buy their information technology, and the health-care providers they will use to serve their students and employees. In a stable political environment in which social issues related to corporate providers are not being voiced, decisions may be largely bureaucratic and cost-based. However, change agents may advocate for CSR with these institutional audiences just as they do with private consumers; they can urge the purchasing or contracting organizations not to enter into purchasing agreements or other contractual relationships with the targeted corporation. Because such institutional purchases often are very large, any success in this respect may have a relatively high payoff with respect to its effect on the corporate target.

In working with consumers, it should be obvious that boycotts tend to be a primary tactical device of pressure-driven CSR initiatives. Change agents can either attempt to convince consumers to completely boycott a type of product if negative practices are seen as widespread in a particular industry, or alternatively to argue that they should purchase a product from another corporation not being targeted.

The simplest external CSR initiatives may only require interactions among change agents, consumers, and corporate officials. In these cases, change agents organize consumers to boycott or otherwise protest against the practices of selected corporations, and simultaneously attempt to convince corporate officials that they will end negative actions as soon as corporate behaviors change in desired directions. Corporate officials then must consider whether they are willing to make changes in hopes of ending the boycott, and in turn may negotiate with change agents concerning mutually agreeable changes. From the change agent perspective, decision making related to corporate offers often revolves around whether the promised changes are credible and sufficiently robust to justify a cessation of actions against the corporation. This in turn also may involve consideration of whether the change agents believe any agreed upon changes will be well enough received by the involved consumer groups to convey a feeling of satisfaction related to the actions in which they have engaged. In addition to ethical considerations, this latter point is especially important to change agents who are engaged in CSR actions on an ongoing basis; being able to demonstrate to consumer groups that they have been effective is likely to be critical to encouraging future engagements around other issues.

Although the preceding discussion illustrates the most basic dynamics of pressure-driven CSR initiatives, other actors are prominent intermediaries in more sophisticated CSR initiatives. As mentioned, the two most important of these are media representatives and government officials, and in some cases competing corporations also may become involved. The media often plays a critical role in bringing attention to CSR initiatives by publicizing socially inappropriate behaviors, as well as the nature of the resulting buycotts or other actions. In fact, some authors make the distinction between CSR initiatives that are mainly consumer driven or primarily media driven (Friedman, 2006).

It therefore is not surprising that both change agents and corporate officials often work hard to influence the media regarding an initiative. For the change agent, the media can serve as free publicity and marketing to extend the reach of an initiative to a broader consumer audience, and also to convey to corporate officials that negative publicity is likely to accompany the

CSR initiative. Corporate officials of course may recognize this and consequently may interact aggressively with the media to offer a more favorable portrayal of their behavior. The interpretations by media representatives of varying change agent and corporate perspectives in turn may play a critical role in the framing of a CSR initiative to the broader public.

Government officials are important in some CSR initiatives in other ways. Change agents may solicit key government officials to support an initiative, with the idea that the endorsement of important public decision makers may signal other community members to participate. In addition, they may lobby government officials to more strongly regulate the offending behavior if corporate officials do not voluntarily alter their practices. It is noteworthy that change agents actually may prefer that governments strengthen the regulation of corporations in some cases, although in others they are more interested in simply convincing corporate officials that a credible regulatory threat exists. Corporations have their own lobbyists and government relations officials, however, and these corporate representatives generally are better financed and positioned with government officials than are change agents. Corporate lobbyists consequently are likely to vigorously counter change agent messages regarding regulation, by attempting to discredit the community standing of the change agents and their arguments and by reiterating the value of the corporation to the constituents and campaigns of government officials. For example, they may argue that the costs of complying with CSR goals may be so great as to diminish employment or other benefits that the corporation provides in the community, or may even force the corporation to leave the community for sites where costs are lower.

Although less well documented and probably less common, a final set of actors merits attention in considering pressure-driven CSR initiatives—corporate officials themselves. Here I am not referring to the obvious role they play in developing reactionary strategies to the pressure brought to bear on their own corporations by external agents. Rather, in some instances corporate officials become intermediary advocates in bringing pressure to bear on other corporations. This may happen due to either one of two differing corporate perspectives, both of which stem from perceptions concerning the position of the corporation in relation to its competitors. First, it is not uncommon for corporate officials to react with somewhat of a "why us" response when they first are targeted by a CSR initiative. That is, they may believe, or at least want to argue, that corporations with whom they compete engage in similar or even worse behaviors, and so they may try to convince change agents or the media that other corporations are worthier CSR targets.

Second, if a CSR initiative proves effective in forcing one corporation to modify its behaviors, officials of that corporation may subsequently believe that they have become relatively disadvantaged in relation to their competitors who were not targeted and who made no such changes. For example, a corporation in a competitive environment that has improved working conditions may now face a higher cost structure than its competitors, and so be concerned about its ability to remain competitive in pricing. In such instances, corporate officials may lobby government officials to develop regulations that force other corporations to adopt practices similar to those which their corporation has been pressured into adopting (Bendell & Kearins, 2005). I should note that, although actions such as these are rational and sometimes used in particular corporate engagements, they also may be considered risky by corporate officials; they not only may further encourage CSR change agents that the corporation would prefer not to nurture, but they tend to run against the grain of opposition to government regulation that is common in the corporate world. So, to the extent that such actions are taken, they can be seen as short-term strategic tactics.

The Use of Positive Reinforcement in Pressure-Based Initiatives

Thus far, I have described pressure-based CSR in terms of the threatened deployment of negative sanctions against corporations if offending behaviors are not changed. As mentioned earlier, there also are many examples of externally driven CSR that instead emphasize positive reinforcements for socially responsible social behavior. The processes through which corporate behaviors are expected to be altered in this more positive scenario are analogous to the negative sanction approach, except that change agent approaches to consumers and corporate officials are made in a manner designed to reward positive behavior.

To take a simple case, change agents may determine during the course of investigating selected corporate social impacts that a particular corporation engages in one or more practices considered desirable. Change agents in turn may encourage consumers with whom they interact to purchase a particular good or service from that corporation or, in some instances, to support the corporation more generally. Similar to the use of boycotts in the negative sanctioning example discussed earlier, such positive tactics sometimes are referred to as "buycotts." Some analysts have argued that positive change overtures generally are more effective than negative ones because they offer the opportunity for cooperative actions between change agents and corporate officials (Vogel, 2006). Of course, change agents engaging in such friendly interactions also may be more subject to cooptation by corporate officials.

Socially Conscious Investing

Another external CSR variation focuses on influencing investment as opposed to consumer decisions as a vehicle for changing corporate behavior. This form of CSR has become increasingly important as stock market participation has grown and diversified and as improving data on corporate activities have become available. For example, it is estimated that in the United States alone, $1.7 trillion was invested in socially screened portfolios in 2005 (Chatterji, Levine, & Toffel, 2009).

From a political development standpoint, such investment-oriented approaches are very analogous to the consumer approaches already discussed. As in the consumer scenario, change agents first identify corporations engaging in practices they consider as socially irresponsible. They then attempt to influence investors not to invest in targeted corporations. For example, there has been increasing attention to convincing individuals and institutions not to invest in tobacco companies, which has led some institutional investors to divest tobacco holdings (Epstein, 2008).

Employing more positive tactics, change agents also may urge investors to buy stocks or other assets in companies that engage in designated socially responsible behaviors. In addition to advocates urging investments in selected corporations, new companies and nonprofit organizations have emerged as conduits for advising investors on how to develop investment portfolios that are more socially responsible. The Calvert group serves as one of an increasing number of companies that advise clients on socially responsible investment portfolios, and indicators such as the Dow Jones Sustainability Index have emerged to provide investors with shortcuts in determining corporate practices. The ratings of Kinder, Lydenberg, Domini Research and Analytics (KLD) have been widely used by institutional investors to guide socially responsible investment decisions, as well as by academics to study the impact of socially responsible performance (Chatterji, Levine, & Toffel, 2009).

The process through which intermediaries influence corporate behavior in investment-oriented CSR initiatives is a bit more complicated than for comparable consumer-related efforts. Although there are countless individual investors who purchase stocks or bonds for themselves, they do so through private brokers or through the institutions where they work. Consequently, CSR advocates must convince individuals not to purchase stocks or other corporate assets, and these individuals in turn must direct their agents not to do so. This can become very complicated, because brokers typically work with their clients to select mutual funds that package corporate stocks into larger portfolios based on criteria that have nothing to do with CSR issues. This difficulty, together with rising interest in socially responsible investing, has led to the just mentioned emergence of firms specializing in identifying more socially responsible options for investors.

Institutional investment employees or agents again may be very important intermediaries in investment-oriented CSR activities, because they are involved in making investment decisions for the institution and for employee pension and deferred compensation funds. Because many such institutions control very large amounts of investments, their decisions concerning corporations in which to invest can have substantial financial repercussions. For example, universities and other large institutions were prominently lobbied to divest from South Africa as part of advocacy efforts against apartheid. In cases of this nature, change agents pressure representatives of institutions to make more socially responsible investments, sometimes with the threat of demonstrations or other sanctions for noncompliance. For example, in the South African example, student groups were influential in pressuring for university divestment, with the organization of campus demonstrations a prominent tool toward this end.

More Advanced Pressure-Based Approaches

I have, for simplicity, described positive and negative consumer and investment possibilities related to CSR initiatives separately. In reality, more sophisticated pressure-driven CSR initiatives skillfully weave together these different advocacy options For example, some initiatives may urge consumers to purchase from corporation X rather than corporation Y based on their differences in desired CSR attributes, and simultaneously may work with investors toward the same end. An interesting recent example of a dual focus of promoting some corporations while boycotting others is the development of the Buycott smartphone application, which allows consumers to determine whether products were manufactured by those with objectionable values or by those with preferred ones (O'Connor, 2013). It has been used, for example, to allow consumers to determine if products were made or distributed by corporations supporting genetically modified organisms (GMOs), such as Monsanto and Koch Brothers.

This more complex calculus brings into sharper focus a fundamental issue facing pressure-driven CSR change agents. That is, they typically must be able to demonstrate for consumers or investors the relative costs of participating in the designated change efforts. If they are fortunate, change agents may be able to refer these intermediaries to other sources of provision with minimal cost implications. However, as discussed earlier, socially responsible corporate behavior commonly carries at least short-term costs, so illustrating the benefits of alternative provision again becomes very important in convincing intermediaries to bear such burdens. This concern points to an underlying principle of importance in CSR and in the fair trade approach described in Chapter 6; the success of each often ultimately resides on the willingness of consumers and investors to pay a price for the values they hold. This is an issue to which I will return in the concluding chapter.

Pressure-Based Case Examples

Examples of pressure-based CSR initiatives are mainly presented in the literature rather idiosyncratically as individual cases, with widely varying descriptive emphases and levels of detail. One of the few attempts to present a set of larger initiatives using a common framework is presented by Kendall, Gill, and Chaney (2007). These authors describe six cases in which advocates have been engaged in pressuring large corporations over long periods; the corporations included are Coca-Cola, Shell, Texaco, Walmart, Nike, and Starbucks Coffee.

Kendall, Gill, & Chaney (2007) describe different tactics and coalition building strategies employed by change agents, varying response patterns over time by the corporations, and ultimate changes that were or were not made. The variability across all of these dimensions probably is what stands out most in their analysis. Among the corporations assessed, it appears that Starbucks most quickly was responsive to pressure from advocates. The company was targeted for protests and vandalism in 1999, and was accused by leading advocacy organizations of using "sweatshop coffee." Starbucks responded by creating a Department of Corporate Social Responsibility, and in turn, by developing annual corporate social responsibility reports as well as brochures on various company efforts in this realm. Starbucks also initiated a partnership with the fair trade organization TransFair USA to promote fair trade awareness and provide some fair trade alternatives in its stores. Despite these efforts, Starbucks continues to be painted by many advocates as providing a largely marginal response, which has allowed the company to promote itself as socially responsible while continuing operations that primarily rely on traditional coffee sourcing.

THE LIMITS OF CORPORATE SOCIAL RESPONSIBILITY APPROACHES

The effectiveness of CSR approaches has been criticized on many grounds. Perhaps most fundamental to these critiques is the recognition that even the most socially conscious corporations are driven primarily by profit motivations. As such, it is argued that socially responsible responses by corporations always must be considered predominantly within a broader profit-making calculus, as opposed to being significantly driven by a heightened orientation to values. In the long run, the socially responsible corporation usually faces competitive challenges to its survival unless it succeeds in convincing consumers to pay more or investors to accept less as the price of socially responsible behavior. Alternatively, even if discretion is sufficient to allow some level of socially conscious engagement without any significant survival risk, resulting actions are likely to be marginal in order to maintain low-risk exposure. As Karnani (2010) has argued, "In circumstances in which profits and social welfare are in direct opposition, an appeal to corporate social responsibility will almost always be ineffective because executives are unlikely to act voluntarily in the public interest and against stakeholder interests."

Perhaps all CSR approaches should be considered as a two-stage process. In the first, corporate officials must become aware of selected social effects of corporate operations, because otherwise there is not even a reason to contemplate changes. If this first test is met, a second stage can follow in which corporate officials consider possible social improvements that can be carried out without being too damaging to the basic corporate profit orientation. In this context, corporate officials must be skillful in assessing the possible effects of selected socially responsible practices on corporate well-being and, in turn, in promoting such practices to the stakeholders on whom they depend for support. Ultimately, in deciding whether to engage in socially responsible practices, corporate officials are tasked with finding a market niche that allows for some level of a targeted behavior without jeopardizing the corporate market position or the well-being of the corporate officials within it.

Viewed in this light, the profit versus social benefits trade-off consideration poses differing limitations or problems for each of the corporate models discussed, with the calculus especially difficult in the internally directed models. In the case of the ethical leader approach to CSR, efficacy may be very limited if the responsible corporate official operates in an environment where competitors do not share or exercise the same social values. The ethical leader in this case faces two related sets of problems. First, he may encounter challenges from within, in which competitors for leadership positions may argue that socially responsible behavior will reduce profits and compromise shareholder interests. Second, even if a supportive internal corporate culture can be established, external competitors may be less socially responsible and thus be able to undercut prices on those that act more responsibly (Bendell & Kearins, 2005). As should be obvious, the problems in the ethical leader approach thus transcend concerns about the goodwill or the intent of the corporate leader. Rather, even if we assume great improvements in the ethical fiber of corporate leaders, the fear is that their good intent will be severely limited by the corporate environments in which they are enmeshed.

The problem for strategic CSR is similar. In the case in which managing potentially depletable supplies is the primary impetus behind socially responsible behavior, corporate officials must convince investors that their long-term interests trump shorter term ones and that lower immediate profits may lead to longer-term growth and sustainability. Officials within the corporation must be convinced of the same thing, because otherwise the most talented employees may leave to pursue more lucrative opportunities. It likewise can be assumed that, barring unusually active and consensual consumer involvement on an issue or alternatively strong governmental regulations pushing corporations as a group in selected directions, some corporations will always gravitate toward short-term profits and thus be able to undercut corporations with longer-term perspectives.

In cases in which customer and community loyalty are being counted on to sustain socially responsible behavior, these audiences must be reassured that any extra costs they bear are directly related to the socially desired corporate behaviors they wish to support. This of course requires very active marketing of the socially responsible ideas being promoted and, ideally, routine reporting on the social impacts resulting from positive corporate behaviors. Ultimately, unless customers and communities sufficiently support the corporate arguments about social practices by providing their tangible consumption or investment support, corporate profits may be sufficiently diminished to require reduction or abandonment of the social effort.

The challenges for pressure-driven CSR are different but nonetheless difficult. Change agents using this approach face the fundamental problem of trying to alter consumer behavior sufficiently to influence corporate decision making. This is extremely difficult for two reasons. First, consumers tend to be diffused and to have a wide variety of tangible and social motivations; in many areas, they also enjoy a great number of purchasing options. Organizing them around a coherent set of social issues consequently is very challenging and requires considerable ingenuity and skill. Second, pressure-based CSR change agents typically are poorly resourced in comparison to corporate officials; if challenged, corporations may be able to bring substantial resources to bear in fighting CSR initiatives. These resources commonly include access to information on corporate production processes not available to the public, high-level marketing capability, and connections with politicians and others of prominence in public debates. In comparison, advocates frequently must rely on the creative use of smaller resource pools and more limited political connections.

Monitoring the effects of CSR initiatives, as well as compliance with any changes that corporations claim to make in response, likewise can be difficult. For example, in the initial stages of a corporate boycott, participants may want to be informed about how many like-minded persons have joined in their effort, or to find out how much sales of a product have been reduced by the boycott. Measuring such changes in a meaningful way often is very difficult, and the corporation has no incentive to share such information unless doing so illustrates the ineffectiveness of the CSR actions.

It also is reasonable to assume that, in reacting to external CSR initiatives, the rational incentive for corporate officials is to bring the external action to cessation while still minimizing costs. This suggests that any concessions offered by corporations are likely to be marginal. Given that corporate leaders in these cases may not be particularly enthralled by such concessions, effective compliance monitoring is critical to assure that agreed upon changes have been made. This again can be problematic because of the superior resources that corporations command, and so successful negotiations of compliance monitoring terms may powerfully affect the extent to which advocates can measure their success. Yet, unless faced with a strong alliance of consumers and other stakeholders, corporate officials may have little incentive to fully cooperate with such monitoring, and in many instances may be well-positioned to subtly undercut it.

A similar but more generalized concern with CSR initiatives is that corporations use them mainly for public relations purposes or image polishing. Critics in this vein argue that corporations will do just enough to gain favorable public attention or to diminish any negative publicity or profit reductions they are facing based on boycotts or other social actions (Hess and Warren, 2008). Utilizing the sophisticated resources often at their disposal, they may employ public relations or other staff to convey information that exaggerates how much is being achieved related to the issue of concern.

Some have used the term "greenwashing" to refer to such efforts with respect to environmental behaviors (Ongkrutraksa, 2007), and corporate "cleanwashing" has been used to capture this sentiment with respect to a wider range of corporate behaviors (Hess & Warren, 2008). In its worst forms, corporate cleanwashing may involve making "socially responsible" changes in behavior in a geographic area in which public attention has focused, while continuing the offending behavior in other jurisdictions. For example, many pharmaceutical companies attempted to garner favorable public attention by donating drugs to developing countries, only to later be exposed for using drugs that had past their expiration dates and so would not be marketable in developed countries (Hess & Warren, 2008).

A similar concern involves corporations that engage in a limited number of positive social activities, but do so in the context of far larger and more damaging production practices or socially irresponsible behaviors. The cigarette industry provides a leading example for this phenomenon. Phillip Morris, which not only manufactures a dangerous product but has covered up possible harmful effects, also has prominently supported community grants for the arts and community services. Cynics not surprisingly suggest that such practices are a shallow attempt to create goodwill and deflect attention from much larger issues regarding corporate activities (Edwards, 2010; Hess & Warren, 2008).

There are at least two important problems for advocates in attempting to respond to cleanwashing or other corporate manipulations of public sentiments. First, as previously mentioned, advocates generally operate with substantially fewer resources than the corporations they target, so corporate officials usually are in a better position to put forth favorable publicity if they choose to do so. Such resource differentials may be especially problematic in monitoring large multinational corporations, because their activities are so multifaceted and geographically spread that it is difficult to clearly assess their activities. Second, through the use of selective benefits such as community grants or other public concessions, corporations may be able to enlist supportive community allies or at least minimize community criticism. For example, perhaps a community behavioral health agency would be reluctant to accept a grant from a gaming corporation, because of the negative effects gambling has on some consumers. However, the agency may need the funding and assume it will be spent on other agencies at any rate, and so decides to accept the grant. In doing so, it may become more reluctant to criticize the gaming corporation, both because it sees another side to the corporation and because such criticism may appear hypocritical. The community agency also may become more dependent on the gaming corporation for future funding support, which again may decrease the likelihood of objectively assessing and responding to corporate actions.

Another difficulty for pressure-based CSR advocates is determining the corporations upon which to target their efforts. In the broadest sense, individual corporation practices regarding any socially important behavior may represent a continuum from very responsible to very irresponsible. In some cases, the expanse of the continuum may be wide, or there may be negative outliers that easily suggest which corporations may be targeted. However, in other cases, such choices may not be obvious, and charges of unfairness may emanate from the targeted corporations.

Advocates of course may avoid this issue by more broadly targeting sets of corporations or even entire industries. Although this approach can minimize charges of unfairness and extend the reach of the initiative, it has important costs as well. It not only may significantly raise the costs of organizing and implementing actions against the offending behaviors, but also is likely to engender a broader and more highly resourced response from a now larger set of corporations. For example, it may lead affected corporations to form allegiances to resist the externally driven change efforts, and these corporations collectively may be able to provide substantial resources. Further, depending on the importance of products or practices being targeted, organizers may not be able to suggest desirable options for consumers who engage in the CSR initiative, aside from total abstinence from the type of product in question.

These challenges in selecting corporate targets, and in adequately monitoring corporate responses, point to a more central strategic concern for outside advocates interested in influencing corporate behavior. That is, many scholars question whether advocates might be better advised to pressure government officials to institute more overarching corporate regulatory requirements, rather than attempting to change the behavior of corporations through direct pressure tactics (Bakan, 2004; McIntosh, 2007). This is a complex issue, and it requires a careful assessment of available resources, political climate, corporate receptiveness, and philosophies concerning government intervention in the economy.

In practice, this issue may be revisited many times as CSR initiatives progress, with changes in strategy resulting from evolving interpretations of interactions and circumstances. It likewise should be noted that this tactical choice is not always a simple either-or situation; advocates instead may pressure corporate officials to change voluntarily while simultaneously lobbying governments to institute mandatory requirements. An example of changing strategy may occur when change agents determine that initial attempts to change corporate behavior through direct pressure tactics are ineffective. Change agents may become frustrated in such circumstances and may decide that their resources would be more wisely invested in influencing government officials to regulate corporate behavior.

More positive renditions of this evolutionary shifting from direct pressure CSR to government regulation also are possible. For example, a central intent of most pressure-based CSR initiatives is to bring broader public attention to adverse corporate practices. To the extent that such initiatives gain public attention, they may serve to elevate the concern to the policy-making agenda of public officials, at which time attention can turn to pressuring these officials to develop stronger corporate regulations.

Measuring and Monitoring Corporate Social Responsibility Behavior

Measuring the impact of CSR initiatives can be very difficult. Although it may be fairly easy to measure and disseminate information about some basic strategies, activities, and outputs, determining the ultimate effects of CSR activities on either social well-being or on corporate profits is much more challenging. As already noted, many such impacts are realized over a longer time period, so short-term effects may be difficult to ascertain. During initial periods of CSR implementation, it therefore is important to report on process steps that document initial actions that are being taken, while also reinforcing that desired outcomes have a longer time horizon. The skill with which communications are carried out is particularly critical in the common case in which short-term costs may increase due to the social engagement.

More fundamentally, there are two basic problems that complicate the measurement of CSR impacts, and each of these can undercut any instrumentally derived support for initiatives. First, like many social program efforts that are preventive or developmental in nature, there is an asymmetry in the timing required for measuring costs versus benefits. This asymmetry results because the costs of such efforts occur immediately and generally are fairly easy to identify and measure in a manner clearly attributable to the initiative. But benefits, especially with respect to ultimate effects on profitability or social well-being, only are likely to be discerned over time. This longer time horizon unfortunately elevates a second measurement problem. That is, even in relatively straightforward operations, many factors determine the profitability of a corporation or of any product line within it. Isolating the effects of any CSR initiative therefore requires very sensitive measurement and analysis, and results may be equivocal even when well-implemented.

A simple example may be useful in illustrating these issues. Suppose that a corporation initiated a strategy to require all of its subcontractors to establish improved working conditions in developing world countries, such as requiring no child labor, setting maximum number of hours worked rules, and establishing selected workplace standards for production facilities. It may be relatively easy to measure the extent to which subcontractors comply with all of these socially responsible requirements, and this in turn could be reported to relevant stakeholders. It likewise may be fairly straightforward to measure the costs subcontractors indicate they are incurring in complying with these new requirements and in turn to estimate the relative short-term costs of the CSR behaviors. However, benefits that accrue in terms of profitability most likely will occur due to increased worker productivity, lower turnover, improved product quality, or greater customer loyalty or engagement of new consumer groups. Each of these potential benefits is likely to take time to develop, and the measurement of each may be affected by factors other than the CSR initiative.

All of the arguments above assume well-intentioned actors involved in the CSR impact measurement process. Yet in many instances, this assumption does not hold. As previously discussed, a central criticism of CSR is that corporate officials have incentives to overestimate the extent of their CSR activities and related benefits. This may most benignly involve overly flowery interpretations of efforts. In worse cases, corporations may use their command of data and communications resources to deliberately misrepresent corporate efforts and impacts. It may credibly be argued that corporations have meaningfully increased attention to CSR issues over the last 30 to 50 years in the face of growing public attention. However, as demonstrated by recent excesses on Wall Street and countless scandals involving bribery, regulatory violations, and deliberate deception of consumers and investors throughout the world, one should not be sanguine about the willingness of corporation officials to engage in disingenuous actions.

It is in this challenging context that attempts to monitor corporate behavior have been instituted. Important progress has been made, as is illustrated by the aforementioned investment rating services and by the emergence of many watchdog organizations to monitor corporate performance along a wide range of socially responsible dimensions. This attention has helped fuel the increasing provision of corporate social responsibility and sustainability reports and other publically available indicators of corporate performance (Epstein, 2008; Gjølberg, 2009).

Yet, the overall impact of socially responsible performance on corporate financial performance remains difficult to measure and is the subject of academic debate. Based on a meta-analysis of research in this area, Margolis et al. (2009) concluded that corporate social performance (CSP) has a mild but positive impact on corporate financial performance. After an extensive literature review, Wood (2010) similarly concluded that "there is no compelling evidence that CSP is too costly, and the preponderance of evidence points to the opposite conclusion: it is costly to be socially irresponsible" (p. 62). The extent to which these relationships continue to hold, or to grow in their effects, will depend heavily on how well change agents succeed in developing more effective monitoring strategies.

SKILLS NEEDED FOR CORPORATE SOCIAL RESPONSIBILITY PRACTICE

It should be obvious from the discussions here that change agents require a range of fairly sophisticated skills if they are to engage effectively in CSR initiatives. When viewed from the perspective of externally driven CSR efforts, at least four skill sets seem especially important. First, change agents must have the ability to identify and measure the costs and the benefits of initiatives, which requires strong training in areas such as cost-benefit analysis, data collection, and in research and analysis techniques. It is highly likely that the corporations to be engaged will have substantial capabilities in these areas, and that they will craft messages intended to portray corporate performance and practices in the best possible light. Change agents thus must not only be able to conduct credible independent analysis, but often to detect and critique flaws in corporate communications.

Second, CSR change advocates must have strong communication skills in terms of being able to clearly demonstrate to potential audiences the harms created by negative corporate practices and the potential benefits of specific CSR initiatives. These agents typically operate in a world of heavy advertisements crafted by corporate communications experts, so effectively putting forth alternative messages is no easy task. Yet doing so both through traditional and electronic media is critical to drawing a large

enough audience to make a CSR initiative viable. Maintaining and growing support over time also is critical to most initiatives, and so being able to
clearly communicate successes and obstacles to supporters is important in
being able to build and continue momentum for an initiative.

Third, change agents must have well-developed political instincts and
related negotiation skills. They commonly will be involved in conflictual
situations with more well-resourced adversaries, and there is the potential
to be either overpowered or misled in negotiations regarding changes that
a corporation can make. A particular concern is that corporate officials will
offer to make changes that are largely cosmetic in nature, and that relatively
unsophisticated change agents will view such changes as more substantial
than they really are. Because the intermediaries on which they depend for
support typically are so diffused, the change agent must sensitively detect
what level of changes are sufficient to generate sustained intermediary participation and satisfaction. This not only is important from an ethical perspective but more pragmatically in terms of change agent abilities to engage
intermediaries in future initiatives.

Finally, CSR change initiatives typically require the skillful organization of many intermediaries. Tactics common to externally driven CSR
initiatives, such as buycotts or demonstrations, require the ability to bring
together large numbers of diverse stakeholders in a cohesive manner. This
organizing focus, which requires many of the skills taught in community
organizing courses or programs, also frequently requires the ability to
weave media involvement and coverage into organized events.

The Internet as a Tool in Corporate Social Responsibility Initiatives

As will be discussed more broadly in the concluding chapter, the rise of the
Internet and other information technology has enhanced contributions
of all of the approaches presented in this book. Nonetheless, technology
advances appear especially noteworthy with respect to externally driven
CSR initiatives, because they have significantly eased the challenges of organizing diverse and widely dispersed audiences and also have made it easier
to instigate media attention across global expanses. In particular, as CSR
change initiatives have become increasingly global in character, Internet-
based communications have allowed the identification of corporate effects
across space while simultaneously improving the ability of change agents

to organize broadscale boycotts or other actions against corporations. For example, when I was living in China in 2010, Western media attention became focused on the high suicide rate for employees working in the production facilities of Foxconn Technology, which produces iPads and iPhones for Apple and which is a supplier for corporations such as Dell, Microsoft, and Hewlett-Packard (Barboza & Bradsher, 2012). This led to investigations and scrutiny of working conditions by change agents, who pointed to factors such as long work hours and poor working conditions as possible contributors to this problem. Facing worldwide criticism, Apple pressured Foxconn to institute changes in working conditions, which in turn were widely publicized. An interesting twist of this story was that attention to this problem in turn spread in China because Internet sources from the Western world reported it widely. That is, a story originating in China was not initially publicized there but eventually was as the news circulated across the new media.

SUMMARY

The pace with which CSR has generated increasing attention in recent years is striking. Not only do nearly all large companies at least consider CSR from a strategic perspective, but consumers are much more likely to attend to corporate performance in this respect. In addition, external advocacy groups have emerged to challenge corporations to perform in a more socially responsible manner, and often have had media representatives as strong allies in these pursuits.

The evidence on the impacts of CSR, both due to internal corporate efforts and external pressure, remains equivocal. Notable case successes have resulted from application of a variety of tactics, but overall effects seem modest and idiosyncratic. Because corporations always must focus first on profits, and because they often hold large resource and power advantages, relying on either the goodwill or supposed strategic interests of business to bring about significant social change through internally directed CSR appears to be a highly questionable strategy.

Externally driven CSR initiatives organized through nonprofit agencies and other advocacy groups seem more promising because these efforts generally are motivated to stimulate meaningful social change. The challenge for these externally driven strategies is to organize sufficient resources and expertise to effectively challenge corporate power, not only in attempting to influence corporate actions but also in monitoring corporate performance and follow through. Although this challenge is large, the vigorous response of social change agents in this area is critical. Corporate power and reach most likely will continue to grow in an age of globalization and attenuated government powers, and external advocates are needed to serve as a check on this power. They can do so not only through organizing consumers and investors around a wide array of social responsibility issues, but also by lobbying governments to institute laws that appropriately limit corporate power, protect employees and consumers, and more broadly protect the local and global communities affected by corporate production practices.

4

Social Entrepreneurship

THERE HAS BEEN GROWING ATTENTION in recent years to social development strategies that collectively may be referred to as "social entrepreneurship" (SE). Although this term often has been very loosely and variably defined, SE at its heart involves the application of principles from business entrepreneurship to innovative social ventures. In contrast to corporate social responsibility (CSR), SE generally is viewed as a more bottoms-up approach in which an individual or small group first develops a small-scale project, which then ideally grows after initial testing and refinement. As in business entrepreneurship, the individual social entrepreneur typically is at the center of SE change efforts, and the particular characteristics of individual change agents in creating and then growing innovative projects in turn is celebrated in the literature. The pioneering development by Muhammad Yunus of the Grameen Bank to support microenterprises for poor persons is a well-known example, and emerging literature has described countless other SE projects, especially in the developing world (Alvord, Brown, & Letts, 2004; Bornstein, 2007; Welch, 2008).

Given the imprecise definitional nature of SE, which will be discussed in a subsequent section, it is impossible to estimate the extent of SE projects around the world. Nonetheless, the number of change agents who define themselves as social entrepreneurs or their projects as socially entrepreneurial has increased dramatically. SE likewise has been adopted by many charitable foundations as a conceptual centerpiece in marketing and in reaching funding decisions, and academic interest in the approach has grown rapidly. Developing a better understanding of SE and attempting to more clearly define and demarcate its fundamental characteristics and boundaries therefore is very important.

THE HISTORICAL DEVELOPMENT OF
SOCIAL ENTREPRENEURSHIP

Although small-scale development projects have a long history, the consideration of such projects under the rubric of SE is fairly recent. The term most often is traced to an influential article written by J. Gregory Dees in 1998. Dees argued that efforts to assist the disadvantaged could benefit from the application of principles from business entrepreneurship, especially by bringing innovative solutions and sound business management to difficult social problems. Dees portrayed the social entrepreneur as much like the business entrepreneur, except that social entrepreneurs were seen as emphasizing the creation of "social value" rather than individual profit seeking. Although exemplars claiming the SE moniker have been promoted in nonprofit and for-profit venues, probably the greatest attention has been generated with respect to initially small nonprofit start-ups that eventually grow to a much larger scale.

The idea of SE has subsequently enjoyed a rapid ascendancy in academic and program development circles. Although there appears to be no single overarching factor that explains this rapid growth, several features of the recent developmental environment appear pertinent. Three of these factors were already discussed in Chapter 1, but they bear brief restating here because of their particular importance to SE. First, the tremendous growth in the nonprofit social service sector in recent years has included both agencies operating solely within countries and those that cross national boundaries. A great deal of this growth has occurred in the social service, educational, and health fields that are fundamental to social development (Forman & Stoddard, 2002; Salamon, Sokolowski, & List, 2003). Many of these nonprofit agencies provide services under government contracts, and competition for constrained public resources has prompted increasing accountability demands in such contracted relationships (Smith, 2009). Nonprofit agencies consequently have been driven to improve management practices and also to develop more innovative service approaches. Competition among nonprofit and profit-making agencies likewise has stimulated greater attention to innovative revenue-generating and cost-saving strategies (Dees, 1998; Dees, Emerson, & Economy, 2001, 2002).

Second, the revolution in computer and other information technology has created new opportunities for innovation in organizations. Discussions and allegiances between social service professionals and those with information processing and business expertise in turn have blossomed and have become critical to agency success. Although the products of these cross-professional collaborations often have focused on improving internal program management, they also increasingly have included interesting innovations in actual service delivery. In addition, the new technology has allowed innovations to much more easily transcend spatial boundaries and has helped create interest in innovations designed to address social issues in developing countries (Murero & Rice 2006). It also has allowed individuals and small groups to communicate and carry out activities with more limited physical infrastructure and staffing, which fits well with the small-scale developmental nature of most SE efforts.

Third, some of the entrepreneurs who made large fortunes through the technology revolutions became interested in addressing social issues, and they brought lessons learned from business entrepreneurship to social concerns. For example, eBay's first president, Jeff Skoll, established the Skoll Foundation in 1999 to promote and support social entrepreneurship. Ashoka, the Schwab Foundation, and Echoing Green similarly emerged as funding organizations that explicitly embraced SE as a guiding approach. In the United Kingdom, UnLtd was set up for similar purposes with substantial government funding support (Nicholls, 2010). These foundations not only seeded many important SE ventures and provided consultation to social entrepreneurs, but also were influential in promoting SE as a change approach.

Fourth, academic and popular publications began advocating for and assessing SE as a social change strategy and sought to articulate various principles and exemplars (see, for example, Bornstein, 2007; Dees, 1998; Dees, Emerson, & Economy, 2001, 2002). In addition, organizations such as the Kauffman Foundation and the Coleman Foundation emerged to promote entrepreneurial education in higher education institutions and among professionals. For example, the Kauffman Foundation invested nearly $50 million in establishing entrepreneurship programs in 19 universities across the United States between 2003 and 2006 (Kauffman Foundation, 2008).

These latter foundation efforts were not geared toward the development of social entrepreneurship, but academics often interpreted entrepreneurship approaches broadly and began to apply them to nonprofit agencies and the social sector. Most SE educational efforts in this respect were initiated in business schools, as opposed to social science disciplines. From the business school perspective, the goal was to engage a subset of idealistically oriented business students to invest at least part of their talents in social ventures.

Although no academic degrees and few courses on social entrepreneurship existed before 2000 in the United States, by 2004 more than 100 courses were being offered, and many universities had fairly aggressively embraced this concept in teaching and service (Brock, 2008). This number has continued to expand rapidly across universities and, in terms of depth, within selected universities. For example, academic minors and certificate programs on SE have begun to be established, with the intent of moving SE well beyond the single course phenomenon as part of a business degree or other major (Brock, Steiner, & Kim, 2008). In addition, leading universities such as Harvard, Duke, and Oxford initiated social entrepreneurship or social enterprise programs, which lent growing credibility and intellectual leadership to the field (Nicholls, 2010).

The number of journal articles focusing on SE likewise exploded. For example, using advanced Google scholar search, only 19 articles with SE in the title were shown in 2000, but this number had grown to nearly 1,500 by 2012. Research and applied journals either solely or largely devoted to SE likewise emerged, such as the *Journal of Social Entrepreneurship,* the *International Journal of Social Entrepreneurship and Innovation,* and the *Stanford Social Innovation Review.*

Finally, as detailed in Chapter 3, the 1990s witnessed increasing debate in the corporate sector about socially responsible business practices (May, Cheney, & Roper, 2007; Reich, 1998; Zadek, 2007). Although such discussions focused partially on the nature of contractual relationships with corporate employees, interest also grew in establishing social ventures that returned some value to the broader communities in which corporations operated. In many instances, the business expertise of these entities was carried over into the social ventures in which corporations became involved, and increasing attention to business and social service partnerships often resulted. I have elected to treat such corporate efforts under the rubric of corporate social responsibility in Chapter 3, because I believe they generally are byproducts of broader corporate efforts designed to maximize profits or to improve corporate images. Nonetheless, increasing corporate attention to social efforts has reinforced a more businesslike approach to social program creation and management, and hence arguably has had notable spin-off effects in stimulating SE.

THE DIFFICULTY OF DEFINING SOCIAL ENTREPRENEURSHIP

Among the many difficulties in assessing SE as a social change model is that it has been imprecisely and amorphously defined. Several critics have noted this definitional fuzziness and have argued that it has limited the possibility of analyzing SE as a coherent approach (Light, 2008; Martin & Osberg, 2007). Martin and Osberg, for example, argue that "the definition of social entrepreneurship today is anything but clear. As a result, social entrepreneurship has become so inclusive that it now has an immense tent into which all manner of socially beneficial activities fit" (p. 28). I strongly agree with this assessment, and hence believe that a useful starting point lies in clarifying some of these definitional issues and in turn presenting a working operational definition to guide analysis.

Returning to my general framework emphasizing that change processes may focus upon behavioral theories or implementation processes, SE should be viewed quite strictly in terms of the latter. These processes typically involve the meshing of innovative service approaches, the application of sound business principles in planning and managing programs, and careful attention to the sustainability of program efforts. Although I will return to these and other SE process features in more detail momentarily, I first will discuss the substance of SE initiatives and what this implies about any undergirding behavioral theories implicit in SE.

The Substantive Content of Social Entrepreneurship and Related Behavioral Assumptions

If one carefully reviews the SE literature, there is little conceptual emphasis on the types of benefits or on any specific behavioral changes that change agents should focus upon as they implement this approach. The countless SE case studies that have been described likewise are wide-ranging in terms of the benefits delivered, such as education, health care, employment, basic food and housing assistance, and many others (see, for example, Bornstein; 2007; Welch, 2008). As such, it does not seem useful to assess SE in terms of its performance on any theoretical underpinnings about how beneficiaries will be affected by programmatic efforts.

The one behavioral component reflected in many SE projects is an emphasis on benefits intended to empower recipients for longer-term self-improvement. For example, many SE projects feature job creation or income generation strategies geared toward sustainable economic development for disadvantaged groups, such as through microenterprise financing (Schreiner & Woller, 2003). An emphasis on empowerment in this respect is not surprising, because it is consistent with the broader entrepreneurial ethos of individualistic development. Nonetheless, it should be reiterated that this focus only is notable in a subset of SE projects. The more important point is that the approach is extremely pliable with respect to the subject areas of change it may encompass, and largely is silent with respect to particular behavioral assumptions or logic models pertaining to how beneficiaries are intended to change.

Although classifying social entrepreneurship efforts according to subject area has little utility, it is useful to consider the particular benefit delivery aspects or situations around which SE cases most often have been documented. First, many social entrepreneurs focus on delivering a new benefit for a group, so the innovation centers on the actual creation of the benefit and the related delivery system. Second, some SE efforts have been more concerned with refashioning the manner in which an existing benefit is delivered, with the intent of improving access to services or timeliness of delivery or otherwise positively affecting service delivery efficiency. Third, a subset of SE initiatives focuses more narrowly on financial sustainability. Such efforts hence are primarily concerned with the development of financing schemes that maximize the likelihood of selected benefits being delivered consistently to designated target groups over time.

Distinguishing Essential Implementation Features of Social Entrepreneurship

Lacking a clear substantive or behavioral change focus, the viability of SE as a development approach instead hinges on its attributes in terms of program implementation processes. A review of conceptual articles in the SE literature reveals a consistent focus on broad implementation features that are viewed as central to this approach. Unfortunately, varying implementation features are emphasized by different authors, and even commonly identified features have been inconsistently defined. Further, no well-recognized standard has emerged from this mix of definitions, with authors alluding to many previously offered vague definitions and usually extending little effort toward improving definitional clarity. In this section, I discuss the most important features that have been emphasized, with the intent of culminating in a working definition.

As previously noted, the SE concept derives from business entrepreneurship, which emphasizes the aggressive identification and exploitation of opportunities that result in productive innovations. The business entrepreneur is viewed as an opportunistic risk taker who creates innovative economic change while pursuing individual profits. This process features the "creative destruction" of previous production or distribution models and their replacement by new and innovative ones (Schumpeter, 1942).

Social entrepreneurs are viewed as similar to business entrepreneurs in that they aggressively seek opportunities and engage in calculated risk taking in pursuit of innovative purposes. However, as opposed to seeking individual profits, social entrepreneurs pursue innovations largely for the purpose of creating social value or social change, typically with the idea of benefiting less privileged segments of society (Bhawe, Gupta, & and Jain, 2006; Dees, 1998). Hence, although they adopt an entrepreneurial mindset in terms of the way they implement project development strategies, they are driven more by altruism than by individual gain.

A primary difficulty with this definition is that "social value" lies in the eyes of the beholder, and consequently can mean almost anything. For example, most profit-seeking business persons would argue that the jobs they create or the products they provide to consumers result in substantial social value, and this undoubtedly often is true. Schramm (2010), for example, has argued that "all entrepreneurship is social," which of course is not a very satisfying idea in terms of applied development or analysis, let alone broader public interpretation.

It therefore should not be surprising that consensus is lacking in the field regarding the definition of social value. Nonetheless, discussions generally point to social value creation as a primary motivating force in SE efforts, as opposed to a spin-off activity associated primarily with profit making.

This distinction creates some separation from most of the corporate social responsibility approaches described in Chapter 3, in which social benefits are primarily a spin-off of the drive for shareholder profits.

A related question is whether ventures that include any individual profit taking should be classified as socially entrepreneurial, even if they profess motivations related to social value creation. Perspectives in the literature on this point again are mixed. Some conceptual articles on SE limit its exercise to the nonprofit sector (Weerawardena & Mort, 2006), with the notion that all entrepreneurial activities support the social mission. However, others have applied the term to for-profit start-ups designed to help disadvantaged groups (Mair & Marti, 2006). A hybrid position is to include profit-making ventures under this rubric, as long as the primary purpose of the venture is to fulfill a social mission (Martin & Osberg, 2007). Although somewhat appealing in terms of incorporating the efforts of entrepreneurs who seek to exploit markets to aid the economic development of poor persons, this hybrid definition raises the additional difficulty of requiring interpretation of an entrepreneur's primary motives.

Beyond this focus on social purpose and social value creation, fairly diverse definitional components pertaining to either the nature or intent of activities have been elaborated by various authors. Three important themes in this respect merit consideration. First, and perhaps most in the spirit of creative problem solving eschewed in business entrepreneurship, some definitions focus on the innovative nature of activities designed in response to a social problem (Dees, 1998). The activities may be commercial or not, as long as they generate innovative social solutions. The test of whether an activity should be considered socially entrepreneurial therefore rests heavily on the extent to which it departs from existing practice, or to which it can be considered "pattern setting" (Light, 2008).

Second, SE definitions sometimes focus more narrowly on the conduct of innovative commercial activities that generate revenues for social purposes (Emerson & Twerksy, 1996). In this sense, the revenue-generating activities may be comparable to a private business, but the intent of profits generated is a social mission as opposed to individual wealth creation. A U.S. example would be the selling of wildlife and nature calendars and other merchandise by the nonprofit Sierra Club in order to generate funds that then are used to support activities consistent with that organization's environmental and conservation mission. Note that under this definition, it is the commercial activity that is paramount, and this commercial activity may be used in support of an ongoing social purpose as opposed to underwriting a new and innovative one. The nature of innovation in this case is not the service or product to be delivered but the means of financing a social activity.

This type of commercial financing activity has been referred to separately in the nonprofit literature by terms such as earned income ventures or earned revenue streams, and such market-based commercial activities have been among the fastest growing revenue sources for nonprofit agencies (Wei-Skillern, Austin, Leonard, & Stevenson, 2007). What may be seen as separating socially entrepreneurial revenue strategies from this more general interest in nonprofit revenue streams is the extent to which such activities can be considered to be innovative or pattern setting. However, many authors tend to view any type of earned revenue strategy in this vein as socially entrepreneurial, which has stimulated attention as to how existing nonprofits can become more entrepreneurial through such strategies.

A third theme is similar to the "innovating for social purposes" emphasis described earlier. However, in addition to a focus on the initial development of a socially innovative activity on a limited scale, the processes through which initial innovations are diffused are stressed (Alvord, Brown, & Letts, 2004; Bornstein, 2007). In this vein, there is a particular interest in social ventures that are "scalable" in the sense that they can be widely replicated. For authors stressing this aspect of development, the size and reach of the innovation matters a great deal. In fact, some would argue that in order to be considered as SE, a social innovation must reach a very large scale in which it can be considered socially "transformative" (Alvord, Brown, & Letts, 2004; Bornstein, 2007). This emphasis has become increasingly important in many foundation and development communities, with the idea that social investments should be clearly targeted on interventions that can become large and hence influence substantial numbers of people. For example, Ashoka founder and leading SE proponent Bill Drayton has consistently emphasized scalability in explicating SE as an approach and in making Ashoka funding decisions (Bornstein, 2007; Drayton, 2003).

Finally, I should note that many SE authors focus on the personal characteristics of the social entrepreneur, and they concentrate on elaborating personal characteristics that somehow distinguish social entrepreneurs from other project developers or managers (Bornstein, 2007). As in any social endeavor, leadership characteristics are of obvious importance in determining success, and defining leadership qualities associated with particular management practices or service outcomes may be helpful. Nonetheless, I generally find it much more useful to focus on articulating the central conceptual and implementation features associated with development processes, with the idea that those with the talents and skills best equipped to lead such efforts then can be identified as a second order consideration.[1]

Toward an Operational Social Entrepreneurship Definition

The relative emphasis given to each of the characteristics described in the preceding section varies considerably in the literature. In addition, as in most social change models, the processes described are ideal types that typically are met only in practice. Nonetheless, they serve as prescriptive strategies and as frameworks for assessing the extent to which social actions may be considered as entrepreneurial.

In this spirit, I will synthesize here key components from the previous literature that I believe are most useful in framing SE as a social program development approach; these features also are summarized in Table 4.1. First and foremost, SE should be viewed as a change process that always involves a venture with a predominantly social mission, regardless of the venue in which it is carried out or the particular content of the change. This implies that an initial step in SE development is recognizing a social need or demand and developing a specific mission in response. The ventures so created may be either profit generating or not. However, if profits are made, they must be used to further the social mission as opposed to being passed on to investors; Yunus (2007) has characterized such profit-making entities as "social businesses." This distinguishes SE from corporate philanthropic efforts or from other socially responsible business activities that, although of possible importance to social well-being, essentially are byproducts of more fundamental profit-oriented motives; I consider such approaches under corporate social responsibility in Chapter 3. It also distinguishes SE from profit-oriented start-up ventures by either corporations or individuals, which I consider in Chapter 5 under the rubric of private sustainable development.

TABLE 4.1 PRINCIPAL COMPONENTS OF SOCIAL ENTREPRENEURSHIP
AS A SOCIAL CHANGE PROCESS

- Requires a clearly defined social mission with creation of social value as principal purpose.

  ◦ May be either nonprofit or for profit, but any profits generated must further the social mission.
  ◦ May occur in either international or domestic settings in a variety of organizational venues, including existing agencies and start-ups.
  ◦ The content or subject area of programs is open and thus may involve a wide range of activities.

- The primary change effort, or a component central to its implementation, should be innovative or pattern-setting.
- Emphasizes the application of business principles to the change effort, including:

  ◦ Aggressive opportunity identification, risk assessment, and calculated risk-taking
  ◦ Utilization of sound business practices in program planning and operation
  ◦ Emphasis on sustainability over time
  ◦ Commitment to process and outcome evaluation, with accompanying product or service revision
  ◦ Scalability or replication of initially small-scale start-up

Of course, all social change efforts involve a planned response to perceived social needs, so additional emphases are necessary to distinguish SE. Perhaps most important is the extent to which any initiated change can be considered innovative or pattern-setting; strictly speaking, simple replications of existing practices in new settings are insufficient to qualify as SE. The attempt to apply business principles to social venture creation and management also separates SE from other social change approaches. In particular, SE explicitly draws on business entrepreneurship in its focus on opportunity recognition, assessment, and calculated risk taking for innovative purposes. In addition, there is a consistent emphasis on the need to utilize sound business practices in planning and implementing the social venture in order to maximize current value and sustainability. Developing financial planning procedures to enhance prospects for sustainability is particularly important in this respect. Such planning efforts often include long-term in addition to shorter-term project planning. A commitment to careful assessment of program processes and outcomes also is embraced, consistent with a stated desire for ongoing product or service improvement.

Unlike some scholars, I do not believe that being able to "scale" a social innovation in a transformative manner is necessary for a program to be considered socially entrepreneurial. Many excellent innovations do not reach a widespread socially transformative stage and yet may be extremely valuable and even pattern setting in the jurisdiction in which they are developed and implemented. I therefore prefer to consider scalability as an indicator of the reach and related impact of an SE initiative, but believe it is sufficiently important to be included as an attribute of the approach.

Synthesizing and summarizing the above points, I view social entrepreneurship as an approach in which change agents engage in missions with a purpose of social benefit creation and with a focus on innovation and utilization of business principles in implementation. Like many other definitions of SE previously offered in the literature, this one requires many aspects of interpretation, some of which I have previewed in the preceding discussion. In addition, as with most broad definitions, key features of this one are not absolute in practice but rather may be viewed as variables against which change efforts can be assessed.

Nonetheless, I would argue that the central features outlined here at a minimum are more easily subject to analysis than most SE definitions offered in the literature. In particular, it should be possible to assess whether a mission is primarily socially motivated or not, as well as the extent to which change practices are innovative and engage in commonly identified business practices. This sets the stage for more thoughtful empirical analysis of the costs and benefits of SE as an approach, and in particular to considering whether change agents who frame engagements around SE are more effectual than others.

One final definitional point merits elaboration. First, there has been some attention in the literature to the issue of whether SE is limited to start-up organizations or alternatively can occur in existing organizations.

This issue presents a tricky analytical problem in terms of the unit of analysis for a change effort. Although many of the better known SE case examples pertain to start-up ventures, prescriptive-oriented SE authors often encourage existing organizations to become more entrepreneurial. My perspective is to consider SE at the program level, with *program* broadly conceived to include any well-designed set of activities central to the delivery of benefits to a targeted group. This definition allows the consideration of particular service programs or fundraising activities within existing organizations, such as the development of a new benefit for an already established target group, a new service delivery mechanism, or an innovative revenue generation strategy.

In this sense, the focus should be less on whether an entire organization is entrepreneurial and rather on whether particular programming efforts fall under this rubric. For example, a long-standing agency with well-established service patterns may engage in a new revenue generation strategy that meets the criteria of SE, and as such, this particular component of the agency's work could be considered as socially entrepreneurial. This would not mean, however, that we would view the entire organization as socially entrepreneurial.

These definitional requirements suggest the directions of greatest importance in attempting to more accurately characterize and measure social entrepreneurship. Measuring SE from my perspective suggests a two-stage process. First, a prerequisite is to determine whether an organization or group operates primarily to further a social mission, which usually can be ascertained by the nature of its mission and whether individual profit taking is allowed. Second, the degree to which any entities meeting this baseline criterion can be considered entrepreneurial then can be assessed according to characteristics more generally associated with entrepreneurship, especially in terms of whether change efforts can be considered innovative or pattern setting and whether selected business practices are emphasized in implementation. Of course, both innovation and business practices are multifaceted and continuous in nature, so measurement should not be considered as absolute but rather as a continuum along these dimensions. Thus, a social change effort would be viewed as highly entrepreneurial if it engaged in a primarily social mission and if it was assessed to be innovative in an important aspect of its approach and to emphasize sound business practices in its planning and operations.

THE POLITICAL DEVELOPMENT OF SOCIAL
ENTREPRENEURSHIP INITIATIVES

Although many SE initiatives are established in existing organizations, and so may represent a particular program effort encompassing many workers, more often the literature points to start-up ventures being led by a single individual or small groups. I therefore will focus on the start-up SE case in framing the political development of this approach. The politics of developing entrepreneurial approaches in existing organizations involves similar challenges, except that they typically must include attention to existing organizational dynamics and related decision-making and resource allocation hierarchies.

Figure 4.1 summarizes this developmental approach. In start-up SE ventures, the change agents usually are individuals or very small groups who become interested in a particular problem for various reasons. These change agents then work to clarify the problem and think through alternative strategies for responding. Given the focus on innovation, these initial steps

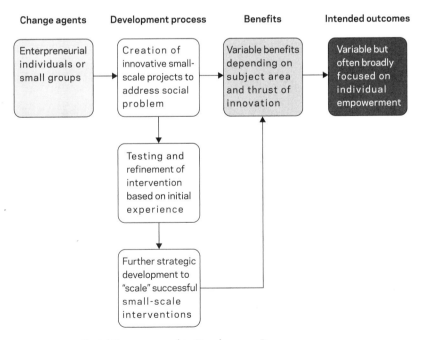

FIGURE 4.1 Social Entrepreneurship Development Process

ideally are characterized by unusually creative thinking about problems and solutions; a common admonition in the field is for change agents to "think outside of the box" as they consider social issues. Thus, in comparison to the other approaches examined in this book, SE emphasizes the process of creating new change ideas to a greater extent—the idea itself is viewed as the principal contribution of many SE initiatives.

Once an idea for responding to a social need has been established, the social entrepreneur ideally will flesh out the behavioral logic associated with it. Because the ideas produced are so variable, there is no particular behavioral logic that can more broadly be said to characterize SE projects. Nonetheless, as in all logic models, the task is to begin by defining the intended outcomes and then to delineate the steps or actions most central to their achievement.

The change agent then must turn to the more concrete implementation of the project, and in these respects, SE mirrors business entrepreneurship quite closely. As with other models, this includes first identifying and recruiting relevant stakeholders essential to model implementation. However, it is notable that many SE start-ups require relatively crude stakeholder development in the initial stages; they often rely on the energy and even private financial resources of their creators, and then branch out in terms of supportive stakeholders after initial development and testing.

The subsequent business of change aspects of implementation again parallel business entrepreneurship quite closely. Although obviously implemented with widely varying dexterity, social entrepreneurs ideally are seen as minimizing costs to extract maximum value for investments, tracking and refining operations based on experience, and as consequently seeking new opportunities to expand or improve their initiative. The main difference between social entrepreneurs and business entrepreneurs in implementing such aggressive business styles again ties back to underlying motives, with the business entrepreneur focused on maximizing profits and the social entrepreneur focused on maximizing social value.

SELECTED SOCIAL ENTREPRENEURSHIP CASE EXAMPLES

Because of the breadth and differing foci of SE as a change approach, presenting some case exemplars should be useful in clarifying its applications. I have selected four examples for this purpose, which will be described briefly and are intended to highlight differing innovative aspects that have gained attention in the literature. The first two of these pertain to start-up initiatives designed to deliver new benefits to previously excluded or underserved groups; these start-ups perhaps best capture the aspect of entrepreneurship in which a determined individual develops an innovative solution to a social problem on a small scale, tests and refines it, and then grows it to a larger scale. The next case exemplifies innovations in a service domain in which considerable activity already was ongoing; the intent of innovation revolves more around improving the manner of service delivery of an existing type of benefit in order to extend service access. Finally, the fourth case focuses on new financing arrangements within an existing entity, with the intent of making service delivery more sustainable and of extending its reach.

Social Entrepreneurship as Innovative New Service Effort

The creation and development of the Grameen Bank in Bangladesh by Muhammad Yunus is perhaps the best-known case example cited by SE proponents. Yunus was an economics professor in Bangladesh who was troubled by the poverty he observed as he traveled to and from work at his university (Yunus, 2007).[2] He thought that many of these poor people could dramatically improve their circumstances if they had access to financial support to start a small business. Yet, poor people could not obtain loans from a bank even if they had a promising business idea, because they were considered bad credit risks.

Yunus found it ironic that the persons who most needed credit to move forward could not obtain it, and he decided to develop strategies for rectifying this problem. He began by lending small amounts of money from his own pocket to poor people so that they could start very small businesses, which commonly are referred to as microenterprises. He charged low interest rates and required no collateral, and he established repayment schedules that were reasonable for recipients. Eventually, he formed the Grameen Bank in 1983 to further this purpose.

Based on his initial experiences, he refined his model to focus on poor women, and also instituted the practice of developing small support groups among borrowers so that peer pressure could be used to improve the likelihood of loan repayment (Yunus, 2007). Because his strategy proved successful on a small scale, he worked to expand it more broadly, incorporating increasingly sophisticated business practices to meet the needs of his growing organization. The Grameen Bank eventually spread across Bangladesh and, by 2007, was operating in 78,000 villages. It had made more than $7 billion in loans to more than 7 million poor people, with 97% of these being poor women. Reported repayment rates have been more than 98%, and the bank has been self-supporting since 1995. In 2006, Yunus was awarded the Nobel Prize for his work. He also has gone on to establish Grameen Phone, which is an innovative attempt to improve access to cell phones by poor women in remote rural areas, as well as other innovative strategies for helping the poor.

The Grameen Bank not only expanded to reach an impressive scale, but it also helped create interest in the phenomenon of financing microenterprise development more broadly. Many other organizations have emerged to provide microfinancing, under both nonprofit and for profit auspices. For example, in 2007, it was estimated that more than 12,000 microfinancing institutions worldwide were providing loans (Swibel, 2007). Yunus's work thus also can be seen as having been very pattern setting in the spirit of innovation emphasized in the SE conceptual literature.

Perhaps illustrating the difficulties associated with growth and sustainability, Grameen Bank came under some criticism as it matured organizationally. First, the repayment rates for Grameen loans have declined over time, and various measures of delinquent loans have risen (Roodman, 2010). For example, repayment rates for all Grameen Bank loans have declined from just over 99% in 2003 to 97.25% in 2013 (Grameen Bank, 2003; 2013). Although still high, repayment rates at slightly lower levels can result in major sustainability problems for microfinance institutions. Second, Yunus became embroiled in conflict with the Bangladesh government, which now owns a 25% share of the bank. The government forced out Yunus as Grameen Bank's managing director in 2011, ostensibly because of age but perhaps also because of political differences (Ahmed, 2012). These recent difficulties notwithstanding, Grameen remains an almost iconic presence in the SE field and certainly exemplifies the creative problem-solving approach on which SE proponents pride themselves.

A second less well-known example of SE as an innovative start-up approach concerns the work of Victoria Khosa in Africa (Bornstein, 2007).[3] Khosa was a nurse who was distressed by the widespread suffering in her community resulting from the acquired immune deficiency syndrome (AIDS) epidemic ravaging Africa, and particularly by the difficulty that those with the disease experienced in getting assistance in their homes. At the same time, she had interactions with young street prostitutes, who were in great danger of becoming infected and of spreading the disease. Khosa believed that the key to moving these young women away from a life on the streets was to develop meaningful alternative employment opportunities, but job prospects in her community were extremely limited.

As she pondered how she might assist these women and the AIDS patients, she was struck by the idea that she could respond to both problems by recruiting and training the street workers to become home care workers. Given her experience as a nurse, she had the capabilities to develop training curricula for home care workers, and she began recruiting small numbers of street workers for her project. She also expanded her efforts by recruiting other community members to become home care workers.

After some initial difficulties, she refined her project and training, and she was successful in recruiting large numbers of workers and clients. She did so without any external financial assistance of note by contributing her own money and by charging clients or family members for services. As her project grew, she recognized the importance of more coherently developing her training materials into a manual, and she did so. Eventually, Khosa's project became well-known to those in the social service community. The government, which was struggling with the AIDS epidemic more widely across the country, learned of her program and eventually modeled similar programs after it.

Yunus and Khosa meet the definition of being social entrepreneurs, and their actions more concretely illustrate several aspects of the previously described SE process. In particular, each of them responded to a very critical social problem in innovative ways, largely by thinking beyond current practice wisdom and by refusing to accept existing stereotypes or limitations. Second, each started on a very small scale, even investing their own money for the sake of testing whether their idea would work. Third, each carefully observed and reflected upon their initial program experience and was flexible in refining their service model based on what they learned. Finally, as they grew confident about the viability of their program model in addressing the social problem they had identified, they worked to expand or "scale up" their programs so that larger numbers of persons in need could be reached.

Social Entrepreneurship as Strategy for Extending New Program Ideas

Although the SE literature most often centers on how change agents identify and then initiate new program ideas, in some cases social entrepreneurs begin with an existing program idea and then work to extend it in new ways. They may do so either by designing strategies for providing an existing benefit idea to new target groups or by substantially altering the pattern of delivery to an existing target group (Alvord, Brown, & Letts, 2004). One way to contrast these two possibilities is to think of the provision of benefits to new target groups as extending the reach or scale of a particular benefit idea, and to consider new benefit patterns to existing groups as extending the impact of change efforts on current recipients. The definitional issue in these "extension" cases revolves around the need to determine whether change efforts are innovative or pattern-setting, as opposed to being merely incremental increases in previous service delivery efforts.

The microfinancing organization Kiva provides a good example of innovating by extending a basic program idea to new audiences, and it is especially useful for discussion here because it builds on Yunus's microenterprise idea.[4] It likewise highlights the value of cross-disciplinary partnerships in SE projects, as well the transformative value of new technology applications.

Jessica Flannery worked for a nongovernmental organization developing case studies on East African villagers who were seeking seed funding for small-scale business projects. Her husband, Matt Flannery, was a software developer. In observing his wife's work, he came to believe that Americans could be convinced to financially support such projects if they could be made aware of their value. But doing so was difficult because of the spatial and cultural gaps between developed world individuals with financial resources and developing world individuals in need of financial capital.

In 2005, they launched Kiva, which posts Internet profiles of low-income individuals or small groups in developing countries that need loans to start or expand small businesses, and which obtains online contributions from persons willing to lend money to these entrepreneurs. Operated as a nonprofit agency, the key innovative features of Kiva are an extensive cross-national network of field partners coupled with creative Internet technology usage.

The process begins with on the groundwork by agencies known as "field partners" in the developing world. Kiva has partnered with 190 such nonprofit organizations in 67 countries; the agencies typically are engaged in developmental and human services work in the geographic areas in which they operate, and so have substantive knowledge of local economic conditions and opportunities. These field partners are responsible for advertising the availability of microloans, screening applications from potential borrowers, developing profiles and taking pictures of borrowers for posting on the Kiva Web site, disbursing loans, and collecting repayments. The field partners charge interest rates on the loans to cover their costs, but neither Kiva nor the individual lenders receive profits from interest payments.

Although these partners make microloans and collect repayments in a manner similar to other microfinance organizations, the innovative aspect of Kiva is how it generates funds to support the loans. The profiles developed by the field partners are edited by volunteers and then posted on the Kiva Web site along with a targeted loan amount. Visitors to the site can review any profile they like and can make donations online; these donations can be for as little as $25. The Web site includes many innovative features to facilitate the process of finding an enterprise to support, such as allowing searches by country, gender, and type of enterprise. For each profile, a viewer is also able to see what portion of the needed loan amount already has been raised.

Once loans have been repaid by the person or small group, lenders can either receive their money back or reinvest it in other microenterprise projects. The site also solicits donations to cover staffing and other overhead costs associated with running the organization. Kiva reports repayment rates of about 99% on more than 541,000 loans to slightly more than one million borrowers. The average loan size is $404. People who visit the Kiva site to make microloans typically provide funding for multiple loans; lenders have averaged slightly more than nine loans during the life of the program.

Kiva thus has taken the fundamental microloan process developed by Yunus and extended its reach through innovative technology and related global linkages. Although all of Yunus's microlending activity focused on Bangladesh, Kiva has been able to reach the poor in many countries. Its other innovative aspect is using the Internet to connect lenders and borrowers through the assistance of field agents and creative Web sites.

Social Entrepreneurship as Innovative Financing Strategy

A final area of SE concerns strategies for financing change efforts, whether the organization initiating them is new or not. Any new change effort has to grapple with how it will secure the funds required for implementation, and this issue often is an essential feature of a new benefit idea. However, the focus here is on how existing change entities try to extend their reach or simply make current operations more sustainable through innovative financing mechanisms. This financing emphasis has been employed prescriptively by SE advocates in arguing that existing nonprofits need to become more entrepreneurial in their fundraising strategies.

The work of Govindappa Venkataswamy and David Green provide an interesting example of how creative financing and related sound business practices can fundamentally extend the reach of a social project. Portrayed in the popular PBS documentary, *The New Heroes*, Venkataswamy is a doctor in India who in his later years decided to focus on performing cataract surgery for the poor. Cataracts can result in blindness if untreated, and this is a very common problem among the poor in India. Dr. Venkataswamy opened the Avarind hospital for this purpose, which in its first year performed about 5,000 surgeries.

David Green is an American with a business background who observed and was inspired by Dr. Venkataswamy's work while visiting India. He discovered that the costs of the replacement lenses implanted during surgery were very high, and that costs could be reduced substantially if the lenses were self-manufactured. He subsequently convinced Dr. Venkataswamy to partner with him in opening a lens factory.

In 1992, Green established Aurolab as a nonprofit manufacturing facility for this purpose. In addition to lenses, the factory produced sutures, pharmaceuticals, and eyeglasses. Aurolab was able to sell lens for $4 to $5, as compared to common prices of more than $100 charged by U.S. manufacturers. With the lower cost lenses, Dr. Venkataswamy was able to substantially extend the number of persons who could afford the surgery.

However, even with these radically reduced lens prices, the very poor still could not afford surgery. Venkataswamy and Green consequently developed an innovative pricing strategy to further extend the number of surgeries. In particular, Dr. Venkataswamy began charging for the surgeries according to ability to pay, making a profit from those who are relatively well-off and reinvesting these funds in free or very low-cost surgeries for the poor. With the advent of the cheaper lens and this differential pricing strategy, Avarind eye hospitals now perform more than two million surgeries a year using products manufactured by Aurolab. At the same time, Green has extended his product distributions to many other doctors and eye care facilities and now manufactures an estimated 10% of the world lens supply. He also has branched out to develop other low-cost products to assist the poor with other maladies; his current work is focused on the development of low-cost hearing aids.

ASSESSING SOCIAL ENTREPRENEURSHIP AS A SOCIAL CHANGE STRATEGY

The preceding discussion hopefully conveys the great enthusiasm SE proponents bring forth in advocating for SE as a social change strategy. The positive support expressed for SE includes wealthy entrepreneurs and related foundations, business academics, and a growing number of on-the-ground social change agents; media accounts likewise have reported many SE change efforts in glowing terms. Further, many of the ideas central to the approach increasingly have been incorporated into related change strategies, such as the attempts by many foundations to consider and then measure the sustainability and reach of the programs they support.

Despite this relatively unfettered enthusiasm, empirical support for the efficacy of SE as a change strategy is essentially absent. Many cases put forth as SE exemplars have provided impressive accounts of individual project success. However, in addition to the wildly differing definitional issues noted earlier, it is impossible to determine the extent to which success is based on model features versus other factors. Discussions of the potential strengths and limitations of SE as change strategy likewise are undeveloped, and literature only has begun to put forward important research questions that may be pertinent is advancing knowledge in this respect. I turn next to discussing some of the conditions that are most conducive to the effective implementation of SE as and, in turn, to an assessment of the approach.

Conditions and Resource Needs for Successful Social Entrepreneurship

Because SE tends to be so amorphously defined, the conditions and resource needs associated with its successful application vary. I therefore will focus here on resource needs and conditions in the start-up SE context, because this is the aspect of SE that has generated the most attention and that is most developmental in nature.

From a needed resources or skills perspective, three features stand out in the literature on SE project development. First, as previously mentioned, the literature is replete with studies that attempt to explicate the personality characteristics of social entrepreneurs and of entrepreneurs more generally. Among the more commonly mentioned traits are persistence, passion, and a propensity for calculated risk taking (Llewellyn & Wilson, 2003; Nga & Shamugnathan, 2010). The underlying fabric holding these characteristics together is the notion that innovative new projects require a certain level of risk taking to generate high rewards, and that risk taking requires both the passion to stimulate it and the persistence to overcome likely obstacles.

If it is to meet the definitional characteristic of being innovative or pattern setting, successful entrepreneurship likewise requires a certain level of creativity. Especially in new project development, social entrepreneurs must be able to examine problems and solutions in fundamentally new ways, and a sense of creativity is a great asset in this respect. It therefore is not surprising that some university-based entrepreneurship programs include teaching related to creativity (see, for example, Program for Innovation, Creativity, and Entrepreneurship, 2013, and Center for Innovation, Creativity, and Entrepreneurship, 2013).

These personal characteristics suggest qualities likely to be associated with the success of a person in creating new projects, but there is a second related technical side that appears important as well. Because social entrepreneurs typically operate fairly independently and begin on a small scale, a keen sense of many aspects of business development and of planning is extremely valuable. Typically, resources are not available to allow widespread specialization at early stages, so the social entrepreneur requires good basic skills in all of the areas of project development. These include common business skills such as market assessment and product marketing, short-term and longer-term strategic planning, management information system development, financial management, and using data to analyze performance and improve operations.

Third, the use of new technology appears heavily embedded in the operations of many SE start-ups, and the social entrepreneurs who create them often are very skilled in new technology applications. In fact, clever new technology use quite often is at the core of what constitutes a particular project as innovative, as is the case with the previously discussed Kiva. It is unclear whether this is due to an increase in technologically trained people engaging in social missions, or if it stems from passionate and creative people seeking new solutions from as many directions as possible. But, at any rate, emerging information and other new technologies are creating possibilities for novel benefit creation, and hence are a critical resource for social entrepreneurs.

Although this discussion points to some characteristics and resources that are conducive to successful SE project development, one of the more desirable features of SE is that the cost of entry into such endeavors can be relatively low. Many projects noted in the literature began as very small-scale start-ups with limited funding, as both the Yunus and Khosa cases illustrate. The common genesis of many of these projects is for a single person or small group to initiative a project on a very small scale, to test and refine it, and then to eventually scale it to greater heights if successful. This allows for more sophisticated resource development strategies after success already has been established in an area.

Given the focus on small-scale start-up and individualistic innovation, the literature on SE contains relatively little emphasis on macro level factors that may encourage or discourage SE initiatives. However, two points are worth noting in this respect. First, the broader interest in SE as an approach has led foundations to be important in terms of seeding many SE efforts; compared to the other market-based approaches, the foundation environment has been particularly important to SE development. Second, and perhaps not surprisingly, SE advocates commonly speak less of any possible external stimulants to SE development and more about creating an environment that lacks developmental impediments. In particular, consistent with its entrepreneurial focus, SE proponents tend to emphasize the importance of not having to face bureaucratic constraints in developing start-up initiatives, such as rigid licensing rules or externally imposed reporting (Dees, 2007). For example, governmental funding streams and related bureaucratic structures sometimes are seen as discouraging innovation, as well as creating a relatively closed system in which small-scale experimentation is difficult.

Governments in turn are encouraged by SE proponents either to minimize regulations or to provide more open or experimental funding streams to encourage SE development (Dees, 2007). However, as has been noted by DeLeon and Denhardt (2000), doing so often creates difficult tensions in governmental organizations and even in large nongovernmental bureaucracies. That is, these organizations often have fairly stringent accountability demands, and allowing relatively unfettered development approaches with little monitoring carries the risk of creating difficulties regarding agency actions. This could occur, for example, if providing relatively open funding streams resulted in a series of uncoordinated and poorly related program initiatives, and the agency in turn lacked the ability to report on any coherent efforts or aggregated impact.

The Strengths of Social Entrepreneurship as a Change Approach

Despite my contention that SE remains largely untested as a change strategy, I do believe it has had some meaningful effects in the social program development world. In particular, despite its frustrating imprecision, SE has served as a useful metaphor in evoking enthusiasm for tackling difficult social problems, and it has done so in a manner that brings new thinking and sound business practices to program development endeavors. In particular, it has helped foster broader public attention on social development. It likewise has created new attention to social development in the business world, and in many university programs that train future business leaders.

The image of the individual entrepreneur engaged in social problem-solving has considerable appeal to many audiences, and people often find stories about creative individuals engaging in such endeavors to be highly stimulating. Many likewise embrace the notion of well-off individuals such as Bill Gates using their wealth and business skills to bring new solutions to social issues. It therefore is not surprising that the work of these individuals has generated considerable press attention to various projects and in turn has fostered discussion even among lay audiences about beneficial social projects and how best to conduct them. That these discussions often lack deeper programmatic or process implementation substance is secondary in this respect—the point is that they may generate new energy among those otherwise not so disposed. This may inspire greater donations of funding and expertise by people well-positioned to do so.

The growth and dissemination of social entrepreneurship perspectives has been particularly notable among two sectors with the potential to seriously impact social development. First, the aforementioned attention by those with business skills has been fairly profound. It has been evidenced by the rapid growth of business literature examining various aspects of SE, as well as by the development of SE courses or even full SE programs in many business schools. This may be especially important in that those with business skills often have been skeptical of social endeavors, because of perspectives that such programs are poorly designed or managed. Second, the SE lexicon has likewise grown substantially in the foundation and nonprofit worlds, so that the term and selected SE process features have gained considerable currency.

This growing attention to SE would not be particularly important if it did not translate into significant differences with respect to how programs are operated. But it may well have that potential through supplying more business-trained personnel to social programs and by stimulating greater attention to business practices in nonprofits and foundations. This may result in substantive improvements in many projects, because the foundation and nonprofit sectors have long been characterized as frequently suffering from poor management. Developmental and execution failures in this respect run the gamut of functions needed to conceptualize and implement a program idea, including faulty program logic as well as weaknesses in marketing, information system development, sustainable fundraising, evaluation, and in stakeholder communication.

Many of the process features previously discussed in my definition of SE can improve implementation practices among those with good program ideas. Thus, I see SE as having the potential to serve as a normative model for guiding the implementation of many social development projects. Such guidance may be especially valuable to relatively inexperienced change agents who wish to develop and implement a new project at the ground level. Operating a nonprofit agency or other social endeavor requires competently carrying out most of the same functions required to run a business. By adapting principles and procedures that have proven to be effective in the establishment and management of businesses, SE offers an approach to development that can enhance the assessment of program ideas and the creation of sound agency operational practices.

Another potential strength of SE is its potential as a bottoms-up program development approach. Interestingly, this feature often is provided limited attention in SE descriptions in the literature, because it is lost in the focus on entrepreneurial risk taking and sound business implementation. Yet one is struck in reading SE case descriptions by how many social entrepreneurs initiate their projects after thoughtful interactions with target groups. More generally, this feature is characteristic of many business models in terms of fully understanding the customers to whom one is expecting to sell products. However, it often has negative connotations among change agents who reflect on business practices, because the nature of this interaction is viewed as exploitive.

When change agents adapt "understand your market" business principles to social missions, which should be standard practice in well-implemented SE models, they essentially are conducting needs assessments with target groups. To the extent that these interactions involve recipients of proposed benefits, which the literature reveals they often do, the basic SE developmental approach tends to dovetail nicely with more traditional human service professional concerns with involving recipients in developmental change efforts. It is especially consonant with social work ideas about empowering recipients through meaningful involvement in social change processes and delivery strategies. I therefore believe that this is a naturally occurring but inadequately articulated facet of many if not most SE change initiatives, especially those that take the form of small start-ups. I will talk further about this phenomenon of bottoms-up recipient engagement in Chapter 5 when discussing private sustainable development, which embraces such interactions more systematically and explicitly.

Finally, within the aforementioned attention to business operations fostered by SE, the focus on innovative financing mechanisms is especially interesting. As previously mentioned, some SE proponents who concentrate on the sustainability or financial aspects of social projects argue that market-oriented financing is at the heart of SE. From this perspective, the extent to which a project is entrepreneurial is heavily tied to whether most or all of its funding comes through commercial or other market exchanges.

Commercial or other market-oriented funding schemes are seen as desirable largely because they are argued to be more sustainable over time, and also because they provide project leaders with greater discretion concerning how revenues are in turn expended. That is, funds from sources such as donors, insurance companies, and the government may come with specific reciprocal obligations, which may limit decision-making discretion and create additional work in terms of reporting and other accountability demands. Such funding sources also may be inconsistent, because they are subject to political and economic factors that extend well beyond the control of change agents. Another possible advantage pertains more narrowly to requiring user fees or other customer payments in return for benefits; it is argued that services in these instances remain more consistent with customer needs. Fees are seen as creating a better forum for client-based accountability demands, in that one who has to pay for a benefit may be more likely to advocate for certain quality aspects than one who is receiving it without cost.

I find the SE literature pertaining to innovative financing strategies to be potentially thought-provoking and useful for change agents struggling to develop sound financing strategies. However, I likewise should note that the actual extent to which market-based financing schemes foster either greater sustainability or greater service responsiveness to consumer demands is an empirical issue upon which there has been little study. Although these are interesting conceptual arguments, it also should be pointed out that there is nothing inherently more stable in market-driven approaches than in other financing mechanisms. For example, markets often change dramatically for reasons that extend beyond product need or quality, and the failure of many private market entities should serve as a constant reminder of this. This problem is even greater in social endeavors, where by definition SE entities have a social mission that may deflect from the proprietary focus viewed as critical to operating successful commercial endeavors. More fundamentally, an important rationale for providing social benefits is to correct for the inability of private markets to deliver such benefits, especially because those in the greatest need are unable to pay. It therefore may seem a bit odd to glorify the types of delivery mechanisms often associated with causing the need for government intervention. However, as mentioned in Chapter 1 and frequently discussed in economics and politics (see, for example, Lindblom, 2001; Stiglitz, 2007), the modern challenge generally is to ascertain the particular functions in which markets provide value, and then to structure exchanges accordingly.

The Limitations of Social Entrepreneurship

One of the fundamental problems of SE to date has been that the enthusiasm of its proponents has deflected attention from careful assessment of its limitations. This of course is characteristic of many new phenomena that generate academic and popular attention, and so should not negatively reflect on the approach itself. However, more balanced assessments do suggest that SE probably is at best a limited and very uneven approach for promoting sustainable change on behalf of the most disadvantaged. The potential limitations of SE occur at both the individual project and at the more macro or aggregate levels of assessing social change. I focus on the aggregate level because I believe this is where SE limitations are most vexing. However, important problems at the individual project level first should be noted.

The prescriptive practices outlined in SE models appear to be sound general developmental advice for most social program efforts. However, the difficulty in assessing SE projects at the micro level basically is two-fold. First, many of these same SE practices are employed at one level or another in projects that do not portray themselves as SE. Further, given the improved teaching on technical planning in social science and related professional programs, as well as more rigorous requirements in this respect by foundations and other funders, the push toward better business planning and management across all types of social programs is likely to proliferate. It therefore becomes difficult to assess if good program results are related to SE as a social development model, as opposed to more general and related changes that are occurring in the nonprofit world. Second, as discussed earlier, the SE concept has been so loosely defined that it has been difficult to clearly determine what qualifies as an SE project, let alone measure the effectiveness of an SE project or the components that may drive success.

Some may argue that this is splitting hairs as long as agencies improve their level of business practices, and in turn that these practices result in overall improvements in social benefit delivery. However, general positive findings on the importance of sound business practices are likely to obscure which features of program development really make a difference, and particularly whether or not the more entrepreneurial aspects emphasized in SE are critical to better performance. There is no easy way out of this dilemma in terms of assessing the relative effectiveness of SE, except as already has been argued to better define and measure its central attributes. This includes not only more rigorously measuring SE program outcomes and comparing them to other program models, but measuring the effects of SE program components.

From a more aggregate social development perspective, perhaps the most troubling limitation of SE concerns the unknown nature of benefits that may flow from its collective application. That is, as with many voluntary efforts, the issues of focus and related social program outputs depend on the inclinations of those who choose to volunteer. On the one hand, this may result in attention to a rich diversity of social problems, and the literature on SE cases surely reflects this. In addition, it is difficult to reduce the vast array of social problems afflicting the world to an easily definable set of priorities for social action, and therefore a diversity of interests and approaches can foster experimentation across a range of issues. To the extent that such experimentation leads to successful interventions upon which to build, the highly decentralized developmental approach characteristic of SE can in theory lead to substantial progress on a host of social issues.

However, the types of social benefits that will result from SE efforts are very unpredictable and scattered. This is true not only in the short run, given the distribution of any set of social entrepreneurs operating at a given point in time, but also over time as the interests of social entrepreneurs may change and as they move in and out of social missions. There are three related and critical distributional issues in this respect, which I will refer to as unpredictable substantive content, uncertainty of reach, and questionable targeting effectiveness.

By unpredictable substantive content, I mean that the aggregate output of all social entrepreneurs in various substantive areas will depend almost solely on their individual interests and proclivities. The distribution of these outputs across subject areas is likely to be very broad and to reflect the diverse interests, experiences, and talents of social entrepreneurs. This obviously can result in considerable attention to some substantive areas and likewise to relative neglect of other important issues. Further, the coordination of attention even within a particular subject area will be limited, because individuals pursue their own favored strategies.

By the term "reach," I mean the extent to which a particular benefit is available across geographic areas and to defined target groups. A common problem of small-scale start-ups and voluntary efforts more generally is that they do well in one particular setting but then do not grow to serve larger audiences. Especially when a social problem is widespread in a population and scattered across many geographic areas, the failure to disseminate successful program ideas more broadly may be criticized on effectiveness and efficiency grounds. Yet voluntary strategies such as SE typically lack the inclination or the broad geographic embeddedness needed to push successful innovations to new areas or audiences, and like many small business entrepreneurs, social entrepreneurs may be very geographically centered and not inclined to enter new jurisdictions.

SE actually may perform better than many voluntary efforts in terms of disseminating good program ideas, because increasing the number of persons served and related social impact is a stated objective of many SE scholars and practitioners. This normative concern generally is referred to as "scaling," and involves first testing and refining a small-scale program to demonstrate effectiveness and then aggressively moving the tested program to new sites to serve broader audiences. This is akin to small businesses, such as Starbucks or Kentucky Fried Chicken, starting small and then using marketing and other rational analyses to expand to new markets. Some of the more prominent funders of SE, such as Ashoka, in fact include an assessment of scalability in making funding decisions on new projects because they ultimately are concerned about the reach of programs they fund. In addition, some excellent examples of SE programs with impressive scaling effects have been described (Alvord, Brown, & Letts, 2004; Crutchfield & Grant, 2008; Elkington & Hartigan, 2008), and the emphasis on transformative or pattern setting innovations similarly suggests that SE efforts may result in changes that have extensive reach (Light, 2008).

Having said this, the problem of reach remains substantial in most SE projects, and there appear to have been no published studies that examine the consistency, timing, or ultimate reach of SE scaling efforts. In the absence of research on these and related issues, the promise of SE in terms of scaling must be considered to be based much more on rhetoric and selected positive case examples than on more rigorous research evidence. Further, even if scaling is found to occur at substantial levels, its particular geographical emphases will be subject to the individual idiosyncrasies of countless social entrepreneurs. Unlike governments or related authority structures with geographic-based scopes of responsibility, social entrepreneurs are free agents who can flow their resources or efforts anywhere they desire and anywhere they have the capability. This can lead to creative expansion to reach new populations in some cases, but there is relatively little impetus to do so beyond altruism or ego; the institutional drivers that facilitate expansion of governmental programs simply are lacking in most instances, as is the profit motive instrumental to driving growth in for-profit entities.

Finally, the extent to which SE activities in the aggregate will distribute a benefit to those segments of a population in greatest need also is highly questionable. Although many important SE examples such as the Grameen Bank indicate that SE programs often do target program activities toward the very disadvantaged, the targeting practices of SE programs more generally are unknown and difficult to assess. This is of concern because there are good reasons to suspect that SE targeting performance will be uneven at best. For example, the emphasis on creation of successful business models and the initial need for sustainable start-ups may skew program efforts toward groups with moderate problems rather than focusing on the most disadvantaged, due to factors such as the relative ability of better-off clients to pay for services or the greater ease of serving people with relatively modest presenting problems. This problem corresponds closely to what is often referred to in the social service literature as "creaming," which refers to the fact that social service providers at times have perverse incentives to attend to relatively better-off clients or to those that are easier to treat successfully.

Of course, unpredictable substantive content, uncertainty of reach, and questionable targeting effectiveness are not unique to SE, but rather are concerns of any development approach. As such, it may be argued that empirical investigations can meaningful assess SE performance against other development models along each of these dimensions. I agree that this is a useful direction in assessing all development approaches, and while difficult, advancing research in this respect would be very helpful.

Nonetheless, a more fundamental problem with SE, as with other voluntary approaches, concerns the extent to which SE development may or may not be reflective of broader social values about needed areas of social change—and how decisions regarding prioritizing needs should be made. Because atomistic social entrepreneurs control the ideas and resources in most SE renditions, an SE dominated system would be one in which broader societal perceptions regarding the most pressing problems and needs could easily be overlooked. Suppose, for example, that among those predisposed to engage in SE, a highly disproportionate share had a parent with Alzheimer's disease. Assuming that the subject of engagement for these social entrepreneurs was heavily influenced by personal experience, it is likely that investments related to Alzheimer's would be great. This would be positive for those interested in and affected by this disease, but might come at the expense of other problems of more pressing societal interest.

The extent to which this is a problem in practice is partially an empirical one that depends on how closely the investment choices and efforts of social entrepreneurs correspond to broader social values. However, even if distributional impacts were determined to reasonably reflect those of society, they may very well occur through a process that is not especially participatory or democratic in its developmental character. This is not a trivial concern, because the process of selecting areas of social investment itself has considerable value in democratic societies in terms of aggregating social preferences; simply turning this process over to a set of individuals acting on their own inclinations is not at all satisfying in terms of democratic theory.

To the extent that SE remains totally voluntary, SE enthusiasts may counter that investments are over and above what is provided through governments and other collective means, and so more democratic decision-making processes should not be a particular concern. However, SE proponents often argue that SE should be the preferred approach to collective social investment (Easterly, 2006). In this instance, the distributional effects across subject areas become very important, as do the levels of societal involvement in selecting the topics of primary developmental interest. Similarly, if SE activities tend to be used as arguments for a less involved public sector, or as a reason not to tax the income or estates of the well-off, it seems reasonable that one should be concerned about distributional impacts and societal involvement.

Free market enthusiasts also may argue that, following economic principles, social entrepreneurs will respond to the problem areas of greatest need, just as business entrepreneurs respond to economic market signals. If the market mechanism worked well in this way, over time social investments would tend to flow to the subject areas and places where they were most needed. However, as SE texts have pointed out, the absence of market signals is among the most fundamental differences between business entrepreneurship and SE (Wei-Skillern, Austin, Leonard, & Stevenson, 2007), so there is no reason to believe that market signals will be effective in ascertaining social needs. Similarly, even a casual reading of the SE literature suggests that personal background, experiences, and place of residence or professional operation often have tremendous influence on the investment choices made by social entrepreneurs.

Another difficulty in promoting SE as a broad-based development approach rests on more fundamental criticisms regarding whether societies should encourage systems in which well-off individuals are allowed to accumulate vast resources and then are glamorized if they decide to redistribute them. This of course is a deeply rooted and more basic criticism of capitalist systems and their related taxation and redistributional policies. It nonetheless has been given new life by those who criticize SE and philanthrocapitalism.

This is an important and complex argument with many facets, but I think two aspects of it are especially provocative. The first relates to the possible motivations of many social entrepreneurs. Critics contend that social entrepreneurs often make huge profits in the private sector that may involve considerable societal exploitation and negative business practices (Edwards, 2008; 2010). Subsequent SE efforts in turn may be viewed as driven by attempts to gain societal approval or at least to diminish societal approbation related to the profit-making activities that generated the fortunes upon which the SE efforts depend. This criticism is comparable at the individual level to what has been referred to as "greenwashing" or "cleanwashing" at the corporate level, in which corporations are viewed as contributing to environmental or other "socially responsible" causes primarily to deflect attention from socially irresponsible production practices.

A related point is that SE efforts headed by the well-off sometimes are viewed as taking on a paternalistic character. That is, those who have made considerable money and then choose to spend it on social causes are seen as using their financial standing to unduly influence social decision making (Edwards, 2008). One could argue, of course, that any charitable spending by the well-off could be subject to such charges, but in this case, high levels of expenditure and high levels of involvement in decision making ironically seem to fuel this charge.

Finally, as with other forms of voluntary development, a focus on SE arguably may serve to deflect attention from more fundamental social problems that SE is not well equipped to address. Even thoughtful SE proponents often acknowledge that the amount of social investment generated through SE efforts pales in comparison to social needs, and that government involvement is critical in achieving the scale of effort needed for meaningful social change (see, for example, Bishop & Green, 2008, Chapter 5). Yet, especially to the extent that SE efforts are glamorized by the media or others, the public may feel that problems are being adequately addressed through such voluntary efforts. In addition, the question again arises as to the nature of concerns that SE is most likely to address. If SE focuses mostly on minimizing the surface problems or harmful effects of a more fundamentally flawed governmental or economic system, it may improperly focus attention on the consequences rather than the causes of social ills. The tendency of many SE advocates to divorce themselves from any connection to governments only serves to elevate this concern.

SUMMARY

The rapid growth in attention to SE in the last 20 years has been an extraordinary phenomenon in social change academic and practice circles. The infectious manner in which it has captured the imaginations of many change agents, media and foundation representatives, and community members has been useful in extending public interest on a host of social issues. It also has served to inspire a growing cadre of social change agents from outside the social sciences, especially those with business experience or training.

From a substantive perspective, SE development has been most important in challenging change agents to think innovatively in developing responses to seemingly intractable problems, as opposed to simply laboring within the confines of existing approaches or working to incrementally extend traditional change models. The attention SE has provided in promoting and thinking through strategies for small-scale start-up development and testing, as well as in refining and scaling up these efforts, likewise has been welcome. Attention to creative fundraising methods is another contribution of this approach.

These contributions, and the promise of SE more generally, are notable. However, one of the central limitations of writing on this approach to date has been a tendency to inflate claims of effectiveness and reach. The empirical basis for claims on SE impact as an approach remains extremely weak, and it often is difficult to disentangle hype from actual programmatic accomplishments in reviewing this literature. This probably is partially due to the newness of the field and the genuine enthusiasm of SE proponents.

But be that as it may, SE clearly has reached a developmental stage where more careful attempts to document and analyze its successes and limitations are sorely needed.

Another limitation in the SE arena is a tendency for its proponents to view it as the end-all of development efforts. This inclination often hints at the naïveté of SE change agents and scholars, especially when SE is couched as a replacement for governmental attention to social concerns. SE remains most notable as a small-scale and highly decentralized approach for encouraging social change and, in this respect, has much to offer in terms of innovative thinking and in the testing and refinement of new program ideas. Emphasizing these strengths, and attending to the limitations just mentioned, will be critical to continuing to develop and understand SE as a change model.

5

Private Sustainable Development

AMONG THE DEVELOPMENT approaches discussed in this book, probably none embraces capitalistic principles as openly or as enthusiastically as what I will refer to as "private sustainable development" (PSD). Although this term has been used to represent a variety of strategies in the development literature, I will use it to refer broadly to strategies designed to encourage the establishment or improved productive capacity of small-scale low-income businesses, or to create and distribute basic products targeted on poor consumers.

This approach differs from corporate social responsibility (CSR) in that it is not oriented to changing the manner in which corporations produce or distribute their current line of goods. Like social entrepreneurship (SE), PSD emphasizes the development of innovative products and services for disadvantaged groups, especially the poor. However, unlike the altruistic and nonprofit-seeking motives characteristic of SE, PSD begins with a profit-making assumption—that it is possible to make money by developing products and services for the poor. PSD also is more narrowly focused on poor persons in the developing world, and as such centers on strategies for improving consumptive and productive opportunities for such persons.

What characterizes PSD as a social development approach, as opposed to simply an unintended side benefit of the more general drive for profit generation, is its intentionality with respect to developing products and services for or by the least well-off. In this sense, the approach is fundamentally different from the movement of existing corporations or businesses into low-income areas to produce existing products more cheaply by taking advantage of lower wage rates, tax incentives, or other cost advantages (DeWinter, 2001; Harrison & Scorse, 2010).

Although there are many variants of PSD, I will focus here on three that have received considerable recent attention from a low-income social development perspective. The first of these, which has been referred to as "bottom of the pyramid" (BOP) development, focuses on encouraging corporations and other business persons to develop products for low-income markets, especially in the developing world. It does so based on the premise that such product development can both be profitable for businesses and advantageous to the well-being of very low-income consumers.

The second approach instead centers on helping low-income persons become business owners through the stimulation of very small businesses known as "microenterprises." This approach, which has been made famous by Muhammad Yunus through the development of the Grameen Bank, actually is somewhat of a hybrid model. As discussed in Chapter 4, micro-enterprise development often has been described as an SE approach at the aggregate level, in that initial development through microfinancing owed much to social entrepreneurs like Yunus in providing primarily altruistic economic assistance to the poor for the financing of microenterprises. However, other microenterprise developments have featured a profit-making financing orientation (Bhatt and Tang, 2001; Cull, Demirgüç-Kunt, & Morduch, 2010), and at the individual business level, microenterprises are very small-scale indigenous business operations. Thus, aside from those microenterprise start-up financing strategies that rely on nonprofit funding pools, the street level development strategy falls more within the rubric of private sustainable development. It differs from the BOP model primarily in its emphasis on the creation of small businesses by indigenous entrepreneurs, as opposed to the creation of products by larger corporations or other outsiders for poor residents.

A third PSD approach, which also has intersections with SE, focuses on developing and producing products that have the primary intent of improving the capabilities of small-scale developing world producers, often through the use of improved production technologies. This approach is not consistently labeled or discussed in the literature, and many examples of it are described as SE. However, I view it as sufficiently important and distinct to discuss separately, although acknowledging that some may consider it simply as a form of SE. I use the term indigenous technology creation (ITC), although I should note this is my own title and that cases I use to exemplify its principles may employ other broad labels. Its emphasis is well-articulated by Paul Polak (2009) in his book *Out of Poverty*, as well as in many other case examples of technology development. Like BOP and microenterprise development, ITC embraces capitalism as the road to prosperity for the poor in the developing world. However, it differs from BOP in its focus on developing productive capacities rather than consumption-based products, particularly with respect to technology-oriented aids that can improve productivity. It also is distinct from microenterprise in its attention to thinking about technology aids that are broadly needed and can be widely replicated, as opposed to merely envisioning how financing will allow poor persons to be more productive given their own ideas and proclivities.

These three approaches are held together by their focus on profit making and belief in the power of private market systems to advance the well-being of the poor. However, the stated or implied behavioral dynamics and strategic development processes are distinct to each approach. I consequently will present each separately, and then will discuss some of their comparative strengths and limitations. Before doing so, it is worth briefly highlighting some important general debates concerning the merits of profit-making approaches in social development.

PROFIT MAKING AND FREE MARKET CAPITALISM IN DEVELOPMENT

The virtues and deficits of relatively unfettered free market capitalism in aiding or limiting the well-being of the poor in developing societies have long been debated. Promoters of "market fundamentalism" have argued that private capitalistic investments are the key to providing the jobs and products necessary to move poorly developed communities forward (Lal, 2006; Friedman, 2000; Hart, 2005; Soros, 2008). Others contend that private development of a sufficient magnitude is unlikely to occur without governments leading development, which may include providing capitalists with incentives to enter relatively disadvantaged markets (Evans, 1995; Kohli, 2005; Stiglitz, 1998). This concern has provided the intellectual impetus for tax abatements or other government economic development policies, and also has fueled the development strategies of many international organizations.

Critics contend that the profit-making focus of most private development efforts often fosters the exploitation of disadvantaged community residents, who lack competitive alternatives for jobs or product purchases (Chua, 2003; Midgley, 1997; Stiglitz, 2007). Subsidization of such development therefore may result at best in relatively minor individual and community benefits; at worst, it may take advantage of poor residents to build profits for unscrupulous investors. It likewise has been argued that if developmental stimulus interventions are not sensitive to local practices and cultures, they may distort more naturally occurring and responsive indigenous development (Escobar, 1997; Pareto & McLean, 2010). The sustainability of subsidizing private development in low-income communities similarly has been questioned because investors continually are driven to maximize profits, and therefore are prone to exit developing areas after subsidies end or profit-making opportunities subside (Korten, 2001). In many cases, this creates bad feelings and dashed expectations in poor communities when seemingly promising development efforts wane as investors exit after initial profit maximization. Furthermore, the benefits emanating from outside assistance in developing countries often have been argued not to flow sufficiently to those most in need, resulting in what Midgley (1997) has characterized as "distorted development."

The PSD approaches considered here are not immune from any of these criticisms. However, PSD differs substantially from traditional private global development efforts that center on employing the poor solely to produce cheap goods for developed world consumers. Rather, PSD emphasizes providing jobs, technology, and productive capacity that result in goods and services for developing world consumers. I turn next to a more detailed description of each of these PSD approaches.

BOTTOM OF THE PYRAMID DEVELOPMENT

Many interesting examples of BOP development can be found in the literature on development, suggesting a bottoms-up etiology of this approach. However, the most influential intellectual articulation of the BOP approach has been presented by business professor C. K. Prahalad, principally in the book *Fortune at the Bottom of the Pyramid* (Prahalad, 2005).[1] This work created a basic framework upon which other BOP variations have built or refined, so I will begin by describing Prahalad's characterization of BOP development before considering some important variations that have evolved from his work.

The pyramid described by Prahalad refers to the income distribution and related purchasing power of the world's population. As a pyramid suggests, world income distribution is highly skewed, with smaller numbers of people with very high incomes at the top and a broad base of the world's poor—about four billion people—at the bottom of the pyramid. Many subsequent renditions of BOP development have viewed the term "bottom" as somewhat pejorative or condescending to the poor, and consequently have instead referred to the "base" of the pyramid. Nonetheless, the emphasis on product development for these persons, who have incomes of no more than two dollars per day, is consistent regardless of the terminology employed.

Prahalad argues that corporations and other capitalists traditionally focus on production for the relatively small number of consumers at the top of the pyramid, based on the assumption that profits are maximized by obtaining high returns on each unit sold. This drives a production process centered on higher-end or luxury goods, and likewise typically fosters considerable attention to style and other nonfunctional features in product design. In terms of global development, this production focus has promoted models in which capitalists primarily seek global expansion to find cheaper labor pools to produce goods for the more well-off. For example, the well-known multinational corporation ventures into China, Vietnam, and other developing countries to produce goods for faraway developed world consumers personifies the global impact of top of the pyramid production.

Although top of the pyramid production tendencies may lead to labor exploitation in some low-income communities, Prahalad contends that the traditional critique of capitalistic exploitation of poor communities is largely misplaced. Rather, the more fundamental problem from his perspective is that capitalists ignore poor consumers in their decision making about product development, and in so doing strip them of access to products. Producers do so largely because of the aforementioned emphasis on profit per unit thinking.

Prahalad consequently argues that a key strategy for improving the well-being of the poor is to get business interests actively involved in poor markets. He contends that it is possible to do so because of the very large numbers of untapped consumers who reside at the bottom of the pyramid. This allows the possibility of making reasonable profits by selling high volumes of goods with low per unit price margins, as opposed to depending on lower volume but higher per unit profit margins. This can be accomplished by clearly focusing on basic product functionality, coupled with paying careful attention to the financial resources available to low-income consumers and to their related purchasing needs. Though not characterized as such by Prahalad, this essentially is an extension of the approach of Walmart and other corporations that have developed high volume, lower cost product alternatives throughout the developed world. However, it differs in its focus on products for bottom of the pyramid consumers, whose incomes are far below the income ranges on which these high volume corporations have concentrated.

From a social development standpoint, the most interesting aspect of Prahalad's approach is its emphasis on a specific process of product development, which involves close interactions between capitalists and poor consumers. In particular, Prahalad assumes that the poor are intelligent consumers who have a clear understanding about their basic product needs. In fact, if capitalists and the broader public at times view the poor as irresponsible or uninformed with respect to the purchases they make, this results less from the irrationality of the poor than from the limited understanding by outsiders of their unique circumstances and context.

Prahalad therefore argues that if capitalists are to develop products that have a reasonable chance of succeeding in the lowest income markets, they need to work closely with poor consumers to identify their needs, resource levels, purchasing practices, and other consumer behavior related issues. This requires extensive interaction and information exchange between producers and consumers. In an increasingly sophisticated world of market identification and data-driven decision making regarding product features and delivery methods, such practices may seem indistinct from those employed more generally by entrepreneurs and corporations in product development and marketing. Yet, the process differs because it is recognized that the unique context of the poor requires a more nuanced and in-depth understanding of their purchasing and consumption patterns, and related attention to different product features and distribution strategies. For example, literacy rates are low in many of the poorest markets, and multiple languages or dialects may complicate communication; strategies for interacting with consumers simply to understand their preferences and needs therefore may be quite complex (Viswanathan, Richie, & Sridharan, 2010; Weidner, Rosa, & Viswanathan, 2010).

Prahalad argues that although these interactions between producers and poor consumers may be time-consuming and challenging, useful products ultimately can be developed and profitably sold in low-income markets. The features of such products will vary across low-income contexts, but they tend to differ from more mainstream product features and related marketing strategies in important ways. First, in response to the limited purchasing power of poor consumers, producers attempt to develop products meeting the minimal or basic needs of consumers, as opposed to building in more advanced functionality or cosmetic design features. Second, because the poor often get paid day to day and have limited disposable income, small or single serving packages frequently are a production focus. Third, creative financing strategies that pool the financial resources, efforts, or use patterns of poor consumers sometimes are needed to stimulate sales of even the lowest cost products. Finally, poor consumers often obtain information through mechanisms that are not well understood in terms of traditional product marketing and sales strategies, and they also may be very distrustful of business agents from outside their immediate community. Strategies for involving local residents in product marketing and sales therefore may be necessary, or at least producers may need to closely interact with residents in developing these strategies.

In practice, the extent to which corporations and other product developers following BOP-related strategies involve poor consumers in the creation and production of goods and services varies considerably, which has led to a further refinement of BOP models. In particular, BOP1 and BOP2 have been elaborated, with the primary distinction being the extent to which poor consumers are involved in development (Arora & Romijn, 2011). In BOP1, involving poor consumers is not considered especially important beyond the normal procedures utilized in testing the market for any product. In contrast, BOP2 proponents advocate for more extensive involvement of consumers in various aspects of product design, production, and distribution (Arora & Romijn, 2011). These two variations may usefully be seen as two end points on a continuum with respect to low-income consumer involvement, with the BOP2 end point engaging consumers quite fully, at least as planning partners. Those favoring more of a BOP2 approach sometimes argue from the altruistic perspective of trying to assist in capacity development among low-income consumers (Subrahmanyan, 2008). However, they also may emphasize that such interactions are crucial to successful product development, and that the engagement will more generally foster positive perceptions about the producers and their products. This implies a belief that the higher short-term costs of active involvement of the poor in product planning will be recouped in the long run due to a more sustainable fit with local consumers.

In BOP development perspectives that gravitate toward the BOP2 model, it is interesting to observe how closely the interactions between producers and consumers parallel those in which community organizers work with local residents to determine service needs in a community. To the extent that the BOP2 process is scrupulously practiced, sensitive and nuanced interactions with poor consumers likewise are central to model implementation and to the chances of success. Altruistic organizers may chafe at this comparison, and point out that the intent of engagement and related interaction objectives vary so much that the analogy is inapt. Yet, clearly understanding the needs and practices of the target audience is a central focus in product development and delivery regardless of whether or not profit is the motive, and its emphasis in these models represents a striking departure from many more top-down or technical expert focused development approaches.

The difficulty from the business side in such models is that the more a business gravitates toward a BOP2 approach, the higher its short-term developmental costs will be. That is, taking the time and effort to involve consumers can be quite costly, and these costs are likely to increase as the social and cultural distance between producers and consumers grows. Some researchers consequently have argued that those companies that already have experience with non-BOP operations in a country are better positioned to initiate BOP development in that location, because they are more likely to have developed useful social and cultural expertise (Schuster & Holtbrugge, 2011).

Many BOP case examples focus on the initial development strategy for various products, and they include small business start-ups that closely resemble SE projects except for their emphasis on profit-making (Hart & Christenson, 2002). However, attention also has centered on the promise of this approach in bringing products for low-income audiences to scale. Prahalad in particular emphasizes the importance of scaling in extending the reach of products to broad audiences of low-income persons. As a result, he is most enthusiastic about encouraging low-income product development by corporations or larger companies, because he believes that these organizations enjoy production efficiencies that will result in higher volumes of goods being distributed to those most in need (Prahalad, 2005).

Although not emphasized by Prahalad, one other aspect of business strategy may support selected BOP efforts. That is, corporate officials or other business agents at times may believe that poor areas have reasonable prospects for growth and economic improvement over the longer term. In such cases, a business may decide to invest in BOP development in hopes of building name recognition and consumer loyalty that may be sustained as incomes grow and capabilities emerge for purchasing higher end products.

A developed world example from the banking sector illustrates this logic. Some U.S. banks are developing low-cost checking and savings accounts and related financial products for low-income immigrants, as well as opening bank branches in the neighborhoods in which immigrants are concentrated. The primary motivation again is profit oriented; the bankers anticipate that large numbers of these immigrants eventually will flourish, and that they will carry a sense of customer loyalty toward the bank when they become better-off (Anderson, Zhan, & Scott, 2007). However, the initial product development strategies for these audiences focus on limited available incomes, and hence incorporate features such as low balance or check writing requirements.

Local job creation also is considered in some variations of BOP, but principally as a spin-off of product creation for low-income markets. That is, the BOP change agent begins by contemplating which goods or services may be successfully produced in a given market, and then may employ some indigenous labor in the resulting production and distribution processes. It also can be argued that the availability of more desirable local products fuels ambitions for further development and income-generating activities, although this argument is made less frequently.

The Behavioral Dynamics of Bottom of the Pyramid Development

The basic behavioral dynamics of BOP development are straightforward. The change agents in this approach are either entrepreneurs or corporate officials. They are viewed as seeking out poor markets that they view as underdeveloped primarily in order to increase their profits. In this sense, they are weakest among the market-based models in terms of altruistic motives. They nonetheless differ somewhat from traditional capitalistic developers in poor countries in their focus on developing useful products for the poor, as opposed to simply pursuing cheap labor to manufacture goods for developed world consumers. Much of this literature also either states or implies at least a secondary motive regarding the social responsibilities of corporations, and in this sense PSD overlaps somewhat with internally driven CSR as a change approach. However, the focus on developing products specifically for poor consumers is unique, and its developmental emphasis likewise distinguishes it from CSR and other approaches.

The primary benefits provided through these BOP efforts are the new products made available to poor consumers. Little attention is given to elaborating the precise logic through which such products are predicted to lead to better outcomes for poor consumers, because the approach leaves it to change agents to determine through collaborative engagement with consumers which products may be most beneficial.

Nonetheless, two points frequently emphasized in the literature merit attention in thinking through the behavioral implications of this approach. First, by developing and distributing products not commonly available in the most distressed areas, BOP is seen as improving the quality of life for poor consumers by making new goods available to them. BOP similarly may foster quality of life improvements by lowering the price of existing goods, or by improving their quality in instances when only limited and high cost alternatives have previously been available. Second, although not always emphasized, the products envisioned often are of such a basic nature that they may be seen as putting poor consumers in a better position to be productive. That is, access to products may improve basic functioning such as nutrition and hygiene, which are critical to furthering educational and employment efforts.

A secondary manner in which BOP may be thought to influence behavioral outcomes is through the creation of indigenous job opportunities related to BOP production and distribution. Especially given that some renditions of BOP emphasize cultural considerations related to distribution of products, local people may be particularly important in the product distribution process. That is, BOP developers may find it advantageous to employ local people in marketing and distributing products to help overcome cultural barriers that may affect receptivity to new products. Although local job creation is not fundamental to the approach, it certainly is an important outcome in such distressed areas to the extent that it occurs.

The Political Development of Bottom of the Pyramid Initiatives

As shown in Figure 5.1, the political development of BOP initiatives begins when a corporation or business person decides to engage in product development in a selected location. These change agents initially interact with poor consumers to determine product needs, as well as to ascertain product features essential to allowing product purchases. Central to this determination is establishment of affordable price levels, as well as the minimum attributes required to make a particular product desirable. The more sophisticated and sensitive examples of this approach involve detailed

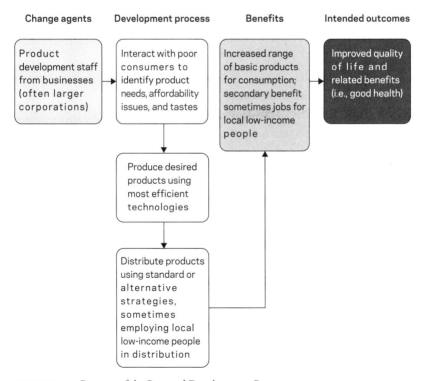

FIGURE 5.1 Bottom of the Pyramid Development Process

considerations of the disadvantaged circumstances of consumers, and related implications for product development and distribution.

Once decisions have been made regarding which products to develop, the change agents produce the goods and arrange distribution systems. Production may occur either in the area in which the initiative was developed or elsewhere. The most important aspects of this process generally involve the determination of profitable pricing strategies that still allow the poor to afford purchases, as well as the consideration of associated trade-offs that may be required between price and product attributes. As products are developed and delivered, the final stage is reviewing and refining products and delivery systems based on experience.

From a political development perspective, BOP strategies are among the simplest of the market-based models. They generally need to involve only producers as change agents and poor consumers as beneficiaries, and the heart of the developmental process is the crafting of interactions between these two groups. Yet, one must be careful not to underestimate the difficulty of these relationships, especially given the great gulf in objective circumstances and perspectives that are likely to exist between the BOP producers and poor consumers.

Examples of Bottom of the Pyramid in Practice

Selected examples are useful in illustrating key features of the BOP development approach. In India, the large salt producer Hindustan Level Ltd. (HLL) has aggressively developed efforts to market iodized salt to the poor (Prahalad, 2005).[2] Iodine deficiency disorder (IDD) is the leading cause of mental illness in the world, and salt generally is recognized as the best vehicle for providing the poor with the iodine levels needed to prevent IDD. Yet most of the salt sold in India is not iodized, and common Indian cooking techniques additionally lead to large losses of iodine during meal preparation.

Through development of its Annapurna iodized salt brand, HLL has engaged in a number of innovative steps to develop and market high quality iodized salt targeted at low-income consumers. Its strategies have included the use of more robust iodine in salt production, development of small unit packages, market appeals to mothers about the importance of iodine to the healthy development of their children, and creation of a direct home sales force in rural areas that features poor women trained as sales agents. Although the expansion of iodized salt to the Indian poor has obvious health benefits, the company's efforts are being carried out within a business context of stimulating product consumption in order to make profits.

The production and distribution of information technologies (ITs) are another interesting area of BOP development.[3] Attention to this issue has been increasingly prominent in international development communities. For example, at the 2005 United Nations World Summit on the Information Society, 174 countries agreed to the Tunis Commitment aimed at reducing the digital divide (Kuriyan, Ray, & Toyama, 2008). As a BOP strategy, information technology distribution has been embraced as a mechanism for promoting sustainable development in multiple ways, including supporting education, health, e-governance, and employment related productivity enhancements (Kuriyan, Ray, & Toyama, 2008).

Kuriyan, Ray, and Toyama (2008) discuss the emergence of personal computer distribution projects in India, and describe the Akshaya Project in Kerala, India, as one interesting pilot that featured government and private partnership toward this end. They indicate that the mission of this initiative was "IT dissemination to the masses." Akshaya established more than 600 Internet-enabled computer centers, with the intent that each of these centers or kiosks would serve 1,000 poor households. The centers were to be run by private entrepreneurs, who assumed some risk for their operation and could make profits through their operation.

The Kerala government initiated the project and selected entrepreneurs to run each site. It then subsidized initial identification of local people to use the kiosks, as well as a 15-hour computer training course designed to provide basic e-literacy to one family member in each participating household. The government paid the entrepreneurs for each person trained, and the participants likewise paid a small amount for the training. According to Kuriyan, Ray, and Toyama (2008), "By the end of the e-literacy phase in 2003, approximately 500,000 people had been trained" (p. 96). After the initial training was completed, the entrepreneurs then were expected to make the centers self-sustaining through fee income and other revenue sources, while still providing development services to the local population.

Based on their research on the project, Kuriyan, Ray, and Toyama (2008) found that the entrepreneurs tended to appeal to a broader income spectrum once the initial government subsidy ended, and so that project services often gravitated to middle-income consumers. In addition, some entrepreneurs ended participation once the government subsidies ended. However, the authors also noted that other entrepreneurs used more balanced approaches that continued to include low-income persons in their target audiences.

MICROENTERPRISE DEVELOPMENT

As mentioned at the beginning of this chapter, microfinancing—as an approach to stimulate microenterprise creation—has been characterized as an example of social entrepreneurship, especially to the extent that it has been nonprofit and altruistically motivated. The case example on the development of the Grameen Bank by Muhammad Yunus presented in Chapter 4 exemplifies microenterprise from this perspective. However, at the individual level where microenterprises actually are created, this approach falls more clearly under the PSD rubric. It is based on the idea that large numbers of poor persons can advance economically through the development of small businesses if they are provided initial financing and limited technical assistance. It is a profit-making approach intended to provide income-producing opportunities for poor persons, while simultaneously creating products and services that will be sensitive to local needs by virtue of the fact that they are produced by indigenous business persons. The following description focuses on this individual level development of microenterprises in the context of considering it as a branch of PSD.

Microenterprise Developmental Model

In developing his financing strategies to support microenterprise establishment, Yunus observed that the fundamental problem facing the poor with whom he interacted was that they did not have money. Although this may seem obvious, his point was that the poor could move forward if they just had better access to financial capital. From an economic perspective, he believed that the poor had the ideas, energy, and talents to establish small businesses if they were provided access to start-up capital. His central contribution was to create aggregate capital financing mechanisms to support such small business development.

It is useful to more closely consider what this emphasis on providing start-up capital for very small-scale business establishment implies about microenterprise as a development approach. For one thing, as compared to BOP development, the focus shifts from poor consumers to the individual microenterprise developer. That is, as opposed to carefully considering how best to develop products for poor consumers assuming the availability of competent production expertise, attention falls primarily on letting individuals develop their own production strategies and then providing the funds that allow them to implement their ideas. Given that microenterprises begin as very small-scale businesses, this suggests a decentralized approach in which the direction of development depends heavily on the decisions of countless poor entrepreneurs about what they believe is potentially profitable in their communities. Similarly, in contrast to BOP, microenterprise development has not been much concerned with the scale of any products or services developed. In fact, microenterprises typically are defined as businesses that employ fewer than five employees (Salamon, 1992), and they generally are focused in informal economic sectors. This is not meant to suggest that microenterprise supporters have no interest in scaling this approach, but rather that the scaling tends to be thought of in terms of the number of microenterprises established rather than in the growth of any particular products or services.

There are interesting economic and social implications to this strategy. From an economic perspective, a focus on microenterprise development signals a belief that small-scale developers can be successful agents in terms of assessing what consumers in their communities will support. Its proponents thus are much less concerned than BOP developers with a consideration of how to identify useful products to develop, and instead rely more on the inclinations of indigenous microenterprise developers. Microenterprise approaches also place greater emphasis on the community benefits that will accrue if more indigenous members become business owners.

In practice, the totally decentralized approach to allowing small entrepreneurs to develop desired products and services often is modified, and several practice variants of microenterprise development have emerged over time to strengthen the approach based on early struggles in some programs. For example, better screening criteria for what is likely to constitute a successful business operation have been established in many programs (Cooper & Kleinschmidt, 1993), and such criteria commonly include an assessment of the potential market available for the goods or services to be produced by the microenterprise. Similarly, just as mainstream banks require business plans that allow bankers to reach conclusions about the likelihood of business success before they make loans, microenterprise lenders often require fairly well-articulated business plans before they make loans. In addition, due to the uncertain prospects of many microenterprises and the limited financial circumstances of their creators, group support and group payback schemes among microenterprisers in specific locales sometimes have been implemented (Mahajan, 2005). Strategies to train or provide ongoing technical assistance to microenterprisers also have been featured in some programs, which may be especially important given the lack of training in basic business techniques among those in the poor areas where microenterprise programs usually are targeted (Edgcomb, Doub, Niebling, Losby, & Williams, 2002). Collectively, orientations such as these are intended to increase the probability of success and related client well-being for those who start microenterprises; Datar, Epstein, and Yuthas (2008) have used the term "client-centered microfinance" to attempt to capture the extent to which microfinancing organizations move beyond basic finance and into a more service-oriented approach.

Taking steps such as these to strengthen technical assistance and monitoring of microenterprises often has been considered crucial to improve the sustainability of microenterprise programs, especially if the microenterprise lender is not significantly underwritten by charitable entities. The cost of bad loans must be reflected in either higher future interest rates or in the inability to sustain the entire lending enterprise, and higher quality screening and support are seen as tools to minimize bad investments. Assistance also is considered to be a positive vehicle for nurturing beginning entrepreneurs with little experience. These caveats aside, microenterprise remains a highly decentralized and bottoms-up approach to development, which at its heart reflects a belief in entrepreneurial capitalism in moving poor families forward.

The Behavioral Logic of Microenterprise Development

As suggested by Yunus and in the discussion here, the driving behavioral assumption guiding microenterprise strategies is that the poor have sufficient motivations and talents to move forward economically largely on their own if only they are provided access to financial capital that more closely parallels what is routinely available to better-off persons. Loans to help the poor establish small enterprises are the vehicle for providing such financial capital, and it is assumed that businesses established with these loans will allow their creators to progress. The precise nature of such projected progress often is loosely stated, but increased incomes and related poverty reduction emanating from the microenterprise endeavors generally are the prominent predicted outcome. As with most approaches, the family consequences of growing income typically are not well delineated, but may include general quality of life improvements as well as some more explicitly articulated behaviors. For example, program effects sometimes are predicted to extend to children, through role modeling, better education, and purchases that higher incomes allow (Cohen & Barnes, 1996). In this sense, it has been argued that children may be freed from more onerous child labor practices and so allowed to continue involvement in school, or that increased disposable income may be used for such fundamental purchases as better health care (Cohen & Barnes, 1996).

Several other outcomes sometimes are assumed to result from the experience of developing and operating a small business. In particular, some have predicted increased self-esteem and self-efficacy as emanating from these experiences (Schreiner, 1999). Because women often have been targeted in microenterprise interventions, it also has been hypothesized that women will become more empowered through this approach, which may have implications in such diverse realms as gender interactions, family life, and community participation (Leach & Sitaram, 2002; Leach, et. al, 2000).

The Political Development of Microenterprise Initiatives

Figure 5.2 summarizes the processes required to develop microenterprise initiatives. Development begins when microfinancing programs are established in an area, and change agents advertise the possibility of loans to create or expand small-scale businesses. Individuals or small groups who have ideas for starting microenterprises then meet with a microfinancing organizational agent to present their business idea and seek a loan. The agent reviews the idea and decides whether to provide funding, based on whatever criteria the organization may use.

If a decision is made to fund the microenterprise, the change agent provides the agreed upon loan, and payback arrangements are made. The microenterprise developers then initiate the agreed upon business activity.

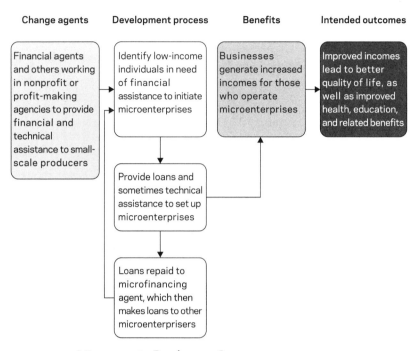

Change agents	Development process	Benefits	Intended outcomes

FIGURE 5.2 Microenterprise Development Process

They often receive technical assistance or training from the change agent, with the intent of improving business management or other areas of expertise considered critical to the success of the microenterprise.

The interaction is completed when microenterprisers repay loans. From an ongoing development perspective, success in repayment is critical to the sustainability of the microfinancing system because otherwise future loans only are possible with donated funding. This of course also implies that start-up capital is required to support initial loans. This initial funding must either be raised by change agents or else be available through existing resources, such as investment funding in banks that choose to enter the microfinancing market.

Research Findings on Microenterprise as a Development Approach

Microenterprise effectiveness ultimately rests on the number and relative prosperity of the businesses it has supported, on income growth and employment stability in the families of microenterprisers, and on work-related spin-off benefits for such families. Of course, many purported microenterprise benefits are similar to those argued to result from other development strategies, which suggests that microenterprise outcomes can be compared to other job creation and income generating strategies.

Empirical examination related to each of these desired outcomes is growing, but results remain equivocal and controversial. Repayment rates are perhaps the most basic proximate measures of initial success in microenterprise development, because positive rates at least suggest that the funded enterprises generated sufficient returns to repay loans. In this most basic respect, the reported loan repayment rates often have been impressive. For example, Grameen Bank has had variations in repayment rates over time. Yet Yunus has reported that at least 95% of Grameen Bank loans eventually are repaid, and this repayment success was critical to allowing Grameen to become self-sustaining after an initial period of partial charitable subsidization (Grameen Bank, 2012; Yunus, 1999). Other leading microfinance institutions, such as the Association for Social Advancement (ASA) and Bandhan Financial Services, similarly have reported high loan repayment rates (ASA, 2012; Bandhan Financial Services, 2011). Nonetheless, problems have surfaced even in this most basic of measures. For example, as discussed in Chapter 4, repayment rates for Grameen Bank have decreased over time, which is of particular concern given the low interest payment returns typically provided through these loans (Roodman, 2010).

Some studies have focused on the ultimate success of the businesses formed through microenterprises, and these findings have been mixed (Green, Kirkpatrick, & Murinde, 2006). Even basic measures such as longitudinal survival rates for businesses established through microloans are rarely reported. However, some scholars have pointed to high microenterprise failure rates and to stagnating growth of those enterprises that do survive (Hoque, 2004; Harvie, 2005).

Studies in many different settings also have found positive microenterprise outcomes in terms of household income and expenditures, as well as decreasing welfare dependency. In addition, some studies have reported positive spin-off effects such as more positive nutritional outcomes among microenterprise participants (Hamad & Fernald, 2010), housing improvement and purchases (Barnes, Keogh, & Nemarundwe, 2001; McIntosh, Villaran, & Wydick, 2008), better education and health outcomes for women and children (Adjei, Arun, & Hossain, 2009; Hamad & Fernald 2010), increased contraceptive use (Littlefield, Morduch, & Hashemi, 2003), and improved human immunodeficiency virus (HIV) prevention for women (Gupta, Parkhurst, Ogden, Appleton, & Mahal, 2008).

These outcomes appear quite promising for participating individuals, especially given the often dismal results of many developmental efforts. However, the validity of such findings increasingly has been questioned, largely because studies rarely have included control or comparison groups. It consequently has been argued that positive findings may be significantly biased due to selection effects (Sebstad, Neill, Barnes, & Chen, 1995; Tedeschi, 2008). In particular, microenterprise participants collectively are likely to be more highly motivated and entrepreneurial than poor persons in general, so it is possible that they may have been among the most likely low-income persons to move forward regardless of whether they received microenterprise support.

Several studies have responded to such limitations by incorporating comparison groups into research designs. Although some of these have reported promising findings for microenterprisers versus comparison groups (Hulme & Mosley, 1996), the extent to which microenterprise positively impacts family incomes, employment, and consumption patterns remains highly contested and unclear. Even some of the more fundamental aspects of microenterprise programs have been questioned based on some research findings. For example, in studying women in India who had received microloans, Garikipati (2008) found that 79.4 % of the microenterprise loans obtained by women were diverted into household activities, as opposed to being used to support the intended business start-ups.

The performance of microenterprise in stimulating women's empowerment likewise has been controversial. Proponents point to the large percentage of microloans that have been extended to women, who often have been disenfranchised or highly disadvantaged in initiating income-generating activities in developing world communities. For example, Deshpanda (2001) reports that 60% of the clients served by 29 surveyed microfinance programs were women, and that about one-fifth of these programs focused exclusively on women.

However, others have reported more equivocal and complex relationships regarding microenterprise effects on women and their family relationships. For example, some researchers have found that loans obtained by women are passed on to male family members, who in turn control any resulting business activity. Although an estimated 95% of the loans provided through the Grameen Bank have been reported to be given to women (Cull, Demirgüç-Kunt, & Morduch, 2009), Goetz and Gupta (1996) found that 63% of these female clients failed to gain control over the loans.

Reports that microenterprise at times has created or exacerbated gender conflicts within families also are troubling. Rahman (1999) reported that 70% of women who participated in microfinance programs in Bangladesh experienced verbal or physical violence by their husbands, and smaller numbers of these experienced violence because they refused to turn over their microloans to their husbands.

The research summarized here suggests that the impacts of microenterprise remain questionable. A critical challenge for those engaged in microenterprise is to more carefully document the effects of these endeavors in relationship to comparable target groups and over time. For example, one critical issue is determining whether income generating and poverty reduction effects are any better for microenterprise initiatives than for other employment development approaches. Establishing what percentage of any population pool represents good candidates for microenterprise development is another important challenge, as is gaining a better sense of the characteristics of those most likely to be effectively assisted with this approach.

Microenterprise Development Examples

As previously mentioned, the stimulation of microenterprise development requires the creation of microfinancing enterprises. Case examples of these are presented in Chapter 4 for the Grameen Bank and for KIVA. It also is worth noting that microfinancing organizations vary considerably in the level of services they provide, and in the extent to which they focus on particular markets or geographic areas.

Microfinancing organizations likewise have differentiated over time to include for-profit enterprises. For example, Sodhi and Tang (2011) describe SKS Microfinance, which was started in India in 1998. SKS has tried to build on the Grameen Bank experience by using a business model that provides attractive financial returns to investors, with the corresponding idea that investors will provide substantial inflows of financial capital that will extend the reach of microloans that can be offered. The business model developed by SKS Microfinance also focuses heavily on the development of efficiencies in the various transactions needed to review, provide, and collect loan repayments. An emphasis on the use of more sophisticated information technology is critical to creating such efficiencies. According to Sodhi & Tang (2011), SKS Microfinance was operating in over 30,000 villages by 2008.

At the individual level, the small businesses created by microenterprisers are incredibly diverse. An easy way to obtain a flavor of this diversity, as well as the very basic nature of many microloans, is to visit the Kiva Web site (www.kiva.org) and peruse the profiles of microenterprisers seeking loans. The enterprises financed include farm equipment and farm animals, small restaurants and stores, transportation services, and many more.

INDIGENOUS TECHNOLOGY CREATION AS A DEVELOPMENT APPROACH

Unlike microenterprise development, indigenous technology creation (ITC) takes more of a guiding hand approach to employment development, but it shares the microenterprise focus on small-scale development. Some consider this form of development under the broader umbrella of social entrepreneurship, and many case examples that I consider as ITC appear in that literature. However, I consider them separately here for two reasons. First, as previously argued, SE tends to be so broad as to not allow meaningful substantive distinctions, and I believe the ITC orientation is important substantively and merits separate classification. Second, the approaches discussed here under ITC often are profit-making in nature, and so straddle the fence of SE for those who believe that SE should be limited to nonprofit development.

Proponents of ITC generally are skeptical regarding the potential of large-scale development projects directed by outside agents. Although the specific nature of these concerns varies, they frequently focus on the poor fit between the development technology employed and the capabilities of local producers. For example, sophisticated pumps, irrigation devices, and electrical systems may be wonderful aids for enhancing productivity, but they may not be easily adopted or sustainable if their purchase and operating costs fall beyond the means of most local producers. Cultural constraints to adopting unfamiliar technology also sometimes are important, especially when newer technology threatens to replace time-honored practices (Polak, 2009). These points fall within broader critiques of large-scale developmental approaches being insensitive to local needs (Easterly, 2006).

The fundamentals of ITC perhaps are best embodied by Polak (2009), who has worked to improve the productivity of poor farmers throughout the developing world. Polak argues that most of those in extreme poverty continue to live on small farms in rural areas, and that developing responsive technologies to enhance their productivity is fundamental to reducing poverty. He consequently has created organizations to work on these problems, and has used both nonprofit and profit-making auspices for this purpose.

ITC proponents view improved technology as critical to helping poor persons in the developing world move forward economically. However, they believe that the employment of technology only will be effective if it is sensitive to local needs, conditions, and capabilities. They therefore favor an interactive developmental approach that features listening to local producers and then developing responsive and affordable aids to enhance productivity. In this sense, ITC developers are similar to BOP proponents in terms of their emphasis on interacting with local people in developing solutions, except that they focus on enhancing the productivity of small-scale producers rather than on improving consumption opportunities.

Another key feature of this approach is the value it places on experts with technological skills, in contrast to the microenterprise emphasis on deferring to the productive inclinations of local entrepreneurs. As Polak (2009) says, using one family with whom he worked as an example:

> But without the help or information they needed, Bahadur's family was stuck. Small-acreage farmers like Bahadur have hundreds of critical problems like this that modern designers with access to worldwide information could solve rapidly. The problem is that 90% of the world's designers spend all of their time working on solutions to the problems of the richest 10% of the world's customers (p. 64).

The Behavioral Logic of Indigenous Technology Creation

The behavioral assumptions behind ITC differ a bit from those of microenterprise development. Both approaches share a basic positive orientation toward poor producers, in that their proponents believe the poor are well-motivated and intentioned but lack key resources critical to moving forward. However, unlike the microenterprise focus on the primary need for financial capital, ITC developers believe that helping poor producers requires interactions with skilled business and technology persons to create more general strategies for development. In this sense, the approach requires initial interactions with skilled developers to uncover critical technology needs, as opposed to merely providing financial capital to poor producers so that they can establish a more diverse range of businesses and products based on their own assessments and inclinations.

The basic behavioral assumptions begin with the idea that improved productivity among the poor can result through the interactions between the poor and those with technical and business skills. This combination of talents is seen to result in a mix of cultural sensitivity to needs and practices on the one hand and technological knowledge on the other. The assumption is that something uniquely productive will result from these exchanges, and will lead to the development and distribution of technology that will increase local productive capacity. This may occur either through the development of new products or by improving the technology used to develop existing products.

With respect to the local producers who are the receivers of the new technology, the assumption is that they are hard-working and will effectively employ affordable technology to increase their productivity. This in turn is predicted to lead to income increases through higher yields. As with most models, ITC proponents do not focus much on the related positive outcomes that may accompany higher incomes. It simply is assumed that higher incomes will result in associated quality of life and other spillover benefits generally thought to accrue from increased disposable income.

From the standpoint of the ITC producer, the assumption is that needed technologies can be produced and sold at a price that will allow at least small profit taking or surplus accumulation. This of course is crucial to sustainability in variations of this approach that are strictly profit making. However, establishing price points above a breakeven level likewise tend to be emphasized in nonprofit organizations that employ this approach, due to an orientation that pricing the products above production costs fosters sustainability with relatively little or no need for donations or other subsidies.

In addition to sustainability, advocates of this approach tend to believe that requiring products to be purchased as opposed to being distributed freely carries other benefits. From a sales and marketing perspective, some have argued that selling products at low price points that include incentives for marketers and sales persons to earn incomes actually is cheaper than giving products away. For example, the technology development organization KickStart sells low-cost irrigation pumps and other equipment to improve agricultural production; its founders argue that the revenue derived through sales not only makes the selling of these items less costly but also more sustainable (KickStart, 2013).

Consistent with more general arguments about the potential value of charging at least nominal amounts to those who receive benefits, it also is argued that those who pay for a benefit are more likely to use it fully than if it is provided for free. The logic is that purchasing creates a sense of investment and sacrifice that does not occur with free goods provision, and so drives individuals to more fully utilize purchased goods. Purchasing also is sometimes argued to foster greater demands for product quality from consumers, in the sense that those who pay are more inclined to demand adherence to quality standards that can in turn drive performance improvements (Dees, 1998).

Finally, the assumptions underlying this approach carry implications for scaling. In particular, ITC developers typically believe that once cost effective technology aids are developed in cooperation with local producers, these products are likely to be adaptable to similar localities with limited needed adjustments. The model thus is argued to be strong in terms of scaling, because persons skilled in developing usable technologies have brought their expertise to designing products and because pricing has been established to foster sustainability.

The Political Development of Indigenous Technology Creation Initiatives

Figure 5.3 summarizes the basic process involved in developing ITC initiatives. The initial development step involves change agents with technology expertise engaging local producers in discussions about their needs, interests, and how they operate their farms or other economic endeavors. Polak, for example, argues that it is important to do so in an unstructured manner and on the home turf of potential beneficiaries, because otherwise the nuances of local situations will not be well understood. He notes that many

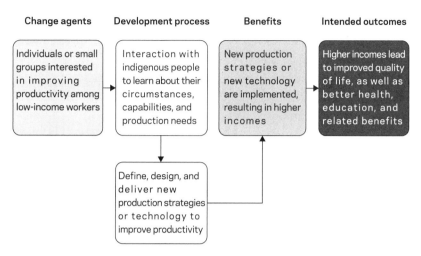

FIGURE 5.3 Indigenous Technology Creation Development Process

people interested in development are disinclined to follow this fundamental step, because they essentially are uncomfortable interacting with people from such different circumstances and cultures. The unstructured conversations essentially constitute an assessment of local needs with respect to economic development, and interacting with local people in thinking through possible solutions to problems likewise is emphasized. As with the more sensitive BOP developers, these discussions also are intended to assure that any proposed solutions fall within the capability of local producers to use well and to afford.

Once these initial interactions have occurred, it is the role of the ITC developers to use their unique skills and financing capabilities to develop products that are responsive to identified needs. This involves all of the various aspects of any new product development: designing the essential products, conducting initial testing, and developing production and distribution schemes. Keeping the costs of producing the technology assistance products as low as possible is critical given the limited financial capabilities of local providers, so ITC production schemes must strive for a high level of efficiency. In some cases, initial technical assistance also may be needed as products become available for the local producers. However, given that basic versus more sophisticated technology generally is emphasized in these approaches, high levels of technical assistance generally are not required.

Selected Examples of Indigenous Technology Creation

As discussed earlier in this chapter, Paul Polak has been perhaps the leading proponent of ITC models, and some of the products he has developed and marketed nicely illustrate this approach. Polak established what has grown into the large international nonprofit organization International Development Enterprises (IDE) in 1982. IDE now has more than 560 employees working in Bangladesh, India, Nepal, Cambodia, Vietnam, Myanmar, Zambia, Zimbabwe, and Ethiopia (Polak, 2009). Its focus is providing technology and related business strategies to help increase incomes for those living on less than one dollar a day. Polak estimates that IDE has helped 3.5 million such families over time, although no information is provided on how these estimates were developed. Polak neatly summarizes the basic approach of IDE as "IDE listens to what its customers, the rural poor, say about their needs and then develops appropriate, affordable solutions that increase their incomes. These solutions include developing and marketing technologies for water access and control, providing expertise and training, and increasing access to markets." (p. 232).

Although Polak and IDE have created a wide array of technology enhancements and tools following this philosophy, they probably are best known for the development and marketing of low-cost pumps that improve the irrigation and related productivity of small farms. Among their other products are low-cost scythes for harvesting crops, steam distillers for obtaining essential oils from harvested crops, and solar dryers for drying tomatoes and banana chips for high-end markets. In addition to developing and distributing tools, Polak and his colleagues also provide technical advice with respect to business strategies in the context of fully understanding local production technologies. For example, they use their expertise to help local farmers select a mix of fruit and vegetable crops that will lead to more productive outcomes, and they also have assisted farmers in improving techniques for marketing goods.

Another interesting example of ITC development is illustrated by the work of KickStart, which specializes in the development of low-cost tools for small-scale African farmers. KickStart is somewhat of a hybrid model, in that it operates as a nonprofit organization. In this sense, it conforms to Yunus's social business definition, in that profits earned by the organization are reinvested to help cover design costs of new products. However, the tools it designs and develops generally are sold to wholesalers, who in turn mark up the products and earn profits when they sell them to local farmers.

The five-step model articulated on the KickStart Web site resonates very clearly with Polak's approach: (1) identify opportunities, (2) design products, (3) establish a supply chain, (4) develop the market, and (5) measure and move along (KickStart, 2013).[4] The opportunity identification step closely corresponds to the principles of examining local needs and culture in thinking through design and distribution strategies; KickStart staff work in local areas to determine the types of low-cost technology enhancements that would allow farmers to increase their incomes. Product design then focuses on developing reasonably priced products that are viewed as promising in terms of helping large numbers of farmers to increase incomes.

Although KickStart has developed many different products, its low-cost pumps probably have generated the most attention. The pumps allow farmers to better irrigate their land, and in their simplest form are highly portable and can be used by individuals to irrigate their entire farms at low cost. KickStart sold about 216,000 pumps from 1991 to 2013. Other products include a manually operated oilseed press to make cooking oil from seeds, and a soil block press that can produce low-cost building blocks for building houses or other structures.

As of 2013, KickStart claims to have helped move 740,000 people out of poverty since its founders, Martin Fisher and Nick Moon, began operating in 1991— mostly in Kenya, Tanzania, and Mali. Although these assertions are not externally validated, KickStart does conduct surveys of farmers before and after they buy equipment, and appears to make an unusually rigorous attempt to ascertain how income changes over time. KickStart also estimates that it has been responsible for the establishment of 150,000 new businesses related to its product development, distribution, and use.

THE STRENGTHS AND LIMITATIONS OF PRIVATE SUSTAINABLE DEVELOPMENT

PSD approaches have presented an interesting mix of strategies to further the economic well-being of poor persons in the developing world. Ranging strategically from improving the productive capacities of the poor on the one hand to fostering basic consumptive opportunities on the other, PSD change agents nonetheless share a common belief that employing capitalistic market mechanisms is central to moving the poor forward. They are to be credited with pioneering many innovative initiatives in the poorest areas of the world, often in locations with especially difficult problems and no clear history of developmental success.

Another interesting contribution of these approaches is that they have helped turn much traditional thinking about product development and the creation or improvement of employment opportunities on its head. With respect to consumption, BOP's powerful focus on developing products with very basic but necessary functionality provides important lessons on possibilities for better serving poor consumers within a profit-making context. This orientation drives the notion that we should focus on what is fundamental in products, as opposed to appealing to stylistic features that add costs but little if any utility beyond psychic benefits. Focusing on basic attributes of product distribution such as portion size, as well as on cultural or other considerations that may affect receptivity to products, likewise can substantially improve prospects for providing needed basic products to the poor. The emphasis in many BOP examples of closely interacting with poor consumers in designing these strategies is a welcome antidote to broader globalization tendencies of simply inundating developing world consumers with visions of developed world styles and brand names.

Although microenterprise and ITC have slightly different developmental emphases, both are based on the refreshing assumption that the poor generally are hard-working and possessed of reasonable capabilities. Poor people are seen as able to move forward largely through their own impetus and efforts if only they can be provided with some fairly basic employment-related assistance. In the case of microenterprise, the key ingredient to success is providing sufficient financial capital to allow poor individuals to initiate their own business visions; microfinancing, sometimes accompanied by basic technical assistance on business management, is the tool that allows this to happen. ITC likewise attempts to unleash the productive capacities of poor producers, but rather emphasizes how those with business and technical skills can provide the poor with improved tools to increase their productivity. Like BOP development on the consumer side, what is novel about ITC is its focus on relatively unsophisticated technology in a high technology world. This focus is driven by the same attention to fit with producer needs and capabilities that underscores BOP product development for consumers.

The features noted here make PSD approaches stronger than the other models examined in terms of their potential to be self-sustaining within the geographic space in which they are established. That is, unlike fair trade and CSR, their success is not dependent on the whims of developed world consumers, nor do they necessarily depend on donations beyond initial start-up investments. Rather, the product development orientation in BOP, the low-grade technology emphasis in ITC, and the focus on small loans to establish small businesses through microenterprise all create the possibility that projects can be sustained over time within poor communities. This is not meant to suggest that they will be universally successful; the success rate depends on many other factors. However, these models at least generally present a conceptual approach to think through the longer-term sustainability of ideas that are well-implemented.

These approaches similarly rate highly in terms of their potential to empower poor persons in development, which is central to developmental perspectives within social work and other community development-oriented fields. None assumes major motivational or character deficits among the poor, and in their strongest forms, each approach recognizes the importance of involving the poor in the planning and design of the products or tools intended to assist them. With its focus on basically leaving it to the poor to define their own economic development projects, microenterprise is especially strong in terms of empowerment, but the participatory developmental nature of many BOP and ITC initiatives also suggests considerable attention to empowerment perspectives.

Despite these notable strengths, PSD approaches have important limitations as well. They suffer from the problems shared by all approaches dependent on voluntary private actions as well as additional issues that market-based profit taking brings to relationships. The profit-related issues are particularly important in many of the developing markets where these initiatives are established, because the market competition and related consumer information required to restrain excess profit making generally do not exist.

Each PSD model also may be susceptible to creaming. The basic problem is that it is very challenging for even well-meaning private developers to provide products or employment assistance to the least well-off and still make a profit. As a result, PSD initiatives often are driven to serve those with slightly higher incomes. Of the approaches discussed here, BOP appears most vulnerable to this criticism (Kuriyan, Ray, & Toyama, 2008; Polak, 2009). Given that even relatively better-off poor persons in the developing world face very real economic difficulties, I am not as troubled as some by this criticism as long as PSD is seen as complementary to other approaches for serving the least well-off. Nonetheless, it is relevant to monitor this concern when assessing these models, especially when claims of high levels of poverty reduction are made.

Some limitations are peculiar to selected types of PSD models. For example, although microenterprise development has been hailed by many for the breadth of its job creation potential, others have questioned its reach and poverty reduction effectiveness (Shaw, 2004). That is, although many businesses have been created, the viability and income generation capacity of these over time remains poorly understood. Even less well-known is whether microenterprises are any more effective in either job creation or income producing capabilities than other approaches, such as having larger businesses train and hire workers. It likewise is doubtful whether the capacity to effectively establish and operate a small business extends beyond a sliver of most populations, again suggesting that microenterprise is best thought of as a complementary approach. The economic and social contexts in which microenterprise are likely to prosper also may vary significantly; for example, in economies with more well-developed production capabilities, it may be difficult for the poor to competitively enter the marketplace (Schreiner & Woller, 2003).

Assuming the existence of technologically savvy developers who work closely with local producers to identify relevant and affordable technologies, ITC is somewhat less likely to suffer from the variable and uncertain prospects of microenterprises. However, some would argue that focusing on sustainable low-grade technology may enhance income and productivity in the short run but also may delay receptiveness to needed large-scale production practices (Leclair, 2002). This is a very interesting question with important intersections regarding productivity, sustainability, and culture, and it requires sensitive philosophical and empirical examination.

Among the three PSD approaches discussed, BOP development is the only one that emphasizes the desirability of involving corporations and other large businesses. Although this is argued to be important in terms of extending product reach and production efficiencies, it likewise may

embed corporations in poor areas in which there are few powerful coun-
tervailing forces. In such settings, it is difficult to effectively monitor the
quality of products or related production practices, and this problem is
reinforced by the relative absence of competitive pressures and the poor
education of local residents. It often becomes incumbent on community
advocates to monitor and potentially check possible corporate excesses, yet
such change agents often are in short supply.

Karnani (2012) has strongly criticized BOP in this and related respects.
He points out that despite the considerable promotion of BOP, there
have been few empirical examples of BOP effectively serving the poor (see
also Frandano, Karamchandani, & Kubzansky, 2009). He also reiterates
the well-known litany of exploitation of the poor by corporations in the
developing world, and on balance suggests that such negative interactions
remain more problematic than supposed gains from BOP.

BOP also may be challenged to the extent it is promoted as a poverty
reduction strategy, as opposed to being a strategy to complement income-
generating strategies. That is, its basic orientation is that people can be
made better-off through providing improved and less costly consumption
opportunities. This assumption probably is true in most poor areas of the
world. However, the extent of its ability to more people forward is likely to
be quite limited unless people have additional income, and BOP developers are relatively silent on this score (Arora & Romijn, 2011).

Taken together, these strengths and limitations suggest that PSD strategies offer useful and diverse opportunities for change agents to consider as
they work in poor developing world contexts. These approaches tend to
be strong in terms of working directly with local populations to improve
income-generating or consumptive activities. However, they are limited in
that they typically either pertain to only subgroups of poor populations,
or else have insufficient power to effect fundamental change unless used in
conjunction with other development strategies.

SKILLS NEEDED BY PRIVATE SUSTAINABLE DEVELOPMENT CHANGE AGENTS

The skills required for effective PSD practice differ somewhat dependent
on the PSD variant under consideration. However, change agents working in any form of PSD will benefit greatly from having well-honed skills

in market assessments, and especially in understanding market possibilities and limitations for low-income producers and consumers. Given the economic and cultural differences that typically exist between change agents and beneficiaries in these interactions, training and experience in working with diverse groups also is very valuable. It is in this area that change agents educated in social work or related human services professional programs may add considerable value to PSD change initiatives.

Given BOP's emphasis on larger-scale production, BOP practitioners must have strong skills in understanding production functions and diverse product distribution strategies. This approach probably best lends itself to persons with strong business backgrounds, and particularly those with experience in designing and producing lower cost goods. Partnerships between those with such production capabilities and those with the ability to sensitively interact with poor consumers around product needs and resource capabilities appear especially promising in this respect.

Microenterprise development likewise requires skills in assessing whether opportunities appear to exist for certain goods or services in communities, but the type of assessment required differs from BOP. Microenterprise change agents are more likely to be assessing whether small-scale plans put together by others have a reasonable chance of success so that payback of loans is likely. The level of business acumen required in this sense is considerably less than is required to plan and operate a BOP initiative. However, as initiatives increasingly have evolved toward providing microenterprisers with some level of training and technical assistance related to microloan receipt, teaching skills on various aspects of small business planning and management have become more important. In addition, training also requires an unusual skill set in that teachers generally are interacting with persons with very limited educations and diverse cultural attributes.

The same teaching attributes suggested for microenterprises are very useful in working with indigenous producers in ITC initiatives, because some training often is required to assure that new technologies are properly utilized. In addition, given the focus of this approach, change agents with the ability to carefully assess production processes and to think through low-cost but sustainable production or distribution enhancements are vital. This suggests the importance of practitioners with sound training in production design, especially those with product invention experience.

CONDITIONS FOR PRIVATE SUSTAINABLE DEVELOPMENT SUCCESS

The broader economic and political conditions most likely to foster the success of PSD initiatives vary depending on which of the three PSD forms are considered. BOP initiatives are most likely to prosper in environments where the provision of basic consumer goods is seriously underdeveloped, and in which it is fairly easy to establish production and distribution operations. Given that low per unit profits are fundamental to BOP development efforts, establishing initiatives in areas in which credible competitors are not projected to enter the marketplace also may be important.

Two cultural considerations also appear to be very important to successful BOP development. First, given that BOP initiatives often focus on communities with limited histories of larger-scale goods production and use, the local cultural receptivity to such production modes is critical to success. Second, the relative ease with which producers can adapt their existing productive, distribution, and other organizational features to local climates far different from the home base is very important. It therefore has been argued that corporations or other businesses that enter BOP markets are more likely to be successful if they have related operations or experiences in a region, even when these other operations are not BOP oriented.

The challenges for successful microenterprise development are much different and perhaps more diverse. From a market perspective, microenterprises are most likely to thrive in areas in which goods produced by larger corporate entities are nonexistent or not well-accepted culturally. In a similar vein, microenterprises may be more desirable in communities in which communal values and indigenous exchange are particularly valued. Success also may be highly dependent on the quality of the microfinancing organization that provides funding for development. For example, issues such as repayment rates and time frames, as well as the quality of technical assistance and training offered, may be critical. Finally, as demonstrated by the previously cited literature questioning how earned income from microenterprises is used in families, social issues such as the relative equality of gender relationships are likely to ultimately affect whether intended microenterprise benefits reach targeted audiences.

The prospects for ITC development are greatest in areas in which productive technology is relatively undeveloped and in which there are large numbers of small-scale producers. As elaborated by Polak, this suggests a focus on rural developing world areas where millions of farmers continue to labor on small farms. The creativity of ITC developers also is likely to determine success in implementation of these models, because they must not only be sensitive to local production needs and capacities but also very skilled in figuring out how to deliver technology improvements at relatively low prices. As with microenterprise development, selecting markets in which goods produced by large-scale business are not competitive likewise may be crucial.

SUMMARY

Although the PSD approaches assessed in this chapter are distinct, they share a common emphasis of embracing profit making to advance development for the poor. In BOP, such progress is argued to occur because the poor are provided increasing access to basic goods at more affordable prices. In contrast, microenterprise and ITC focus on improving the capabilities of the poor to increase incomes through engaging in small businesses or by improving the technology they use in their productive endeavors.

Of the three approaches, BOP is the most decidedly capitalistic because it stresses profit making in the production of consumer goods, with the profits often accruing to large businesses or corporations. Microenterprises and ITC are much more likely to straddle the fence with nonprofit development strategies, with microenterprises commonly financed by nonprofit microfinancing organizations and ITC initiatives sometimes operating as social businesses in which all profits are reinvested in the social endeavor.

The research base regarding the effectiveness of microenterprises as a development strategy is much more developed than for the other two approaches. Little sound research has been done to test BOP as an approach, and ITC study has been limited to a relatively small number of case examples. Some of the research findings on microenterprises have been encouraging, but even here studies generally have been limited by lack of control or comparison groups and by other methodological issues.

As with other market-based approaches, all of the PSD approaches have been criticized for deflecting attention from a more fundamental developmental focus by governments. These criticisms have been most striking with respect to BOP, in that BOP is posited by some to be little more than a form of "greenwashing" or "cleanwashing" by corporations. The other two approaches are more likely to be criticized as marginal, or as being mired in the intentional or inadvertent support of fundamentally flawed capitalistic systems.

6

Fair Trade

THE FAIR TRADE approach to be considered in this chapter falls within a more general developmental orientation often referred to as the fair trade movement, which includes macroeconomic and political development policies and strategies for engaging consumers in more fairly paying for the value of goods produced. Fridell (2004) uses the term fair trade network to distinguish the latter consumer-based approach from the broader fair trade movement, and it is this consumer-based facet of fair trade that I will focus upon here. This approach also has been characterized by some as alternative trade or ethical trade. However, I will simply use the term fair trade or fair trade approach in this chapter, and I will only briefly touch on broader fair trade movement orientations in the historical development section that follows.

THE CONSUMER-DRIVEN FAIR TRADE APPROACH

In simplest terms, the consumer-based fair trade model is a development approach that seeks to improve well-being for low-income workers and communities by appealing to consumer social and economic justice sentiments. The intent generally is to improve returns to indigenous producers in the developing world through more responsible consumption patterns by consumers in developed countries (Fridell, 2004). As such, fair trade initiatives involve the coordination of efforts by participants crossing the developing and developed worlds, with production efforts centered in poor developing communities and marketing and product distribution focusing on consumers in developed countries.

Fair trade parallels many corporate social responsibility (CSR) initiatives in appealing to the altruistic sensibilities of consumers as a primary strategy for conveying economic benefits to poor workers. However, it differs in that it usually features a much more grassroots, bottoms-up developmental genesis, and because it emphasizes establishing markets for smaller-scale entrepreneurs and producers rather than modifying the practices of large corporations (Renard, 2003). Fair trade also is unique in articulating an equitable production and consumption system more holistically, as opposed to attempting to encourage or force large corporate entities to make marginal changes in the way they do business. It also is somewhat more narrowly focused than CSR, given its consistent orientation toward developing world producers.

Fair trade initiatives have grown rapidly in the last 30 to 40 years, but still constitute a very small portion of world markets. The extent of fair trade development to date can be considered from several different perspectives. Important measures include overall sales, number of producers and other employees engaged in certification and distribution, number of sales outlets, and types of products included. Fair trade development has been more extensive in Europe than in North America and other places, but has received rising attention in most developed world countries.

Although data for many aspects of fair trade are limited, by the early 2000s there were about 10,000 stores specializing in fair trade products in Europe and North America, and nearly 57,000 supermarkets were carrying fair trade products in Europe alone (Moore, 2004; Krier, 2006). The value of fair trade merchandise was estimated to have exceeded 2.9 billion Euros in 2008, with accompanying rapid annual growth (Fisher, 2009). For example, Fairtrade International (FLO), the leading fair trade standard setting and labeling organization, recently estimated that FLO labeled goods with an estimated value of 4.9 billion Euros were sold in 2011 (Fairtrade International, 2012). FLO further reports that the United Kingdom ranks first internationally in terms of the value of goods purchased, followed by the United States, Germany, and France. These sales include more than 300 different products that have met FLO certification standards.

It is estimated that there are more than 1.2 million fair trade producers and nearly 1,000 producer organizations worldwide, with fair trade organizations in at least 66 countries (Fairtrade International, 2012). The most commonly traded fair trade products include coffee, cocoa, teas, fresh fruit, sugar, rice, art and craft works, and other food products (Fridell, 2004; Renard, 2003; Moore, 2004; Wilkinson, 2007).

Coffee has been the most widely traded fair trade product. For example, about two-thirds of all fair trade sales in 2000 in the United States and Canada were for coffee (Moore, 2004). Coffee is particularly important to fair trade because of its prominence in developing world economies; it is second only to petroleum in terms of developing country export value, and at the same time, coffee consumption is heavily centered in the developed world (Haight, 2011). In addition, in many countries, coffee is still commonly produced by small growers, and hence provides opportunities for the development of fair trade cooperatives (Haight, 2011). Various fair trade organizations purchase the coffee directly from such cooperatives and then market it in mainstream coffee shops and stores and through alternative outlets.

HISTORICAL DEVELOPMENT OF FAIR TRADE

Fridell (2004) describes the broader fair trade movement as follows: "This unofficial movement—led by various Southern governments, international organizations, and NGOs—has sought to use market regulation to protect poorer nations from the vagaries of the international market and the unchecked power of rich nations and giant corporations in the North" (p. 412). He traces the development of the broad fair trade movement between the two world wars to dissatisfaction with prices received by developing world or "Southern" countries for commodities. In particular, the returns developing countries received for raw materials and other products requiring unsophisticated production processes were viewed as paling in comparison to prices received by developed or "Northern" countries for manufactured goods. Experimentation with schemes to raise basic commodity prices followed, but generally these were not viewed as successful in raising economic returns for developing world countries.

Subsequent public advocacy related to fair trade after World War II concentrated on two issues (Fridell, 2004). First, developing world countries argued that developed countries should weaken protectionist economic policies, such as tariffs and export controls, so that developing country goods would become more competitive. Second, they contended that developmental assistance provided through the International Monetary

Fund, World Bank, or other lending institutions should offer production subsidies to primary producers in developing world countries, as opposed to other forms of assistance. The idea was that providing subsidies to improve developing world trading capacities ultimately would be much more beneficial than simply offering cash assistance. Developing world countries also increasingly turned toward strategies of economic nationalism and self-reliance during this period, while continuing to argue in international forums for more equitable treatment in economic exchanges with developed world trading partners.

Despite this vigorous advocacy by developing world governments, as well as the support of some key international organizations, the macroeconomic and political approaches described here generally were opposed by developed world countries. Such ideas also increasingly flew in the face of growing neoliberal political policies and globalized economic production, which tended to decrease state regulation of economic interactions and to increase the power of multinational corporations to transcend traditional governmental decision-making boundaries (Stiglitz, 2007). As a result, the success of these efforts was limited, and many persons and organizations interested in fair trade instead pursued more direct consumer-based strategies that are the focus of this chapter.

This consumer-oriented approach to fair trade had separate roots stretching at least to the 1940s, when churches and other altruistically driven groups in Europe and the United States began working to distribute goods produced in poor countries to more affluent consumers. Among the most well-known of these efforts in the United States was initiated by the Mennonite Church, which founded the Ten Thousand Villages project in the 1940s to sell handicrafts from developing world artisans in specialty stores. In Europe, Oxfam UK also began selling goods produced by Chinese artisans in its Oxfam shops (Archer & Fritsch, 2010), and several organizations arose to employ similar strategies. In many instances, these efforts grew from other voluntary charitable and relief work in which organizations were engaged in poor communities, such as church mission work (Tallontire, 2000).

The modern fair trade movement then began to emerge more systematically in Europe in the 1970s and 1980s. European fair trade development proceeded much more quickly and extensively than in the United States, but in both places increasing numbers of nonprofit organizations established fair trade initiatives (Fisher, 2009; Moore, 2004). Early fair trade projects usually involved grassroots efforts by change agents to find indigenous developing world producers not believed to be receiving a fair return on their labor, and then developing connections through alternative distribution networks with developed country consumers. Nonprofit agencies often developed alternative trade organizations (ATOs) to arrange for the distribution and sale of the goods produced by indigenous workers. These ATOs typically were seen as separate from mainstream market systems, and as providing consumers with an ethically superior alternative.

Tallontire (2000) argues that fair trade initiatives during this period typically appealed heavily to political motivations, without sufficient attention to the needs of consumers and related product standards. The principal appeal to consumers was to demonstrate their solidarity with producers in developing world countries. This strategy proved limited in terms of attracting a broader consumer base, and attention in the 1990s increasingly shifted toward more careful consideration of consumer needs and interests. As Tallontire writes, "The producer focus of earlier periods was associated with the neglect of the consumer. As profits dropped and some ATOs faced bankruptcy many ATOs began to look toward consumer needs and to balance these with those of the producer. Consumer marketing, product development, and product quality all became important concerns of ATOs, marking increased commercial awareness" (p. 168).

The creation of a certified fair trade labeling process was perhaps the most important development fostering fair trade expansion. Early fair trade initiatives had relied on their own means to convince consumers of the benefits of purchasing the fair trade products they sold. Certification and labeling was viewed as a more consistent and institutionalized process for assuring consumers and distributors that fair trade products met selected standards. The idea was that conventional importers would become more involved in distributing fair trade goods if they could assure consumers of the value associated with these goods; inclusion of these larger and more established importers in turn would allow significant expansion into more traditional markets. From the consumer perspective, a label would provide assurances that the ethical criteria central to their decision-making processes in fact were being applied.

The creation of certification first required independent and unbiased organizations to develop production and distribution standards, and then to assure that these were met in practice. The initial step in this direction occurred with the 1988 establishment of the Max Havelaar Foundation in the Netherlands as the first fair trade labeling organization. Fridell (2004) indicates that by the late 1990s national fair trade labeling initiatives were operable in 17 countries under several different organizational auspices; in 1997, the Fairtrade Labeling Organizations International (FLO) was established in Germany as an umbrella organization for these initiatives. FLO, now known as Fairtrade International, includes 24 members operating in 26 countries, including 3 producer networks, 19 labeling initiatives, two marketing organizations, and one associate member (Fairtrade International, 2012).

In order for products to be certified through FLO, producers must adhere to strict labor and other standards, which have evolved over time and include standards related to four different aspects of production and distribution. These include small producer organizations, hired labor, contract production, and trade. For example, the standards pertaining to trade require companies trading FLO certified products to:

- "Pay a price to producers that aims to cover the costs of sustainable production: the Fairtrade Minimum Price.
- Pay an additional sum that producers can invest in development: the fair trade premium
- Partially pay in advance, when producers ask for it
- Sign contracts that allow for long-term planning and sustainable production practices" (Fairtrade International, 2012)

Among other things, FLO also has emphasized democratic participation by growers in the organizing and decision making of producer organizations as a means of empowering indigenous producers and communities. For example, the FLO committee that sets fair trade standards includes representatives from producer networks, and cooperatives democratically engage in decision making regarding how to distribute the premiums to benefit local communities. Consistent with these directions and a focus on fairer prices for labor, FLO emphasizes empowerment of poor farmers and growers as a central goal of the organization.

In return for meeting certification standards, companies selling fair trade products and the consumers who purchase them receive verification concerning the standards that have been used in production. These include "no child labour, no forced labour, freedom of association, collective bargaining for plantation workers, and non-discrimination policies" (Fridell, 2004, p. 420). These assurances come in the form of a fair trade label, which only can be attached to products certified by one of the fair trade organizations.

As support for fair trade developed, mainstream retailers became more interested in selling fair trade products. They in turn began negotiating agreements with fair trade organizers to distribute fair trade products along with their other goods. As this occurred, some retail corporations also began developing their own fair trade product lines, by making more direct agreements with indigenous producers. For example, the international retailing giant Walmart has partnered with the fair trade organization TransFair USA to offer fair trade-certified coffee at its stores, and sales of this product have grown rapidly at competitive prices. The coffee is sustainably grown by farmers who receive a living wage, and the beans are roasted in a specially designed carbon-neutral roaster (Walmart, 2008; Holahan & Trebilcock, 2011). This "mainstreaming" of fair trade products has allowed significant growth of fair trade sales, but has been controversial in fair trade circles due to fears of co-optation by traditional markets and dilution of the more clearly defined ethical nature of fair trade origins (Nicholls & Opal, 2008; Renard, 2003; Raynolds, 2008).

Corporations moving in this direction largely are responding to tastes among a segment of their consumers, and also are likely to view fair trade offerings as being part of more socially responsible branding in which they are attempting to engage. From the corporate perspective, fair trade overlaps considerably with CSR planning. However, fair trade focuses more specifically on related production and distribution features than the amorphous and poorly defined CSR field; in addition, both historically and presently fair trade relies heavily on noncorporate production and distribution processes.

The possible involvement of governments and large public organizations in fair trade has been a final interesting development of the fair trade movement. Consumer-oriented fair trade models generally have been conceptualized with marginal if any consideration of government roles. However, interactions with governments have received increasing attention as fair trade has grown. For example, in the United Kingdom, government procurement policies allowing fair trade purchases have been adopted in some jurisdictions, and initiatives to increase the use of fair trade products in U.S.

universities also have emerged (Nicholls & Opal, 2008). Campaigns to develop "fair trade towns" additionally have gained momentum, especially in the United Kingdom. Towns must follow established criteria to receive this designation; these include passage by a local council of resolutions supporting fair trade. More than 100 United Kingdom towns had received fair trade town designations by 2004, and similar campaigns had begun in other developed countries (Nicholls & Opal, 2008).

THE BASIC ELEMENTS OF FAIR TRADE
AS A DEVELOPMENT MODEL

Several variations of fair trade approaches have been promoted, but in general, at least five developmental steps are important. The first two of these involve the conceptualization and initial planning of the initiative, while the latter three focus on its implementation. During the conceptual stage, fair trade initiators must first decide what constitutes a fair trade product (Fridell, 2004). Fair trade attributes may include factors such as establishing reasonable wages for the producer of the product, production standards concerning working conditions, quality control standards to assure product reliability, and monitoring procedures regarding the environmental impacts of production. In the modern fair trade era, if fair trade developers want to receive certification through FLO, the attendant standards are already established by FLO, and so developers must determine how producers will meet them. However, specific initiatives also sometimes consider additional production or distribution features in addition to required FLO standards, and there also is some discretion with respect to how FLO standards will be met. In addition, some initiatives considered as fair trade do not seek FLO certification; in this case, they must establish alternative standards and procedures for assuring consumers about the quality of goods.

Second, fair trade developers must select a viable set of producers so that a reliable stream of fair trade products can be available for market (Wilkinson, 2007). Perhaps most fundamental in this respect is determining a targeted group of producers with whom the fair trade developers want to collaborate. In addition, to enhance the chances of success and sustainability, fair trade developers must carefully assess whether the desired group has the capability to produce selected products. This may include a determination of the level of training or technical support needed to ensure sustainable production. The developers must determine whether there is a likely market in selected developed world locations for the goods to be produced—from the standpoint of the viability of the product and in terms of likely support for the producing group. In most initiatives, the agreements with producers are not made with individual farmers or producers but rather with local producer organizations, which often operate as cooperatives.

In practice, these first two steps are not sequential, and in fact the second often precedes the first. That is, many fair trade initiatives are started by promoters who either are working with an indigenous group or who have consumed or observed the production of their products. Such observations or working relationships lead fair trade initiators to think through how they may be able to help indigenous groups expand markets for their products or the returns they receive for their work, and fair trade efforts are promoted as a viable means for doing so. In this process, the initiators in turn may alter current production or distribution practices so that the initiative can fall under the more general fair trade rubric.

After initial decisions have been made to establish a fair trade initiative, three broad implementation tasks must be accomplished. First, a product and payment distribution process, which typically differs from the mainstream production process, must be established (Wilkinson, 2007). Initiators must determine operational aspects such as developing production schedules and amounts, establishing relationships with those who will sell products, creating procedures for shipping products and obtaining payments, and implementing other detailed practices critical to the successful operation of any business.

Second, consumers must be educated about the availability of the fair trade product and about why purchasing it provides economic and social value (Wilkinson, 2007). Given that fair trade products not only often use nonmainstream distribution outlets but also may be more costly than similar goods, solid marketing in this respect is especially important. In addition to the general concerns about product quality that are fundamental to most marketing, fair trade initiators must identify an audience that is likely to be sympathetic to the product and its producers on ethical or altruistic grounds. Such marketing efforts often involve the construction of stories about the producers that are designed to appeal to these consumer motives.

For those initiatives tied to larger fair trade groups such as FLO or Fair Trade USA, producers may benefit from larger scale and more sophisticated advertising by these organizations (Haight, 2011).

Finally, to assure that fair trade products in fact have incorporated all of the relevant components that allow them to be considered as fair trade goods, monitoring of agreed upon production practices is required. This monitoring process generally is referred to as the "certification process" that was described earlier. Systematic engagement in such monitoring is necessary to receive a "certified" label from one of the major fair trade organizations, which serves as a short-hand for fair-trade-oriented consumers that a product actually meets widely accepted fair trade standards. In instances in which fair trade certification is not sought, fair trade initiators nonetheless typically engage in monitoring practices designed to assure consumers that the advertised fair trade features actually are met by producers.

The Behavioral Dynamics of Fair Trade Initiatives

The behavioral dynamics of fair trade approaches are somewhat complex. The ultimate goal of these initiatives is to increase productive behaviors by—and related economic returns to—indigenous producers in developing world countries, as well as more broadly to improve the economies of the communities in which these producers live. Indigenous producers generally are viewed as rational individuals with useful skills who are struggling to make a decent living; however, the international market systems through which most goods and services are distributed tend either to exploit their labor with low wage returns or else ignore them. Fair trade initiators believe that these indigenous producers will respond in productive ways if markets for their products are enlarged, and if their economic returns through higher wages or other forms of compensation are increased. As this occurs, indigenous producers and their families will enjoy improved economic or other circumstances that will contribute to their overall well-being.

Communities in turn are expected to prosper, through indirect effects resulting from better-off families and because initiatives often reserve a portion of profits more directly for community development efforts. For example, FLO certified products are priced in a manner to include a "social premium" component, which is intended to be set aside to support community development (Nicholls & Opal, 2008). This social premium may be used for a wide variety of community development purposes, such as education, infrastructure improvements, and housing. Fair trade, thus can be seen as improving not only tangible living circumstances for producer families, but also the environmental contexts in which indigenous workers engage in productive labor.

Within this developmental framework, initiatives vary in the particular outcomes they are most interested in promoting. For example, the Good-Weave initiative described later in this chapter has a primary focus of eliminating child labor in the production of rugs. Most generally, however, fair trade initiatives focus on increasing the incomes the producers receive.

Many initiatives also stress providing technical consultation and support to indigenous producers, cooperatives, or other organizations (Ronchi, 2002). Such support is consistent with the economic improvement behavioral dynamic described earlier, but differs slightly from the narrow focus on improving prices as a means to increasing prosperity. Rather, it assumes that technical assistance will enhance the capabilities of producers in poor communities in diverse ways, so that organizational functioning is improved and communities become more skilled and self-determinative not only in production but in broader development and decision making. In this sense, not only production workers but others in local organizations and the community may be seen as the beneficiaries of fair trade initiatives.

The other key behavioral dimension of fair trade initiatives involves consumers. In simple terms, fair trade is based on the assumption that consumers are interested or can be made interested in the well-being of those who produce the goods they purchase, as well as about related socially oriented production practices. Fair trade change agents therefore attempt to modify the purchasing decisions of consumers in directions that are viewed as positively affecting disadvantaged producers. The motivations behind consumer behavioral changes in this respect are similar as for consumers in the CSR models described in Chapter 3. That is, they are driven primarily by altruistic motives related to wanting to assist or to be fairer to disadvantaged producers; hence, acting upon such motivations is viewed as providing psychic rewards. If consumers are convinced that their actions indeed have resulted in improved well-being for disadvantaged producers, a virtuous cycle may be created in which consumers seek further psychic rewards through additional fair trade purchases. In general, consumers are agreeing to pay a price premium in order to be more comfortable that the goods they consume result in fairer returns to producers. Archer and Fritsch (2010) have characterized this consumer behavioral process as deviating from more traditional notions of economic rationality, and as instead incorporating ethical social norms in economic decision making.

Some fair trade initiatives include appeals to other consumer motivations as well, with two perhaps of greatest frequency. First, fair trade proponents at times argue that the quality of fair trade products is higher—because products are more carefully produced, use higher quality raw materials, or are made by more skilled or motivated workers. In this instance, change agents are appealing to consumer self-interest motivations for better products. Second, many fair trade initiatives emphasize the sustainability of the processes used to produce products and, in particular stress that such processes are more environmentally friendly. This again is intended to appeal to altruistic motives of consumers regarding environmental sustainability, and hence to provide another form of psychic reward.

The Political Development of Fair Trade Initiatives

Viewing the fair trade process outlined here from the perspective of the political framework introduced in Chapter 2, there are several possible pathways in developing fair trade initiatives. For simplicity of presentation, I will focus on change agents working at the grassroots level to engage new producers in fair trade. Figure 6.1 summarizes the basic fair trade development process from this perspective. However, fair trade is a process that involves people actively working to establish fairer trading practices across the production and distribution processes, and people working in these organizations likewise could be viewed as change agents.

At the local level, where producers are first engaged, change agents representing several different organizational types may stimulate fair trade engagement by producers. First, nonprofit or voluntary organizations may initiate fair trade projects, which either are established as the sole organizational purpose or as only a part of what the organization does. For example, in the previously mentioned Ten Thousand Villages project of the Mennonite Church, the church organization would be seen as the primary change agent behind this development, which obviously is only a small part of the Church's mission. Alternatively, a change agent or small group of persons might establish a nonprofit organization explicitly to develop fair trade

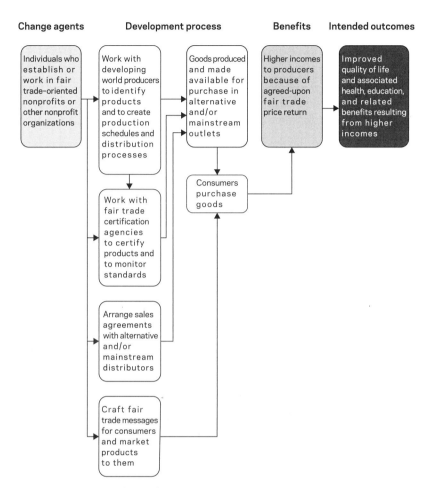

Change agents   **Development process**   **Benefits**   **Intended outcomes**

Individuals who establish or work in fair trade-oriented nonprofits or other nonprofit organizations

Work with developing world producers to identify products and to create production schedules and distribution processes

Goods produced and made available for purchase in alternative and/or mainstream outlets

Higher incomes to producers because of agreed-upon fair trade price return

Improved quality of life and associated health, education, and related benefits resulting from higher incomes

Work with fair trade certification agencies to certify products and to monitor standards

Consumers purchase goods

Arrange sales agreements with alternative and/or mainstream distributors

Craft fair trade messages for consumers and market products to them

FIGURE 6.1 Fair Trade Development Process

projects in a locality or set of localities, and once established, may grow this initiative into an organization that stimulates fair trade project development more broadly. It also should be noted that in addition to being the primary beneficiaries, workers also may be seen as change agents in fair trade, because they often collaborate closely with nonprofit organizational staff in the developmental process. I nonetheless will view them here as being beneficiaries of these efforts.

These workers and their families are almost always the primary beneficiaries of such efforts, although consumers may be seen as secondary beneficiaries to the extent that they derive benefits from being able to obtain higher-quality goods. In addition, many fair trade initiatives consciously target indigenous organizations and community leaders as beneficiaries, in the sense that the intent is to improve organizational skills and collective decision-making capabilities.

Consumers are the most central intermediary actors, and the process of convincing them to purchase fair trade products is crucial to the success of fair trade initiatives. Consumers usually must be enticed to pay a premium price for a good that may be of no better quality than the non fair trade alternative. In this case, they essentially are agreeing to pay for social values they hold beyond the more utilitarian value of the product. Therefore, the ability of change agents to sway consumers in this respect is critical to fair trade success, and it requires the development of solid and well-packaged information on the benefits that flow to producers and indigenous communities as the result of fair trade purchases.

In some cases, especially early in the fair trade movement, change agents were tasked with developing their own alternative distribution networks to sell the products of their producers. However, as the movement has grown, change agents are more likely to work with intermediary organizations for this purpose. If goods are to be sold through alternative markets, the change agent is likely to become a member of an ATO, which then assumes a primary role in product distribution through its networks. In the increasingly common case of selling fair trade goods in mainstream markets, the change agent must work with the appropriate fair trade labeling organization in its area of operation, so that products can be certified. Even when products are not mainstreamed, certification has become increasingly important as part of the product distribution process. These fair trade intermediary organizations also may provide important technical support to change agents, and even may instigate and encourage change agents to develop fair trade projects as well. For example, based on extensive experience with other initiatives, fair trade organizations often can consult with neophyte change agents regarding pricing policies, and also may be in the position to offer advice on expanded distribution networks.

As previously discussed, fair trade projects initially relied heavily on alternative distribution networks, including special stores and mail ordering systems. However, mainstream stores—including many large corporate entities—now are purchasing and selling fair trade products (Fisher, 2009;

Wilkinson, 2007). Like consumers, these corporations and other main-stream stores may be seen as important intermediaries. Corporations may agree to enter into agreements to sell fair trade products for one of two reasons. First, they may become convinced that their customer base is desirous of the fair trade product, and so they provide it just as they would any other good. This again emphasizes the importance of consumers in this form of social change, for their voice regarding desired products must be expressed to the corporate entity (De Pelsmacker, Driesen, and Rayp, 2005). Second, and related, the corporation may be convinced that including fair trade goods in its portfolio will convey positive benefits in terms of corporate branding or imaging (Renard, 2005). In this sense, the corporation may choose at least limited fair trade marketing as a CSR strategy.

FAIR TRADE CASE EXAMPLES

Fair trade initiatives commonly share adherence to a set of principles and practices related to paying producers fair prices and to assuring quality standards. However, they also differ substantially with respect to where they operate, the products they sell, their distribution and financing methods, and their organizational auspices. The following examples illustrate three fair trade initiatives with differences across selected aspects of these features.

The nonprofit organization Ten Thousand Villages is among the oldest and most well-known fair trade initiatives.[1] Founded in 1946 by the wife of a Mennonite Church administrator, Ten Thousand Villages became a Mennonite-sponsored project to help poor developing country artisans sell their crafts. Initial efforts focused on finding developing world artisans and making agreements to purchase their work for sale in the United States. The primary distribution outlets have been small stores run directly by Ten Thousand Villages. In the early years, the stores were staffed almost exclusively by volunteers to reduce costs, but paid managers were added to enhance efficiency and management quality in later years. The project was spun off from the church as a separate nonprofit in 2000 but remained wholly owned by the church until 2012, when a new partnership agreement was reached that continues extensive church involvement without exclusive ownership. The initiative also expanded from the United States to Canada.[2]

Ten Thousand Villages emphasizes several key principles consistent with the fair trade approach. Among these are establishment of fair prices in cooperation with developing world artisans, cash advances to artisans for their products and prompt final payment upon delivery, the establishment of long-term and consistent trading relationships, collaboration on product design, and attention to environmental considerations in product development. The design collaboration is an especially interesting aspect. Ten Thousand Villages attempts to select handcrafted products consistent with cultural traditions. However, its staff simultaneously consults with artisans about refining their goods and production practices, so that products are appealing to developed world consumers and are produced in more efficient and environmentally friendly ways. The organization also conducts ongoing audits to assure that agreed upon fair practices are followed. Prices are kept reasonable despite the higher than usual wages paid to the artisans, because most of the workers in Ten Thousand Villages stores are volunteers and because the Mennonite Church has provided substantial facility donations for the stores.

In 2013, Ten Thousand Villages was operating 78 stores in the United States and had agreements with more than 300 other retailers to sell its products. It additionally has built an extensive online sales capacity in recent years, and collaborates with organizers to sell at a substantial number of art and other festivals each year. It is engaged in agreements with producers from 37 countries in the Caribbean, Latin America, Africa, the Middle East, and Asia. U.S. sales totaled nearly $28 million in fiscal year 2012, nearly double the sales from ten years earlier.

GoodWeave International is using fair trade practices in an attempt to end the use of child labor in the handmade carpet weaving industry in India and Nepal (Welch, 2008).[3] It was founded by Kailash Satyarthi in 1994 in India and was originally known as Rugmark; a U.S. affiliate was established in 1999. These dual locations combined a developing world focus on producers with a developed world focus on importers and consumers. As the initiative grew, it expanded to include a producer focused organization in Nepal and consumer focused organizations in the United Kingdom and Germany. These organizations all operate as nonprofit entities. The Rugmark name was changed to GoodWeave in 2009, although essential features of the model remain similar. In addition, GoodWeave efforts expanded into Afghanistan in 2011.

Rug design or import companies working with GoodWeave sign contracts agreeing to produce rugs without child labor, including agreeing to allow random inspections by GoodWeave staff to verify that child laborers are not in the workforce. Participating companies also pay licensing fees to GoodWeave. In return, GoodWeave labels are placed on rugs produced by the participating companies to certify that child labor was not used. In the consuming countries, GoodWeave organizations work to obtain agreements from importers to sell GoodWeave certified rugs, as well as to educate consumers about the value associated with purchasing these rugs.

A portion of all GoodWeave licensing fees are used to fund the rescue and rehabilitation of children who have been exposed to child labor in the rug-making industry. If children are found to be working in the factories during the agreed upon random inspections, they immediately are removed and provided with alternative services. It is estimated that more than 3,600 children have been removed from factories due to GoodWeave efforts; in turn, they have been offered rehabilitation, medical, educational, and other services.

Nearly 30% of the handmade rugs made in Nepal now carry the Good-Weave label, and nearly 11 million GoodWeave rugs have been sold. The United States is the world's largest consumer of handmade rugs, and about 5% of the handmade rugs imported into the United States are GoodWeave certified. The U.S. affiliate estimates that if the portion of U.S. purchased handmade rugs that are GoodWeave certified could be increased to 15%, child labor in the southern Asia rug industry could be ended (Welch, 2008).

The organization Cafédirect illustrates a more complex development example.[4] Founded in 1991, it represented a unique joint venture among four well-established United Kingdom alternative trading organizations: Oxfam Trading, Equal Exchange, Traidcraft, and Twin Trading. Its objective initially was to obtain fairer coffee prices for small Latin American growers—to improve grower incomes and to foster community development. However, it quickly grew and now is involved in the distribution of more than 40 specialty coffee, tea, and hot chocolate products, and its geographic reach has extended to Africa and Asia. It purchases products from 38 small-scale producer organizations in these developing world locations, which represent more than 280,000 local farmers referred to as "smallholders."

Each of the four founding organizations contributed financially to the development of the initiative, and as the organization grew, venture capital to support operations also was raised. These financial investments allow Cafédirect to provide advance payments of 60% to growers for products, with remaining payments made with interest as products are sold. Each of the four founding organizations is certified as a fair trade organization, which allows Cafédirect to easily certify products and sell them primarily through alternative trading networks. Purchase agreements are made directly with producer organizations so that no additional traders must be paid.

As the organization and the fair trade market more generally evolved, Cafédirect increasingly moved toward mainstream distribution networks, which extended its reach but subjected it to scrutiny and competition from mainstream suppliers. After a meteoric rise in sales for many years, the company has experienced sales difficulties in recent years. It nonetheless remains a leading fair trade company, with 15.7 million Euros in sales in 2010.

Cafédirect has a history of consulting with local producer cooperatives to improve their practices in working with local growers. In this sense, it has focused on the dual fair trade objectives of providing higher economic returns to local farmers while also providing technical assistance on business development. In addition to establishing fair prices for growers, Cafédirect has included these producers as shareholders and has grower representatives on its board. It estimates that more than 50% of Cafédirect profits have been returned to growing communities for programs intended to improve skills and related product quality, improve environmental standards, and enhance community development.

SKILLS NEEDED BY FAIR TRADE CHANGE AGENTS

Fair trade change agents are mostly concerned with developing viable strategies for producing and distributing fairly developed and traded products. The previously elaborated steps in creating such initiatives suggest that the most important skills for these change agents pertain to business management and development. Fair trade initiators must be skilled in assessing both potential markets and the capabilities of indigenous producers to provide goods for such markets in a consistent and sustainable manner. Furthermore, they must possess the practical management skills needed to successfully run any small business, and they also frequently must play an important teaching role in inculcating skills and relevant attitudes to the indigenous producers with whom they work. To the extent that they move beyond alternative distribution networks of their own to working with mainstream retailers, they must also be skilled in negotiating reasonable prices with entities that are likely to have considerable expertise.

As with any business, effective product marketing is critical, and this is especially true of fair trade goods. Fair trade initiators face special challenges if they use alternative distribution systems, in that they must create or tap into networks for connecting with consumers who may be most interested in the ethical values being promoted through fair trade. They also must be able to effectively package and present fair trade messages. This requires skill in concisely presenting factual data related to production processes and product quality, as well as in creating more emotional appeals highlighting the personal circumstances of poor producers assisted through fair trade efforts.

At the community level, fair trade agents must be able to effectively communicate with local producers who often have had extensive histories of being exploited by business entities. This requires not only clearly articulating the fair trade process and how it can work to the advantage of indigenous producers, but also building trust and demonstrating that the fair trade initiative actually will produce the benefits it promises. A great deal of cultural sensitivity is required in these trust-building efforts, as well as in developing communications strategies with local populations more generally. It is in this realm that those with training in human services related professional programs such as social work may be especially well-positioned to contribute.

THE CONDITIONS FOR FAIR TRADE SUCCESS

Fair trade initiatives only are likely to be successful if certain market conditions can be created or stimulated. Product cost issues probably are most fundamental in this respect. In some cases, fair trade initiatives may be able to develop production innovations or other efficiencies that allow fair trade products to be competitive price-wise with products produced in more mainstream ways. However, this generally is not the case; given that fair trade purposefully intends to raise wages, fund community development, or otherwise more fully reflect actual production costs, fair trade goods of comparable quality generally cost more. Some fair trade initiators also will argue that the products produced through their initiatives are of higher quality than similar types of goods, so that higher prices actually are reflective of the tangible quality of the product. However, this typically is debatable, and often is difficult to establish irrefutably at any rate. The actual price premiums for fair trade goods vary considerably depending on the particular products. For example, Fairtrade International (2012) suggested that the social premium for fair trade coffee in 2011 was 20 cents per pound.

Fair trade goods, thus, generally have cost disadvantages, and are mainly sold in competitive developed country markets having many mainstream product distribution networks. Fair trade initiators consequently face challenging market environments, and they must be very creative as they seek to establish and sustain successful operations. There are two nonmutually exclusive general strategies that fair trade initiators may employ in these respects, with one of these focusing on production costs and the other on marketing.

First, higher costs usually will result for that part of production related to labor due to the intent to provide fair returns to workers. With this starting assumption, the only way to make costs more comparable to goods produced without such higher labor costs is to minimize costs in other areas of production and distribution. This requires fair trade change agents to be efficient and innovative in developing their operations. For example, nonprofit organizations may become involved in product distribution, and hence may provide considerable volunteer labor and other resources that reduce distribution costs. Even with such practices, fair trade products are likely to cost somewhat more than similar nonfair trade goods, but keeping such cost differences from becoming prohibitive to consumers is critical to the success of fair trade efforts.

Second, because consumers of fair trade products usually are being asked to pay a price premium to support selected social values in consumption, the marketing of the social values being promoted through fair trade purchases is extremely important. Therefore it is critical that fair trade change agents are able to effectively permeate mainstream marketing networks, or else are able to establish an alternative marketing niche of sufficient size to attract a large and sustainable group of consumers. This condition can be very challenging, especially in a mass market consumer world involving very sophisticated advertising by heavily resourced companies. Faced with generally inferior advertising resources, fair trade initiators must demonstrate considerable creativity in this respect, and clear comparisons with nonfairly traded products may be among the most effective techniques available.

THE POSSIBILITIES AND LIMITS OF FAIR TRADE

The growth of fair trade initiatives over the past 40 or so years has been impressive in terms of the number of new initiatives, the increasing sophistication of fair trade organizational structures such as those developed for labeling and certification, and in terms of increasing market shares. Although the effects of fair trade on producers remains contested, some results indicate improvement in family incomes and in community capacity building (Bacon, 2005; Hayes, 2006; Becchetti & Costantino, 2008; Smith, 2008, 2009). The movement has stimulated not only concrete market-based initiatives on behalf of poor producers, but has encouraged change agents and consumers to carefully think through the production processes associated with consumption. This growth of more politically oriented consumers may have profound implications for development and social justice if it can be extended to wider audiences.

Yet, critics have raised important concerns about the depth of change that is possible through this approach, as well as some possible harmful side effects, and there are many interesting debates among fair trade proponents about the best strategies for extending fair trade development. One criticism of fair trade pertains to the extent of its reach. For example, Fridell (2004) indicates that despite very rapid proportional growth increases, fair trade products represented only about 0.01% of all global trade in 2001. Although fair trade products often show impressive growth patterns when they first are introduced, some empirical research also suggests that this growth plateaus rather quickly (European Fair Trade Association, 2001).

This has led some critics to question whether fair trade initiatives ever will constitute anything more than niche markets. Selected products have captured impressive market shares in some countries, such as an estimated 42% of the bagged sugar trade in the United Kingdom and 55% of the banana market in Switzerland (Fairtrade International, 2012). More commonly, even in countries with relatively high levels of support for fair trade, market shares for products fall well below 10%. For example, MacGillivray (2000) reported that most ethical labeling initiatives regarding fair trade products, organic food, and products free from child labor constituted less than 1% of market shares. Even for fair trade coffee in Europe, which has been at the forefront of fair trade development, De Pelsmacker, Driesen, and Rayp (2005) found very low fair trade market penetration rates in most countries. Furthermore, initiatives to date generally have been limited to a fairly narrow group of products, which raises concerns about fair trade reach as a broader economic development strategy.

The reason for fair trade goods reaching thresholds at relatively low market penetration levels is not well understood. Some critics contend that, by providing artificially higher prices for selected goods, fair trade encourages others to produce more of the goods on which fair trade focuses. This may tend to distort effort and lead to oversupply of these products, which can result in price reductions (Henderson, 2008; Sidwell, 2008). This in turn may not only distort prices generally, but could lead to fair trade sales thresholds as price differentials between fair trade and nonfair trade products grow. Although this contention appears plausible, empirical support for it is not well established. Another possibility is that a relatively limited set of consumers prefers to shop according to ethical values, or at least to pay the commonly resulting price premiums for fair trade products. In that case, it would make sense for fair trade product growth to increase fairly dramatically when products are first introduced before stabilizing as additional consumers with such orientations become scarce. Determining the extent of support for fair trade, especially in terms of actual purchasing practices as opposed to general philosophical orientations, is an important area for further consumer research. It likewise is critical for fair trade proponents to gain a better understanding of this issue, particularly with respect to thinking through how to appeal to a wider consumer base in marketing.

Of course, this criticism only is meaningful at the aggregate level of considering change on behalf of poor producers, and should not detract from successes of fair trade within the narrower margins in which it operates. However, some researchers have also questioned the extent to which fairly traded products actually benefit workers and their families. For example, Henderson (2008) has argued that employee treatment is a relatively minor consideration in obtaining FLO product certification, and Sidwell (2008) contends that fair trade benefits relatively well-off producers while neglecting more disadvantaged ones. However, Smith (2009) counters that the International Labour Organization conventions that serve as the basis of FLO standards actually are quite extensive in the principles and benefits they convey. I agree, and believe that the appropriate basis of measurement is the benefits received by fair trade producers from their labor as compared to other workers producing nonfair trade products of the same basic type. This is an area where more direct comparative research would be very useful.

Other criticisms with respect to the effects of fair trade on producers pertain to equity and to short-term versus longer-term economic benefits. With respect to equity, Leclair (2002) argues that, given the small portion of goods sold through fair trade, the approach essentially selects winners and losers among indigenous producers of many goods. That is, the producers with whom fair trade organizations choose to engage will receive higher prices than other producers of similar goods, even though their circumstances may be similar. The only way to address this issue is to significantly extend the reach of fair trade markets so that greater numbers of producers are included, which runs counter to the previously raised issue concerning market thresholds for fair trade goods.

The short-term versus long-term effects of some fair trade efforts are more subtle. On the one hand, fair trade has been commended as a process that helps preserve traditional products in developing communities, as well as important cultural traditions and values that are being lost in the face of globalized, mass-market-oriented production. However, by encouraging the production of such goods, fair trade may inhibit the responsiveness of these communities in moving production toward goods with higher economic returns (Leclair, 2002). At the same time, Leclair suggests that fair trade may be a viable shorter-term strategy in aiding poor communities as they transition to more modern economies.

At the aggregate level, a more troubling criticism pertains to the growing involvement of corporations in either selling fair trade products or developing their own fair trade product lines. Critics fear that savvy corporations will be inclined to offer a narrow range of fair trade products for branding or positive imaging purposes, while simultaneously focusing most of their production and distribution efforts on unfairly traded products (Archer & Fritsch, 2010; Doherty & Tranchell, 2006). For example, Fridell (2004) indicates that only about 1–2% of the coffee sold by Starbucks is fair trade certified, even though the corporation has received considerable favorable publicity for selling fair trade coffee in its stores. Fair trade thus is viewed as serving as little more than a vehicle through which corporations deflect attention from more fundamental concerns about their operating practices. As discussed in Chapter 3, this corporate tactic sometimes is referred to as "cleanwashing" (Murray and Raynolds, 2000), and it corresponds to similar concerns environmentalists have expressed about "greenwashing" through symbolic corporate attempts to show environmental improvements in selected production practices (Laufer, 2003). In the worst cases, fair trade initiatives may camouflage more unscrupulous production or distribution practices for other products in the same corporation. For example, Doherty and Tranchell (2006) highlight the case of the Nestle Corporation, which introduced fair trade coffee constituting 0.2% of its coffee line while simultaneously occupying "the top spot in the Ethical Consumer organization's list of boycotted products, largely thanks to its aggressive marketing of baby milk powder in Africa" (p.4).

Such concerns about corporate involvement and motivations have fueled a related debate regarding the advisability of "mainstreaming" the distribution of fair trade products. On the positive side, mainstreaming clearly has allowed the expansion of fair trade sales well beyond what would be possible without it. For example, Nicholls and Opal (2008) indicate that sales through supermarkets or other mainstream retail outlets already have become very important for many products, and it often is argued that developing competitive alternative trade systems in the face of increasing mainstream competition is so difficult that further expansion of fair trade will require additional mainstream distribution.

Some fair trade advocates have contended that pursuit of mainstreaming promotes making fair trade considerations an everyday occurrence as consumers are confronted with fair trade alternatives in the places where they do most of their shopping (Doherty & Tranchell, 2006). Penny Newman of Cafédirect nicely summarizes this sentiment: "The fair trade movement must become a mainstream movement, not viewed as a charitable exercise by the minority, but as an everyday consumer choice made and understood by the majority" (Doherty & Tranchell, 2006, p. 19). Doherty and Tranchell further contend that mainstreaming contributes to network building with important community stakeholders who often are influential in the political world, such as supermarket officials; this can lead to the development of stronger coalitions to more broadly advocate for fair trade. They argue that the media also may be more inclined to cover fair trade stories when they can point readers to larger and well-known outlets where fair trade goods may be purchased. Engaging these community stakeholders is considered essential if fair trade practitioners are to simultaneously lobby for broader fair trade policies as they engage in consumer-oriented fair trade; Doherty and Tranchell (2006) refer to this dual focus as "radical mainstreaming."

However, some fair trade proponents fear that fair trade products will lose their distinctive character as mainstreaming proceeds, and likewise are uneasy about the aforementioned co-optation of the fair trade movement in support of corporate imaging. In a related sense, the development of completely alternative production and distribution processes is viewed by some as among the most important contributions of fair trade. They see fair trade not just as a mechanism for improving the well-being of poor developing world producers—it more fundamentally is an approach that can demonstrate the viability of more humane and sustainable economic models. It may be difficult to demonstrate this adequately if consumers only make rapid choices of fair trade versus alternative products in the context of mainstream food purchases. In other words, what is gained in terms of more expandable markets may be offset by a lack of depth of commitment or understanding about fair trade (Nichols & Opal, 2008; Renard, 2003; Raynolds, 2008).

The mainstreaming debate, and the related issue of how broadly corporate participation in fair trade should be encouraged, was brought into sharp focus with the 2012 withdrawal of Fair Trade USA from FLO (Sherman, 2012). Fair Trade USA has long been the FLO certification organization in the United States, and as such was subject to FLO overarching certification policies. But the organization has an aggressive goal of doubling fair trade coffee sales in the United States by 2015. To do so, it wants to include plantations in its fair trade standards, as opposed to the narrower inclusion of democratically oriented producer cooperatives allowed through FLO. This opens up fair trade certification to corporate entities, which is in opposition to FLO certification standards. Fair Trade USA will instead develop its own standards, which of course may confuse consumers further about the meaning of fair trade and also may dilute the distinctive values often associated with it.

A closely related but broader argument has been emphasized by Fridell (2004). He fears that the extensive attention to the consumer-oriented fair trade model described here has deflected attention from the broader fair trade movement, and in particular the more aggregate political economic focus of that movement. As he starkly puts it, "While public institutions in Europe and North America have shown increasing support of the fair trade network, they have also continued to reject the greater demands of the fair trade movement and have pushed forward with neoliberal reforms. This suggests that to these institutions, the fair trade network is increasingly being employed as an 'ethical fig leaf' to mask their devotion to a broader neoliberal agenda" (2004, p. 424). In short, he argues that the growth of fair trade production and consumption has simultaneously been marked by the decline of other and perhaps more important aspects of the fair trade movement.

Both the mainstreaming versus alternative distribution and fair trade network versus broader macroeconomic policy focus debates are very interesting, and there are persuasive advocates on both sides of these issues. These arguments of course are not unique to fair trade. For example, the fair trade network versus broader macroeconomic development issue is similar to many in public policy regarding the desirability of smaller incremental changes versus more sweeping ones—a debate that never has been persuasively resolved in political science or economics. The mainstreaming versus alternative distribution discussions likewise resonate with more general concerns among social movement leaders and nonprofit organizations about the possibilities of being co-opted as they gain traction and engage with wider audiences.

My view is that progress in developing the consumer-oriented fair trade approach described here does not necessarily come at the expense of advocacy around developing more just macroeconomic trade policies between developed and developing world countries. Although the trade-off argument of one versus the other certainly is plausible, there really is no convincing empirical support for it. It seems more likely that the ineffectiveness of advocacy around macroeconomic trade policies has had little to do with the growth of fair trade consumerism, but rather has been a casualty of broader neoliberal thrusts in governmental policies together with the increasing globalization of economic production and distribution.

Although I share the concerns of alternative trading system advocates about the possible dilution of fair trade that may accompany mainstreaming, on balance I think mainstreaming is important if fair trade is to move beyond the niche status it now enjoys. The large majority of shopping for most products continues to occur in mainstream outlets, so using these to sell products seems critical to educating a growing audience about the importance of fair trade and, in turn, to increasing fair trade purchases.

On a great many social issues, advocates with differing perspectives on the most productive strategies for change march hand-in-hand toward a greater purpose, and I think this is a useful direction in thinking about the aforementioned fair trade debates. The nature of political coalitions often allows such groups to simultaneously pursue these different strategic directions while still striving for a common goal. Although deflection or "cleanwashing" is a legitimate concern, it is the role of fair trade advocates to raise this point in policy debates, and to detail the extent to which cleanwashing is occurring. There also is no obvious reason that fair trade advocates cannot continue to lobby aggressively for more just macroeconomic trading policies for developing countries at the same time that fair trade consumerism proceeds. Their effectiveness in doing so is likely to have much more to do with complex economic and power relationships than with the relative success of consumer-oriented fair trade.

Finally, the effectiveness of fair trade ultimately resides heavily on the willingness of better-off consumers in the developed world to pay price premiums to support ethical developmental values; fair trade is very similar to CSR in this respect. Concerns have been raised that such support will be inconsistent and subject to the vagaries of economic prosperity in the developed world (Leclair, 2002). This is a reasonable point, and one to which I will return in the concluding chapter. However, it is worth noting that any efforts to affect the returns to producers and consumers from trade are subject to debate, whether this occurs through laws and regulations in the governmental arena or through appeals to the ethical values of consumers in the marketplace. As such, attempts to provide fairer returns to developing world producers always will involve the willingness of the developed world to pay more for products, so the issue becomes whether this can most effectively occur through consumer appeals, expression through democratically elected governments and international organizations, or by other means.

SUMMARY

With its coupling of grassroots economic development and appeals to consumers to pay fairer prices for the goods they consume, fair trade has become an appealing approach for many social activists. The sale of fair trade goods correspondingly has grown dramatically in Europe and North

America, as has the sophistication of fair trade development and distribution processes. Fair trade initiatives commonly are framed to promote ethical values related to consumption, and so are of particular interest to change agents with a social justice orientation.

Of the approaches examined in this book, fair trade initiatives are most similar to the externally driven CSR model described in Chapter 3. Each requires consumers to consider the consequences of their consumption as they ponder purchases and, in many cases, to pay a price premium to promote social values. However, fair trade is much more focused on the development of alternative production and distribution mechanisms, as opposed to influencing consumers to purchase from one mainstream corporation versus another.

Despite rapid growth, fair trade goods continue to represent a very small portion of nearly all markets in which they are traded, which has fostered criticisms about the relative reach of this approach. This has led some proponents to advocate for the more mainstream distribution of fair trade products, and recent years have witnessed large corporations such as Walmart entering into fair trade agreements for selected goods. Yet such mainstreaming also has become controversial as other fair trade advocates argue that it perverts the fundamental values that were established with alternative trade processes.

At any rate, it appears very likely that fair trade initiatives will continue to grow. Fair trade advocates have gained increasing experience with identifying and offering technical assistance to indigenous producers. Furthermore, the Internet and other improved communications technologies have rapidly expanded the capacity of change agents to frame fair trade appeals to diverse consumer audiences. The term itself has assumed a high moral ground in many countries, which can play a vital role in extending its reach.

Market-Based Social Change Models

THE PRECEDING FOUR CHAPTERS HAVE described and assessed the potential contributions of leading models that emphasize diverse market-based strategies to improve the life circumstances of disadvantaged groups. If one considers the internal versus external corporate social responsibility (CSR) approaches discussed in Chapter 3 and the bottom of the pyramid (BOP) versus microenterprise and indigenous technology creation (ITC) approaches presented in Chapter 5 as essentially distinct models, a total of seven approaches have been considered. In this concluding chapter, I will discuss the most important lessons to be derived from my assessment of these approaches. I do so in the spirit of generating further debate and research concerning their merits, in addition to offering more practical guidance to academics and practitioners who may be considering their use in various social change contexts.

First, I will comparatively highlight key similarities and differences among the approaches described in earlier chapters. I then will discuss some overarching strengths and limitations of these approaches. Given the prominent roles that governments continue to play in social provision, and the frequent absence of thoughtful discussion of governmental involvement associated with these models, I also will offer ideas about possible collaborations between governmental agents and change agents engaged in these approaches. Finally, I will conclude by assessing the potential contributions of these models in broader orientations to social change.

COMPARING MARKET-BASED MODELS OF CHANGE

As discussed in Chapter 1, each of these models primarily utilizes nongovernmental strategies in attempting to facilitate change, and each typically embraces business principles and/or intersects with corporations and businesses as a central operating feature. However, the similarities across all seven approaches tend to end here, so comparative analysis involves coupling selected overarching observations with assessments more peculiar to particular models. I will attempt to do so in the following sections, with respect to a multitude of issues that typically interest academic policy analysts and applied policy practitioners.

For purposes of discussion, and consistent with key aspects of the general model framework presented in Chapter 2, I have selected nine aspects of model development and operation that seem especially useful in thinking comparatively about approaches.

- Who are the intended beneficiaries?
- Who are the principal change agents?
- Who are the key intermediaries?
- What benefits are delivered and with what intended outcomes?
- What is the nature of political interactions?
- What is implied about innovation?
- What is implied about sustainability of projects?
- What is implied about scaling of projects? and
- What is implied about management?

Table 7.1 highlights what I view as the most important model characteristics along these nine dimensions for each of the seven approaches described; the following sections will offer some basic comparative insights concerning each dimension. The table is intended to summarily compare and contrast major features as opposed to providing detailed information. It may omit aspects of models that readers will consider pertinent, so referring back to earlier chapters for more detailed information may be useful. I also should stress that I am trying to make very broad-brush comparisons among models that often have been very loosely defined, which requires considerable latitude in interpretation and which may do injustice to the perspectives of some supporters of a given approach. In particular, for many

TABLE 7.1 Summary Comparison of Attributes of Market-Based Change Models

	CORPORATE SOCIAL RESPONSIBILITY		SOCIAL ENTRE-PRENEURSHIP	PRIVATE SUSTAINABLE DEVELOPMENT			FAIR TRADE
	INTERNAL	EXTERNAL		MICRO-ENTERPRISE	INDIGENOUS TECHNOLOGY CREATION	BOTTOM OF THE PYRAMID	
Beneficiaries	Corporate employees, consumers, community members (within and outside corporate sites)	Corporate employees, consumers, community members (within and outside corporate sites)	Variable	Low-income individuals with small-scale business idea	Low-income developing world producers	Low-income developing world consumers	Low-income developing world producers
Change Agents	Corporate officials	Advocacy organizations	Individuals or small groups	Microlenders and individuals with small-scale business idea	Individuals or small groups oriented toward developing indigenously sustainable productive technology	Profit-oriented entrepreneurs or businesses (especially corporations)	Nonprofit organizations or groups of individuals

(continued)

TABLE 7.1 Summary Comparison of Attributes of Market-Based Change Models (continued)

| | CORPORATE SOCIAL RESPONSIBILITY | | SOCIAL ENTRE-PRENEURSHIP | PRIVATE SUSTAINABLE DEVELOPMENT | | | FAIR TRADE |
	INTERNAL	EXTERNAL		MICRO-ENTERPRISE	INDIGENOUS TECHNOLOGY CREATION	BOTTOM OF THE PYRAMID	
Intermediaries	Other officials within corporation, consumers, and community members	Consumers, community members, corporate officials, media, and government officials	Variable	Minimal, except for volunteers to assist organization, funding efforts, and technical assistance	Minimal	Minimal	Developed world consumers
Benefits	Variable but often focus on benefits to communities with corporate sites	Variable but often focus on wages and other benefits for corporate employees or on local/broad environmental impacts	Variable	Income generation for small-scale producers, largely in developing world	Income generation for small-scale producers, largely in developing world	Improved products for low-income developing world consumers	Income generation for small-scale developing world producers

Innovation	Variable	Variable	Central to approach—emphasis on creative thinking about difficult problems	Variable—depends on businesses created by individuals	Central focus—developing new technologies consistent with producer needs and capabilities	Central focus—developing new products consistent with consumer needs and capabilities	Variable—innovations tend to focus on marketing and distribution strategies
Sustainability	Variable but not primary focus of most initiatives; some strategic approaches stress longer term use of resources or friendlier environmental impacts	Variable—employee and environmental outcomes sometimes framed in terms of more sustainable production	Often emphasized with respect to longer-term financial viability	Not primary focus, except as sometimes emphasized in microenterprise project selection by funders	Central to approach—developers seek technology that can be afforded/maintained by producers	Central focus—product development and distribution strategies emphasize ongoing use by poor consumers	Central focus—interest in pricing and distribution strategies that allow ongoing production and sales
Scaling	Not primary focus	Variable—selection of corporate targets sometimes intended to set precedents for all or larger subset of corporations	Variable—emphasized by some as fundamental to being considered as an innovation	Variable, some have stressed moving models successful in one community to new sites	Variable—some emphasize to extend reach of promising technologies	Variable—some emphasize extending availability of tested products to large numbers of poor consumers	Variable—debates about mainstreaming focus on extending market share

(continued)

TABLE 7.1 Summary Comparison of Attributes of Market-Based Change Models (continued)

| | CORPORATE SOCIAL RESPONSIBILITY | | SOCIAL ENTRE-PRENEURSHIP | MICRO-ENTERPRISE | PRIVATE SUSTAINABLE DEVELOPMENT | | FAIR TRADE |
	INTERNAL	EXTERNAL			INDIGENOUS TECHNOLOGY CREATION	BOTTOM OF THE PYRAMID	
Political Interactions	Consensual	Conflictual with corporations, consensual with other and intermediaries	Consensual, except for occasional social advocacy efforts	Consensual	Consensual	Consensual	Consensual, except for competitive aspects with mainstream producers
Management	Not primary focus but may benefit from internal ties to corporate business resources and practices	Not primary focus but skills in research, organizing, and media communications often stressed	Focuses on entrepreneurial business model, including marketing, testing, evaluation, refinement, and replication	Many projects provide training and technical assistance on sound business operational practices	Not primary focus, except technology developers often provide training and technical assistance on proper use and maintenance of products	Not primary focus, except for emphasis on product design and distribution that allows profit-making with small per unit price margins	Focus on alternative distribution and marketing strategies, as well as technical assistance to improve product development by indigenous producers

of the dimensions, I have attempted to classify each model as "high," "moderate," or "low" with respect to the relative emphasis the literature places on that attribute, and these classification judgments are admittedly impressionistic. I nonetheless believe that such comparisons are needed given the current state of discussion of these models, and I welcome criticism and re-formulation of my interpretations.

Who Are the Beneficiaries?

As stated in Chapter 1, my primary purpose in examining these change approaches was to consider their viability in assisting poor persons in the developing world. My analysis suggests that variations of each model have focused on this purpose, but the extent to which they explicitly do so varies considerably.

Fair trade, microenterprise, ITC, and BOP development approaches center on ideas for improving the economic circumstances of low-income persons, and so tend to be strongest on this criterion. Microenterprise, ITC, and fair trade each offers a different approach for stimulating primarily small-scale, grassroots-oriented economic development in poor communities. In contrast, BOP development attempts to improve the consumption choices that are available in poor areas where basic products have not been readily accessible. BOP secondarily at times promotes job opportunities for poor persons, either through aiding in the production or in the selling of goods developed by BOP producers.

Among the CSR approaches considered, externally driven models are most likely to focus on poor persons in the developing world. For example, externally driven boycott and buycott campaigns often have an objective of improving economic benefits for poor workers, such as by advocating against Nike sweatshop wages in Southeast Asia or more recently to improve Foxconn working conditions in China. However, even external CSR approaches often have other objectives, such as altering corporate environmental practices and other effects on communities in which corporate production is concentrated. Internal CSR approaches are even less focused on the poor, except to the extent that environmental or sustainable resource use and production efforts may spillover into poor communities.

Finally, many innovative projects directed at the poor in the developing world have adopted the moniker of social entrepreneurship. These have included novel approaches for delivering educational and health-care benefits to the poor and in some cases creating jobs for them. However, given that social entrepreneurship is very broad and not subject limited, it does not focus on improving the well-being of any particular target group. Although its principles thus can be useful to change agents in thinking through the strategic development of a project, social entrepreneurship should not be viewed as an approach that primarily targets society's most disadvantaged members.

Who Are the Change Agents?

I believe that social workers and other human services professionals can play useful roles in any of the market-based models described in this book. Nonetheless, the usual organizational venues for different models and the related level of organizational sophistication required to foster initiative development vary considerably. The types of expertise required also differ substantially, and so suggest the type of actors with which change agents most likely need to partner in order to be successful.

Given that social entrepreneurship (SE) projects most commonly involve start-ups instigated by innovative individuals or small groups, SE is the most variable and open to entry of the approaches discussed. Any individual with an idea and fairly limited resources can initiate a social change project incorporating developmental principles highlighted in the SE literature, and such individuals likewise may engage with diverse actors. If one interested in SE engagement wishes to pursue this approach in a more organized setting, social nonprofits embracing SE as well as a few established social businesses probably are the most likely venues.

Private sustainable development (PSD) approaches likewise are fairly open to entry on a small scale, but the business creation nature of this developmental approach suggests the importance of partnering with persons with strong business skills. Within the PSD umbrella, many initially small-scale microenterprise initiatives have grown into larger organizations, most often under nonprofit auspices. Change agents interested in contributing to more established efforts therefore may find a home in these settings. ITC projects usually are initiated by individuals or small partnerships with technical expertise; although size is not particularly important, technical developmental capabilities and business skills are critical to creating basic technology products. Larger for-profit BOP initiatives such as those promoted by Prahalad (2005) more often require corporate production and distribution capacity, and thus change agents favoring this approach should expect to either work within or interact closely with corporations or larger businesses.

CSR approaches likewise require considerable interaction with corporate officials, although the nature of these interactions varies considerably depending on the type of CSR model employed. Internally driven CSR efforts emanate from within corporations, and so the leading change agents generally are corporate leaders or other corporate staff with strategic planning and product development responsibilities. However, corporations increasingly have created "social responsibility" or similarly titled units to focus on social concerns, and individuals interested in social change through internally directed corporate responses may find these units appealing. In contrast, external CSR approaches generally are carried out through nonprofit agencies or ad hoc organizational efforts. These initiatives generally require change agents with a variety of skills, but they are more likely than internal CSR approaches to require strong research, communications, negotiation, and advocacy skills consistent with the more conflict-oriented nature of externally driven CSR.

As the most narrowly focused of the market-oriented approaches, fair trade also has perhaps the most developed organizational structures for engagement. That is, there are many fair trade labeling and certification organizations that provide well-structured opportunities for change agents, and faith-based and other large nonprofit entities have initiated fair trade projects. At the same time, the approach remains a fairly open setting for small groups of individuals to initiate new projects with producers in developing markets. In these cases, change agents can benefit from the mentoring and technical assistance available from more developed fair trade organizations as they establish new initiatives.

Who Are the Key Intermediaries?

Intermediaries are defined in this book as those groups central to whether a change approach is successful but falling outside of the basic program operations of change agents. In this sense, persons who directly contribute to the operation of the change initiative, such as funders, volunteers, and technical consultants are not viewed primarily as intermediaries. Rather, intermediaries are those whose actions change agents need to influence if the change they envision is to succeed.

There are four principal types of intermediaries that are important in these models: individual consumers and investors, institutional agents making purchasing and investment decisions, corporate officials, and government officials or community leaders. Consumers are essential intermediaries in external CSR and fair trade models because influencing consumer purchasing decisions for the benefit of others is at the heart of each of these approaches. Consumers also are important in internally driven CSR models, although not quite to the extent as in the other models. Consumers also may be important in some SE initiatives, although they are not central to that approach.

The nature of the consumptive linkage between change agents and consumer intermediaries is similar for CSR and fair trade approaches. Consumers generally are asked to alter their purchasing decisions to improve the circumstances of others; this requires consumers to consider outcomes that are independent of whatever direct benefit is derived from a product. Consequently, the challenge for change agents is to convince consumers of the importance of their purchasing decisions on the well-being of targeted beneficiaries.

It is noteworthy that consumers also play important roles in BOP, ITC, and microenterprise approaches, but not primarily as intermediaries in the sense envisioned here. Rather, consumers in these approaches are primarily low-income persons themselves. In BOP development, the challenge is to design, produce, and distribute products that meet the needs and capabilities of low-income consumers. In microenterprise work, change agents fund poor producers, who are the main beneficiaries in that the funding allows them to establish small businesses. But consumers obviously are of critical importance, because the microenterprises only can prosper through their purchases. The change agents, however, generally are not directly engaged in trying to influence consumer purchases. In ITC initiatives, poor persons must be convinced as consumers to purchase technology devices that will improve their productive capacities; in this sense, they are the beneficiaries of their purchases rather than the intermediaries.

Individual investors are important intermediaries primarily in externally driven CSR models. Just as consumers are asked to alter consumption decisions on behalf of CSR objectives, investors are asked to use such criteria in selecting investments. Direct investments in terms of donations are important to nearly any other change model as well, but note that when persons or institutions provide funding as a donation or gift they are not expecting a return, while in CSR investing some return is expected.

Institutional consumers and investors tend to be important in the same models as individual consumers and investors, but differ largely in terms of scale. Essentially, they are bundling decisions on behalf of very large numbers of consumers or investors. Because of this bundling capability and the related scale of their purchases and investments, they may be especially valued as intermediaries by change agents.

Corporations are key intermediaries in externally driven CSR and fair trade models. Change agents engaging in externally driven CSR models must convince corporate officials to change selected practices in a manner that will positively impact targeted beneficiaries. As intermediaries in this sense, corporate officials react primarily based on their assessment of the impact their response or nonresponse will have on the consumers and investors the corporation depends upon for support.

Corporations are much less central to fair trade but nonetheless play an important role in some fair trade conceptions. In particular, corporations are critical if trade advocates pursue mainstreaming strategies, because mainstreaming generally requires convincing large corporate retailers of the usefulness of selling fair trade products. In some cases, corporations move beyond merely selling fair trade goods produced through other initiatives and instead develop their own fair trade product lines, in which case corporations move from being intermediaries to being fair trade change agents.

In internal CSR and BOP approaches, corporations play the role of primary change agents. They likewise are of lesser importance as intermediaries in microenterprise development and ITC, and are of little importance in SE. That is, as largely bottoms-up community development processes, microenterprise and ITC initiatives do not tend to engage corporations, although large banking institutions have been involved in some microfinancing ventures. SE likewise most often is characterized by small-scale efforts not dependent on corporate ties, although in some cases social entrepreneurs pursue corporate actors as intermediaries to support scaling or other activities.

What Benefits Are Delivered and with What Intended Effects?

I have argued that most change models include explicitly articulated or at least easily implied perspectives regarding how circumstances will be improved for those who receive benefits. Although the benefits to be delivered through these market-based models most often pertain to economic benefits for poor producers and consumers, there are important variations among approaches, as well as in the underlying logic concerning how such benefits will move individuals and families forward.

SE is least relevant in comparatively thinking through these benefit provision and behavioral logic implications. It is very broad-based with respect to the types of benefits that may be delivered, and relatively silent concerning how such benefits are intended to stimulate behavioral change. Perhaps the most that can be said about SE in a behavioral logic respect is that its proponents often emphasize how program benefits will increase recipient capabilities and empower them to become more self-sufficient, as opposed to relying on continuing consumption benefits over time. However, this tendency is not fundamental to the model, and so I hesitate to give it much importance in assessing SE as an approach.

The other market-based models all are more well-defined in terms of intended benefits, and in turn the behavioral logic behind them is much easier to discern even when not described. Fair trade begins with the straightforward assumption that producers in the developing world are inadequately compensated for the goods they produce, and likewise that their ability to sell goods is undercut by the manner in which larger corporate sellers purchase and distribute goods. The benefits that fair trade purports to deliver are higher payment levels for any goods produced, as well as opportunities to sell higher quantities of goods. An accompanying belief often is expressed that these benefits will lead to improved qualities of life for indigenous producers and their families due to higher incomes, and that higher incomes will have important spillover benefits in terms of improved education, health, and community development. In addition, the portion of profits reserved for community development in many initiatives is intended to stimulate well-being for a broader subset of community members.

The PSD approaches likewise have fairly well-defined benefits and relatively tightly defined behavioral logics. Microenterprise development is much like fair trade in its primary focus on improving incomes for poor individuals in the developing world, and the expectation that such improvements will result in quality of life improvements and the related spillover benefits noted here. It varies primarily in the economic development strategy employed toward this end. That is, as opposed to fair trade's well-defined production and distribution strategy for organizing groups of workers, as well as a quality related certification process, microenterprise programs generally assume that small-scale producers who receive financial assistance are responsible for their own marketing and distribution.

The logic behind ITC initiatives is similar, in that they largely focus upon increasing productive capacity so that the economic circumstances of poor producers are improved. ITC differs from microenterprise by concentrating on developing specific basic technologies intended to move small-scale producers forward, as opposed to simply financing diverse individually developed microeconomic projects. Yet, it remains a bottoms-up approach in which local people work with change agents to define production needs, possibilities, and capabilities.

BOP benefits flow primarily to poor consumers rather than to poor producers. There is no specificity regarding what products should be produced, but the basic premise is that poor developing world consumers lack access to a wide range of products. The key to development in this approach is to provide products that these consumers need and can afford. The implications of providing a wider range of more affordable products are twofold. First, better access to goods should allow more competitive pricing, so that exploitation by unscrupulous providers can become less common. This in turn leaves consumers with more discretionary income for other purchases. Second, more active engagement of consumers by BOP producers is intended to result in a wider range of products being available to poor consumers, which not only can improve their quality of life but in some cases may increase their productive capacities. A secondary benefit of some BOP production models is that they employ indigenous persons in their production and distribution operations, although this benefit is less often stated and not central to the model.

The benefits intended to result from CSR initiatives are variable and tend to differ in emphasis between internal and externally driven CSR models. Important benefits include improving employee incomes or working conditions, providing safer products, minimizing production impacts in communities where goods are produced, minimizing depletion of natural resources, and minimizing broader negative environmental impacts of production or distribution processes. A focus on improving worker compensation or conditions generally parallels fair trade and microenterprise logic with respect to the benefits of higher incomes for workers. Product safety and efforts to minimize adverse local community impacts are intended to protect consumers on the one hand and nonparties to production and consumption on the other. More recent attempts by CSR advocates to focus on broader environmental impacts have less well-defined beneficiaries, in that the intent is to be part of a larger movement to sustain the global environment over time. In some cases, especially with respect to attempts to move corporate production processes toward better management of depletable resources, such environmental concerns also may have tangible impacts on specific geographic locations. For example, a CSR initiative focusing on limiting depletion of fish may have the broad intent of leading to longer-term sustainability of aquatic populations, but also may have more immediately tangible effects on local populations heavily engaged in fishing.

A final note on the benefits and logic of internal CSR models needs to be made. Although I am focusing here on the intended articulated and direct beneficiaries of change efforts, it is clear that the logic driving many internal corporate initiatives is self-interest. That is, although benefits to consumers, producers, or the environment are articulated, the ultimate hope is that these efforts will result in a better public image or other results that will improve corporate profitability. This is particularly true of strategic CSR initiatives.

What is the Nature of Political Interactions?

As discussed in Chapter 2, the politics of change requires not only identifying the roles of change agents, beneficiaries, and intermediaries, but also structuring the most important interactions among them. Although these interactions can become quite variegated and complex in selected projects, at a broad level perhaps the most fundamental question is the extent to which approaches are consensual or conflict-oriented. Another interesting question concerns how central are strategies to engage beneficiaries in development and decision making—or to what extent are these approaches consciously oriented toward participatory empowerment. I will focus on these two issues here.

With respect to the nature of political interactions, nearly all of the models are largely consensual in orientation; they rely primarily on developing supportive interactions with intermediaries for the mutually agreeable purpose of servicing targeted beneficiaries. This is not to suggest that the motivations for such friendly interactions are always the same. For example, fair trade developers may promote working with indigenous producers largely from altruistic considerations, although large mainstream stores may do so to capture a larger market niche or to establish public goodwill. Nonetheless, these two diverse stakeholders often find common ground despite differing motivations, and may work well together. Similarly, most social entrepreneurship initiatives, all forms of private sustainable development, and internal corporate social responsibility initiatives rely primarily on the development of consensual interactions.

The exception to this consensual orientation is external CSR initiatives. These naturally gravitate toward conflict, with the main variation revolving around the nature of the conflict. That is, some merely involve implied threats to encourage consumers to do business elsewhere, while others involve active engagement in boycotts or media campaigns aimed at discrediting corporate adversaries. The only other model that may be seen to engage in at least some conflict is fair trade, in that in many instances fair trade advocates actively contrast their products to mainstream producer products portrayed as ethically inferior. However, the conflict in this case typically is less fundamental to the approach than in external CSR initiatives, and as mentioned, some fair trade initiatives reach out to mainstream distributors as outlets for their products.

The extent to which these models structure interactions to assure that beneficiaries are actively involved in decision making varies considerably. The three PSD approaches discussed generally are strong on this score; BOP, microenterprise, and ITC all feature active involvement of participants in framing the outputs of initiatives. They do so for different purposes and in different ways, yet they share a belief in the importance of participant involvement in decision making. Fair trade initiatives also often involve beneficiaries in decision making—in choices about fair trade standards and in decisions about how to invest price premiums to improve communities. However, fair trade organizations also have been criticized for failure to live up to their participatory rhetoric. Jaffee (2009), for example, argues that "the key institutions setting the rules for commodity fair trade are functionally controlled by Northern interests. In FLO, for example, importers and retailers exert the predominant influence on policy, while Southern producer groups hold only a minority of votes" (p. 253).

Some social entrepreneurship initiatives likewise emphasize beneficiary involvement in framing interventions, but this is not central to the approach. The same can be said of CSR; there is little consistent emphasis on beneficiary involvement in internal CSR models, and even participation in most external CSR initiatives focuses more on purchasing decisions than on helping to frame broader initiatives.

What Do Market-Based Models Imply About Innovation?

The creators of all social change approaches typically view the path they initiate as innovative in some important sense, and this claim often is true. However, my concern here is less with the model itself than with its subsequent emphasis on stimulating new innovations by its practitioners. That is, how central is innovation by change agents and/or beneficiaries in the implementation of the model?

Of the models assessed here, social entrepreneurship clearly places the most emphasis on innovation by its practitioners. With a central focus on stimulating problem solvers to "think outside the box" in developing solutions to often seemingly intractable problems, SE places innovation at the heart of strategic development. Although SE's relative success in this respect remains unproven, its promoters are consistent in attempting to stimulate innovative thought.

PSD approaches likewise often consciously push innovation, although the extent to which they do so differs somewhat among the three PSD approaches examined. The ITC approach exemplified by the work of Paul Polak (2009) is highly focused on innovation in technology development, and in fact fuses the previously discussed beneficiary participation principle with attention to new approaches to production. Beneficiaries work actively with those more skilled in technology in search of new production tools or methods that fit within their economic and cultural circumstances. BOP production likewise depends heavily on recrafting products or distribution processes in innovative ways, so as to be responsive to the unique needs and capabilities of poor consumers. The final PSD approach, micro-enterprise, is more sporadic with respect to innovation. With its stimulation of indigenously developed small businesses, microenterprise initiatives doubtlessly have resulted in many small-scale innovations in diverse communities. Yet the primary focus of microenterprise is to provide capital for low-income persons to develop enterprises, and the extent to which these are innovative new business approaches is a secondary consideration.

Fair trade and CSR initiatives may result in new productive innovations, but this again is not a principal focus. Fair trade primarily is interested in providing an expanding market for indigenous producers, so innovations from such efforts mainly reside in the generation of new ideas about how to distribute products and to compete successfully with mainstream corporate products. CSR initiatives again may or may not emphasize innovation. The focus of many internally driven CSR initiatives is extending social considerations in decision making, which may only require incremental production or decision-making adjustments as opposed to dramatically new approaches. Externally driven CSR approaches perhaps are most likely to be innovative, in that their originators must be creative in developing strategies to overcome the considerable resource advantages held by their corporate adversaries. But again, the benefits ultimately delivered are not necessarily innovative in nature.

What Do Market-Based Models Imply About Sustainability?

Ideas about the sustainability of initiatives can be found in most of the market-based models examined here, although the centrality of this concept and the manner in which it is emphasized vary. In particular, considerations of sustainability tend to arise in two primary ways. First, sustainability often is considered in a narrow fiscal sense concerning whether initiatives or projects have a high likelihood of being maintained over time without the ongoing infusion of donated resources. That is, sustainable initiatives are those in which originators think through and present plans for allowing the initiative to continue over time without substantial nonmarket based support. Second, sustainability sometimes is considered much more broadly in terms of whether production processes or market exchange relationships can be lasting in a manner that is mutually rewarding to exchange partners or to others affected. Sustainability in this sense pertains to issues such as the environmental impacts of production, the productivity and stability of workers given wage rates and working conditions, and the loyalty of customers given their perceptions about products and how they are produced.

Fiscal sustainability in the narrower sense probably is most notable in social entrepreneurship. Many SE proponents stress the importance of creating initiatives that are not overly dependent on donations, due to the belief that donation-heavy projects are subject to donor whims and hence are relatively unstable. This attention to fiscal sustainability has led many SE proponents to stress the importance of earned revenue streams in project development.

Among the other models, fair trade, BOP, and ITC all share perspectives of careful attention to fiscal balance. Each is similar in that project developers must carefully think through the price points necessary to balance the costs of production and incoming revenues from consumers.

These latter three models also share with some versions of CSR a more careful consideration of the broader sustainability issues mentioned here. Fair trade proponents, for example, argue that premium prices paid by developed world consumers are needed to allow developing world consumers to be stable producers and in turn to foster viable, stable communities. With their attention to local capacities and cultures, ITC producers tend to be sensitive to technology development that will fit with local circumstances and hence be better embraced and maintained. The most skilled BOP developers attend to consumer tastes and capabilities, with the conscious notion that doing so is likely to impact sustainability even beyond narrow considerations of price.

Finally, strategic CSR approaches place broadly conceived sustainability at the center of development. In some cases, this reflects careful considerations of production impacts in areas such as depletion of sustainable resources or pollution effects. In others, CSR developers are more concerned with social issues and their effects, such as whether providing selected wage or benefit levels facilitates a more loyal and stable work force or customer base. As mentioned in Chapter 3, this attention to broader sustainability is largely self-interested. But nonetheless, it drives a consideration of longer-term impacts and related sustainability prospects that often is neglected in social service models.

What Do Market-Based Models Imply About Scaling?

Although sustainability refers mainly to the ability to maintain an initiative over time, scaling is concerned with its ability for replication and growth. The idea that change agents should consider scaling potential has received increasing attention due to the notion that great needs require large-scale solutions, and that important efficiencies can be gained if program ideas can be widely replicated. Some proponents of each model featured here have argued that their approach should emphasize scaling in project selection, or else that the approach has the capability to be widely scaled. However, this directive is not generally followed or clearly documented in practice, so I will highlight some of the prospects and limits of scaling associated with each approach.

SE proponents perhaps most often refer to scaling, and many view it as fundamental to the approach. They argue that something is not entrepreneurial unless it is pattern setting, and to be pattern setting implies that a project must be scalable. ASHOKA founder and leading social entrepreneur Bill Drayton has made this argument, and has systematically incorporated scaling potential in considering which projects ASHOKA will fund (Bornstein, 2007). Academic depictions likewise have sometimes portrayed scaling as necessary if projects are to be considered socially entrepreneurial (Alvord, Brown, & Letts, 2004; Light, 2008). Nonetheless, this prescription has not emerged as a commonly agreed upon requirement of SE, as is evidenced by the fact that most of the literature focuses little on scaling.

PSD approaches likewise are variable in attention to scaling issues. Some proponents view scaling as fundamental to this type of model. Prahalad (2005) perhaps pushes this issue the most in articulating his BOP approach. Although he portrays BOP initiatives as beginning on a small, almost grassroots level featuring interactions between poor consumers and producers around needed products, he argues that scaling is critical for extending reach and is best attained by the involvement of corporations in production. He feels that corporations are best equipped to achieve production efficiencies, and that they also have the distribution capabilities to affect large numbers of consumers. In comparison, early microenterprise developers were not particularly concerned with scaling as they created and extended this approach. Yet, Yunus and others were able to reach impressive scaling levels as this small-business development model was replicated across communities. Polak (2009) likewise has emphasized the importance of scaling in promoting various ITC interventions, but again this focus receives varying attention from other ITC practitioners.

Although scaling is not central to most CSR initiatives, it is implied in the thinking of many CSR advocates. For one thing, the decision by advocates to choose corporations as their focus for change often reflects recognition that corporations are especially influential societal organizations, and hence changes within them are likely to have considerable reach. In addition, although many CSR initiatives focus on practices within only one or a few corporations, the intent of bringing about such changes often is to be pattern setting across an industry or even across all organizations. For example, efforts to get corporations to provide the public with social responsibility "report cards" typically are intended to eventually affect all corporate practices, and so can be seen broadly as being sensitive to scaling concerns.

Finally, arguments about the potential of scaling have been important in debates among fair trade change agents, and they often have been framed within discussions about the desirability of mainstreaming in product distribution. That is, because of the competitive advantages of mainstream markets in distributing goods, it has been argued that relying totally on the alternative distribution channels significantly constrains fair trade scaling (Doherty & Tranchell, 2006). Mainstreaming has been advocated largely as a response to these concerns.

What Do Market-Based Models Imply About Management?

Management of course can have many meanings, but here I view it broadly as the philosophy and related practices through which organizations implement ideas or, alternatively, by which they take selected inputs and shape them into final products or services. Beginning with this broad definition, it is not surprising that market-based models do not have a unique lexicon upon which their management practices can be well-articulated. Unlike the other questions discussed earlier, there are not very clear lines of demarcation with respect to management philosophies among the market-based models, and perhaps what is notable is less their differences than commonalities. In particular, there is consistent attention to careful execution of strategies, as well as a focus on results measurement and refinement of practices based on experience.

This process perhaps is best articulated in selected conceptual SE writings, such as those of Dees and Drayton (Dees, 1998; Bornstein, 2007). These SE proponents emphasize a rigorous planning approach, with attention to initial small-scale testing, careful review of results, practice refinement, fiscal sustainability, replication, and scaling. Although not always as clearly articulated in other models, the market-based literature does commonly convey consideration of these and other features of sound management. I will describe in more detail some specific management features that I see as strengths of many of these models in the next sections, with the most interesting of these being a strong focus on creative technology use, attention to establishment of cross-professional linkages to enhance specialized expertise, and the aforementioned concentration on implementation execution.

STRENGTHS AND LIMITATIONS OF MARKET-BASED MODELS

Market-based models have been subject to glowing reviews and to biting critiques. Some of these pertain to the entire group of market-based models, while others center on specific approaches. I turn next to highlighting my perspectives on the most important strengths and greatest limitations of these approaches as a broader group of social development strategies.

STRENGTHS OF MARKET-BASED MODELS

In considering market-based models generally, I find the two most compelling aspects are a strong emphasis on innovation coupled with a focus on how to most efficiently and effectively deliver benefits to targeted audiences. Market models often are criticized for focusing too narrowly on efficiency issues, and exemplars of many of the approaches considered here are subject to that shortcoming. Nonetheless, proponents of these models often have brought forth new ideas concerning how best to help people with very difficult problems. In addition, thorny questions regarding how to provide service access to the most disadvantaged have received thoughtful attention, which extends well beyond what are commonly viewed as efficiency issues. Innovative thinking about benefit delivery also often has included creative attention to the utilization of emerging technologies, which is particularly important in light of still evolving revolutions in this sphere. The following sections provide more detailed discussion of these attributes, as well as other strengths of these approaches.

Innovation in Change Efforts

Perhaps what has been most notable to me in learning about these change models has been the emphasis on innovation. This feature is most broadly characteristic of literature on social entrepreneurship, in that thinking about long-standing problems in new ways is a basic imprimatur. However, it is commonplace in the literature on the other models as well. Scholars and practitioners working with each model recognize that they are enmeshed in deep and often complex problems facing highly disadvantaged groups. In fact, what often seems to push change agents toward one or the other of these models is this recognition, coupled with a frustration with respect to the efficacy of other approaches.

This set of circumstances typically leads model explicators or advocates to promote these approaches as something "new" in terms of bringing different approaches to difficult problems. This view of course is not unique to these models or circumstances, because most change proponents articulate the circumstances that require or stimulate a new approach. Nonetheless, this type of "stage-setting" for model articulation or advocacy fills the literature with a sense of needing to start something from the ground up. The term often used in the social entrepreneurship literature—"thinking outside of the box"—perhaps best captures this emphasis on creatively assessing and then attacking social problems in new ways.

Although this term is metaphorical and abstract, a real sense of innovation is reflected in countless of the market-oriented initiatives instigated through these models. Further, portions of the literature associated with promoting particular market-based approaches through the training of students emphasize teaching about creativity and innovation in problem solving. Although the performance of such training in inspiring creativity remains relatively untested, this to me is a useful direction to encourage. It often is very difficult to recognize and move beyond long established biases and routines as we respond to social issues, and approaches that vigorously pursue doing so have much to offer in thinking through social development.

Incorporating New Technology

Nearly all realms of society are in the midst of ongoing technological revolutions that are reshaping the manner in which we interact with each other and carry out all sorts of sustenance and leisure activities. The literature on a wide range of topics consequently includes substantial introduction of ideas concerning the use of new technology, and so its emphasis in the models examined here perhaps is not unique.

Nonetheless, it is difficult not to be taken by the attention given to new technology in these models. As with society in general, the application of technological advancements in these approaches has been critical in improving the efficiency and performance of existing operations. However, the more interesting aspect is its more fundamental application as the cornerstone of particular interventions. The question either explicitly or implicitly posed is "How can we use the new technology to create interventions that would not be possible without it?" Creative programs such as Kiva could not exist without Internet technology, nor could the globe-spanning nature of many corporate social responsibility and fair trade initiatives (Andersen, 2011).

One other important technology related focus of many initiatives, especially in the social entrepreneurship literature, has been the development of innovative strategies for improving access by disadvantaged groups to various new technology applications. For example, the Committee for Democracy in Information Technology (CDI) was developed by Rodrigo Baggio to distribute low-cost computers to poor persons in Brazil (Welch, 2008), and Yunus established Grameen Phone to bring cell phone access to persons living in remote rural villages. Again, approaches to improve the poor's access to technology are not unique to the models described here, but many leading program examples indeed do fall under this rubric. This is likely to have resulted from the fact that many prominent SE developers came from new technology business backgrounds and hence found it natural to bring such expertise to their analysis of social problems. Regardless of origin, these initiatives are critical to arming the poor with the tools needed to advance in increasingly sophisticated and information-oriented societies, consistent with the capabilities approach articulated by Amartya Sen (1999).

Linkages Across Disciplines

Another interesting feature has been the tendency of these approaches to bring together persons from diverse disciplines to address social issues. Many initiatives are very bottoms-up oriented, and hence initially may include little specialization due to resource limitations. However, program originators often recognize the improvements possible through obtaining specialized expertise, and in turn devise strategies to bring in assistance from a variety of disciplines. In some cases, this leads to minor but nonetheless useful improvements for relatively young agencies that are at the margin of productive functioning. In others, the partnerships may be quite transformative. For example, the partnership between Dr. Govindappa Venkataswamy and David Green described in Chapter 4 allowed Dr. Venkataswamy to fundamentally scale his efforts to help the blind in India, due to Green's business acumen in finding cheaper production processes for the lenses needed for Dr. Venkataswamy's surgery patients (Public Broadcasting System, 2005).

The partnerships observed in examining market-based case examples can serve as a normative primer for those considering program development. They include but are not limited to persons with information technology backgrounds, financial planners and fundraisers, marketing specialists, lawyers, engineers, agricultural experts, literacy specialists, community organizers, doctors and nurses, and social workers. Although again not unique to market-based models, what is noteworthy is the ease with which many of these program initiators cross disciplinary boundaries. There often is a spirit of aggressively seeking out whatever it takes to bring programs to fruition and to maximize their functioning. That is, the innovative thinking extends beyond initial idea generation to the pragmatics of operationalizing a problem, and this thinking often transcends blinders that inhibit collaboration across disciplines. As those who have been involved in interdisciplinary efforts probably will recognize, this is not a trivial accomplishment given turf issues and the common tendency to view one's own professional domain as superior.

Executing Business Skills

Especially in comparison with much of the development literature from the social sciences, there is a relatively high level of attention to business planning and operations in these market-based initiatives. This again reflects the backgrounds and training of many program initiators, as well as the nature of the interactions with which some models are involved. For example, fair trade initiatives are involved in competition with mainstream profit-making businesses and must be skilled in business execution to minimize needed price differentials required to accomplish their social objectives. Advocacy-based CSR proponents likewise must become sufficiently schooled in understanding business motivations and operations to effectively target and carry out their advocacy activities.

More specifically, common business parlance and practices are typically employed, such as developing a business plan and conducting market assessments. Some social service advocates may be taken aback by the manner in which a focus on business practices in these models seems to trump more fundamental attention to client or customer issues. However, although acknowledging that such tendencies do exist, I think in general this is a misunderstanding of the difference between intention and operations. There is nothing inherently inconsistent about strong client-centered program goals and objectives coupled with well-developed and business-focused implementation strategies. In fact, thinking carefully about the latter can be very important in maximizing the performance of client-related goals and objectives. By explicitly focusing on the business skills associated with better operational performance, these models can encourage change advocates to carefully attend to general business practices useful in improving program performance.

Focusing on Sustainability

Although definitions often are loose, much of the market-based literature brings healthy attention to issues related to the sustainability of social programs. Thinking about sustainability is not unique to proponents of these models. Nonetheless, when compared with much of the literature to which human services change agents are exposed in professional programs, the focus on sustainability is notable in the core of many of these model discussions.

As mentioned previously, two different facets of sustainability merit attention. The first concerns the extent to which the operating model of the initiative lends itself to sustainability over time. That is, if one is developing a social service initiative, has serious forethought been given to basic issues such as whether an ongoing market of clients or customers exists or whether sufficient revenue streams will be available to support program operation or growth? Consideration of such issues may seem like foregone conclusions to those not well-schooled in social program development efforts in the public and nonprofit sectors. However, the history of development in this respect is littered with examples of failures that are attributable to planning deficiencies with regard to seemingly basic issues such as these. There are many reasons for this, but my own experience is that lack of adequate program development training, coupled with great enthusiasm for a program idea, are prominent.

The second aspect of sustainability pertains to the broader targeting of program development efforts, as opposed to the operation of the change entity itself. Many program initiatives that fall within the change models considered here are oriented to affecting the sustainability of economic or other endeavors in the communities in which they operate. For example, CSR initiatives often focus on stimulating corporate entities to engage in production practices that are less damaging to the environment, and hence are more sustainable in terms of their impact on natural resource use and/or human health. Similarly, fair trade initiatives attend to providing adequate wages to allow production in a manner that is just for workers and nonexploitive of the communities in which goods are produced. This broader sustainability focus is consistent with social justice orientations common to social program development discussions in the social sciences and in human services professional programs, but the market-based models often bring more rigor to discussions of this type of issue due to their tendency to focus on longer-term economic considerations.

Encouraging Scaling

Among the primary concerns in a world of heavily decentralized change efforts is the extent to which innovative ideas take hold and are extended following initial success. This issue has increasingly been discussed under the rubric of scaling. The diffusion of innovations in this respect has two related but distinct components. The first is more internal in nature and pertains to the extent to which initially small-scale program ideas are brought to a larger scale by their originators. This is akin to the person who starts a single coffee shop or pizza parlor and then subsequently opens additional sites or franchises to more broadly capitalize on their initial success. The second aspect refers to how an innovation created by one person or group eventually diffuses to others in a manner where reach is extended and useful product or service adaptations emerge around a core idea.

As discussed here, market-based models often provide explicit attention to the scaling of innovations by program initiators. From a program development perspective, the primary scaling issue concerns how we can best encourage the spread of ideas that have worked successfully in one location to another geographic area. Given the large numbers of persons in the developing world affected by fundamental benefit provision issues, thinking about scaling in this manner should be a very important concern to change agents.

Scaling considerations have taken hold at a serious level in the development world in the work of private foundations and in governmental contracting with nonprofits. For example, foundations have increasingly required those applying for grants to provide a plan for how they will grow a project if it proves to be successful, and they likewise often are consolidating their funding efforts into more focused areas of development (Bishop & Green, 2009). These trends reflect dissatisfaction with a tendency of foundations to jump from one topic to another and to not have an overarching strategic focus, and so to fail to adequately consolidate and extend promising program results (Fleishman, 2009).

Just as extending businesses to new locations requires thinking that differs somewhat from the creation of a new business, the scaling of social innovations likewise requires special attention. Perhaps most interesting of these challenges is the need to attend to cultural aspects as products or services are introduced into new areas. The central question here, for example, is whether cultural differences among target groups or broader community environments are sufficient to require modifications in benefits, marketing or delivery mechanisms, or other aspects of importance in successful benefit provision.

It is my belief that the attention to scaling in this literature can be very useful for social change agents engaged in a wide array of change activities, especially by detailing advantageous steps and possible associated pitfalls. In addition, given that scaling is strongly influenced by successful adaptation to varying social circumstances, those trained in social work or allied human services fields may find meaningful roles in working with business-oriented colleagues to extend products and services to new geographic areas or slightly different target groups.

Indigenous Community Development and Empowerment

Most change agents trained in the social sciences or related professional programs probably would not think of market-based models as being particularly strong in terms of social justice and participatory community aspects of development. This is a reasonable inclination, because an efficiency focus characteristic of market thinking often flies in the face of these important philosophical traditions. Many business-centered advocates likewise are quite technical and top-down planning oriented in their developmental approaches, based on rational planning training or backgrounds that emphasize the identification of a single best solution to any articulated problem.

Despite these broader tendencies in the business and market worlds, practitioners of many of the market-based approaches examined in this book are well-attuned to social justice and participatory considerations, and these concerns are fundamental to some approaches. For example, fair trade is largely premised on social justice ideas, in terms of assuring fairer returns to low-income producers in the developing world. Externally driven CSR initiatives frequently are motivated by similar considerations, and many iterations of SE involve actively engaging targeted beneficiaries in assessing needs, capabilities, and workable program solutions. By providing poor persons with the financial capital necessary to initiate their self-created economic strategies, as well as often providing one-on-one technical assistance, microenterprise approaches are heavily focused on empowering disadvantaged persons to improve their own economic circumstances. In addition, ITC initiatives commonly work intimately with local producers to determine technologies that appear most needed and feasible. Even BOP development, which is among the most aggressively capitalistic of these approaches, often features a developmental process in which BOP producers work very closely with indigenous populations to assure product compatibility with their customers.

I am not implying that these models should be the cornerstone of thinking about social justice, empowerment, or participation for social change agents. I rather believe that social science-trained change agents may find aspects of these approaches much more compatible with their philosophical orientations than they may think. I likewise believe that seeing these critical social change aspects framed in different ways within diverse developmental approaches is very useful in enriching the thinking of change agents. This is especially true given that these approaches simultaneously expose social science-trained change agents to the business-focused aspects of program development on which they may not be as well-trained.

In summary, the attributes described here suggest why market-based approaches have captured the attention of many change agents and why such approaches have become increasingly influential in social development thinking. These strengths collectively provide a useful set of ideas to consider as change agents engage in new initiatives. The contributions these models have made in stimulating critical thinking about social program development and operational issues have been even more notable.

LIMITATIONS IN MARKET-BASED APPROACHES

Although market-based models have impressive strengths, they likewise have substantial limitations to which I will turn next. These also require scrutiny by change agents, especially in a current context characterized by often wildly inflated claims of model performance. More fundamentally, thinking through the possible benefits of these models should include careful consideration of their potential contributions within broader systems of social provision. I mention this because none of these models should be viewed as an all-encompassing development approach, and yet the enthusiasm of many proponents leads them to view particular approaches as such. The following sections discuss more specific limitations of these approaches or of the literature surrounding them.

Advocacy Without Evidence

The enthusiasm of market-based proponents has been important in promoting attention to these approaches, and also for helping to bring new actors with important developmental skill sets into the realm of social development. Perhaps such relatively unbridled advocacy is a prerequisite for creating interest and excitement about emerging approaches. Yet somewhat paradoxically for models framed in the rubric of business-like development and results-oriented management, the lack of careful attention to documenting program outcomes is a striking limitation. It often is difficult to untangle actual performance from hype in reading this literature, and although many fine program exemplars have been put forward, the knowledge base regarding performance of all of these models remains extremely underdeveloped.

In fairness, many of these approaches have emerged recently, so some limitations may derive from the relative newness of development and inquiry. However, all now are relatively well-established, so they should have moved beyond the stage of simply promoting interest. The next steps for considering these approaches within a broader portfolio of social development models are to more clearly demarcate contributions and limitations. This can only occur if those who write about market-based models do so in a more balanced manner, and if related practitioners carefully define their work and evaluate program processes and outcomes more rigorously. It is encouraging to see increasingly sophisticated outcome-based research studies beginning to emerge, and additional research that includes control and comparison groups is needed to place these approaches on more solid empirical footing.

The Tension Between Service Provision and Profits

One of the greatest potential limitations of market-based models flows from what often is regarded as among their main strengths. That is, market models typically emphasize the need for social interventions to be sustainable, which implies designs that stress financial viability. This often leads to pricing strategies that require recipients to pay relatively high rates for benefits. This fiscal sustainability orientation has many desirable aspects, not the least of which is to encourage program developers to think rigorously about issues such as benefit pricing and service delivery efficiencies. However, to the extent that market exchange becomes the primary funding vehicle, incentives also are created to focus benefits on those who are not in the greatest need.

This well-known phenomenon is known as "creaming." It falls within a broader debate among philosophers, academics, and social program practitioners concerning the extent to which the benefits from any program reach those most in need. Although there are important arguments that call into question whether it always is best to target benefits primarily on the most needy,[1] it is fair to say that philosophical proclivities generally favor provision to those with at least relatively high need levels. Yet if efficient and "sustainable" operations are more fundamental to market-based than other program development models, creaming becomes more acute and potentially problematic. This problem appears more endemic to some market-based models than to others, and thus I first will discuss it generally before turning to the models in which the issue appears most vexing.

Two distinct dimensions of creaming have received attention, and the dangers of creaming in any given program model depend substantially on which of these is being considered. First, clients or customers have varying financial resources, and hence differing abilities to pay for a benefit. Creaming in this respect refers to focusing benefit provision on those most able to pay, which may lead agencies to underserve comparable or even worse-off clients with more limited financial means. Even if agencies are willing to serve highly disadvantaged clients, high co-payments or other strategies to increase customer cost-sharing may lead those with the greatest need not to seek services.

Second, finances aside, individuals vary with respect to the relative effort that is needed to serve them, based on the characteristics and capabilities they bring to any service encounter. This aspect is complex and multifaceted, and can operate much more subtly than creaming based on finances. However, the core of this issue is that it is more "costly" to serve some clients than others, in a financial and in a psychic sense. For example, in a high school completion project, it may be tempting to target persons who need three rather than six courses to complete their degree, on the grounds that students with shorter times to completion will be less likely to drop out and because fewer agency resources will be required to obtain a "completion" or successful outcome.

It readily can be seen that these two sets of factors together determine how costly it is to serve particular clients, with higher costs driven by limited ability to pay on the one hand and by greater case complexity or need on the other. Unfortunately, an agency focus on fiscal viability or sustainability creates pressures to minimize financial or other client need considerations in favor of cost issues. This dilemma is commonly recognized in discussions of public benefit provision, and those receiving government contracts consequently may be pressured or incentivized to care for those with higher levels of need.

Of the models discussed here, creaming probably has received the most attention in the PSD and SE literature. With respect to PSD, the criticism has been that BOP model practitioners have found that it is very difficult to make a profit producing products for the least well-off (Polak, 2009; Arora & Romijn, 2011). Many BOP developers instead focus on those who are somewhat better-off, resulting in useful mass products but not necessarily addressing more fundamental poverty issues. Similarly, in their drive not to rely on "donations" and hence to become financially sustainable, many nonprofit SE initiatives emphasize developing services and products that require high levels of cost sharing by beneficiaries. This again may require high enough pricing to drive purchase costs beyond the means of the worst-off, even when no profits are taken.

The issue of service versus profits extends beyond the creaming issue, which is narrowly related to who is targeted to receive benefits. Another issue is the relative richness of service delivery given any projected revenue stream. For-profit social service agencies sometimes are glamorized as being able to provide superior services for similar costs, due to efficiencies developed in the drive for profits. However, empirical evidence to support this notion largely is nonexistent, and realistic concerns exist that any such cost savings may accrue largely to shareholders rather than to clients. In particular, profit motives create incentives for agencies to skimp on services in order to drive higher profit margins. For example, a recent federal government study has highlighted the poor performance of for-profit universities in serving students. These universities on average spent 23% of revenues on marketing, as compared to only 17% on instruction; profit margins were about 20%. Perhaps not surprisingly, the drop-out rates from such universities are more than 50%, and related public impacts include taxpayer costs as students in turn default on government-backed loans (Stratford, 2012).

For-profit service advocates will counter that competitive markets will minimize such effects, because service consumers will assess the quality of services received and move to new providers if they are dissatisfied. However, competitive markets do not exist for many services of critical importance to the most disadvantaged in the developing world. In addition, competitive markets require the availability of high consumer knowledge levels, as well as the ability to freely make choices. These assumptions are violated in many service situations, and the violations tend to be most profound among the highly disadvantaged.

There are countless examples of these factors working together to produce very unfavorable outcomes from profit-making social service initiatives. The government regulation that market-based proponents decry in fact often arises in response to such problems. For example, repeated care abuses have been found in the heavily privatized U.S. nursing home industry, and government regulations have arisen in response (Winzelberg, 2003).

These criticisms are not intended to convey that high quality profit-making service entities do not exist. However, change agents need to be aware of the dangers inherent in profit-making provision, which constitutes an important subset of market-based approaches. Doing so requires critically analyzing any purported benefits from such provision in relation to possible liabilities and costs.

Marketing Versus Market-Based Provision: Monitoring Performance

Accurate measurement of program performance constitutes another difficulty with the market-based approaches discussed here. Monitoring performance is a difficult undertaking in all types of benefit delivery systems and programs, because of issues such as needed expertise, costs, and accountability structures. This difficulty, however, appears especially taxing in market-based models for several reasons. First, due to the fact that all of these models are loosely structured and tend to have evolved from many different sources and perspectives, simply defining the core aspects of different approaches is very challenging.

Second, even to the extent that such definitional agreements can be reached across many diffuse practitioners, the organizational structures needed to adequately assess performance typically are lacking. This makes data collection and analysis beyond the individual program level very difficult, in terms of common definitions and data collection practices and with respect to establishing incentives for cooperation in data collection and evaluation. Fair trade perhaps has gone the furthest in creating overarching structures conducive to evaluations, with groups such as the Fair Trade Labeling Organization at least setting the standard for more common measurement and assessment. This has largely been possible by developing certification processes, through which fair trade project developers must agree to engage in selected data collection and verification in order to be certified as fair trade organizations.

However, comparable organizations generally do not exist or are weakly developed for PSD, CSR, and SE, and there are structural and competitive reasons to believe they will be difficult to establish in a meaningful way. On the competitive side, PSD and CSR focus on profit-making entities, which may have limited incentives to open themselves up to comparisons with established standards or with their peers. In addition, the diffusion of SE efforts and the economic power of corporations suggest that fairly well-resourced and sophisticated organizations are needed to meaningfully monitor the practices of these change approaches. Developing such complex organizational structures in essentially voluntary sectors is a difficult undertaking that requires substantial time and energy in addition to tangible resources.

The greatest hope in this respect probably involves the creation of consumer-oriented organizations to monitor and assess these entities. This has been done, for example, in the auto industry, where the rating of cars is common, and some types of social services such as child care similarly are experimenting with rating systems (Tout, et al., 2010). However, what is more challenging in the current context is that a strong, educated consumer base often does not exist or is highly diffused, and hence the pressure required to drive cooperation from providers must largely be organized and led by activists for the disadvantaged.

The need to monitor and measure program performance again is not unique to market-based initiatives; it has received growing attention in public policy, public administration, and other academic programs concerned with social program development. However, it is particularly acute in some market-based approaches, especially those engaged in profit-making. That is, there may be a tendency by some profit-making organizations to establish social initiatives primarily for marketing purposes—to demonstrate to their customers and to community stakeholders that they are socially responsible and good citizens worthy of consumer support. This becomes a problem from a social development standpoint when the substance of program development efforts is minimal and serves largely as a vehicle for self-promotion. This not only can have the obvious effect of wasted support for programs with little impact or meaning, but more insidiously can foster wider community cynicism about development efforts.

This issue is of particular concern in approaches such as CSR and BOP, because these strategies typically center on larger-scale profit-making entities that have well-defined profit motives and large amounts of resources. Unless the social change initiative in question represents an unusually large focus of the organization's profit-making strategy, which in most cases it does not, it is likely to receive relatively limited attention and resources in the broader sphere of corporate activity. At the same time, these larger organizations often have sufficient resources to widely publicize their more socially oriented practices, and the incentive to do so in order to promote a favorable public image. For example, I am writing this page in a Starbucks coffee shop, and as I purchased my coffee was confronted with a sign announcing that if I purchased a particular Starbucks product a portion of the proceeds would be donated to create American jobs. Yet, this of course is a very narrow slice of Starbucks' corporate strategy, most of which focuses on maximizing profits.

As discussed in Chapter 3, this phenomenon has been described as "greenwashing" or "cleanwashing" in the CSR and fair trade literatures—in the sense that corporations have an incentive to engage in selected socially responsible practices in order to wash away consumer concerns with the broader social and environmental impacts of corporate operations. Whether a CSR initiative is environmental, worker-related, or involves some other aspect of corporate activity, this image polishing issue merits careful scrutiny in assessing CSR, as well as in fair trade initiatives in which corporate mainstreaming is involved. It similarly is reflected in the literature on corporate BOP development, especially to the extent that the BOP initiatives represent a relatively small portion of overall corporate operations.

Given these potentially perverse incentives, there is a continual need for an outside organization without a stake in corporate profits to monitor claims and inform consumers about the extent to which initiatives and broader corporate practices meet some agreed upon standards. As discussed earlier, given the high level of resources available in larger corporations, such monitoring requires considerable energy and relatively sophisticated skills.

Limited Social Interaction Skills

I recently attended a meeting that was attempting to establish social development initiatives between Native American tribal communities and an individual who regarded himself as a social entrepreneur. The conversation concerning ideas and possibilities was proceeding somewhat slowly as a Native American woman presented some ideas, and it was evident that the social entrepreneur was frustrated and desired a faster pace. He finally turned to the woman and said "What is the major pitch you would make to me in a two-minute elevator speech?" The woman fidgeted and looked a bit irritated and then responded, "That is part of the issue. No one in our community gives elevator speeches—that is a foreign concept to us. It is not the way we think about things."

This anecdote hopefully rings true with any reader who has worked with tribal communities or worked with other groups whose culture and environmental circumstances are significantly different from their own. It illustrates the fundamental importance of cultural sensitivity and related sound social skills in developing initiatives. Although this may seem obvious to some, the development literature is filled with examples of initiatives that failed at least partially because developers did not clearly understand the norms and practices of communities with which they worked.

This problem is not unique to the market-based models considered here, so I do not want to overemphasize it. In fact, in criticizing larger-scale development efforts, social entrepreneur proponents such as Easterly (2006) have argued that small-scale SE initiatives typically stress careful development work with communities in understanding and responding to social problems. As discussed in Chapter 5, the same case can be made for some of the leading PSD work, which emphasizes thoughtful interactions with potential consumers to learn about their product needs and their capabilities to pay for products. On the conceptual level, I am in agreement with these characterizations, and this feature is a significant reason I view many initiatives falling under these market-oriented rubrics to be promising. If such community awareness exists, and if skill in interacting with community residents to determine needs is exercised by program developers, market-based models have much in common with community development approaches promoted in social work and other human services fields.

However, I fear that the anecdote presented here reflects a common phenomenon, and that it is one to which many market-based social initiators may be especially susceptible. That is, those with training, experience, and success in the business world often may convey an attitude of knowing what is best for indigenous communities—if only the communities will trust in their expertise. Such paternalistic tendencies, even if born of the best motives, are likely to lead to flawed or failed interventions. The bottom line mentality so critical to survival in competitive business environments similarly may come across as crass and self-serving if instigated in communities in which change agents are not well-established.

Some market-oriented proponents are likely to recoil at my characterization, and rightly may point out that success in business is highly predicated upon correctly recognizing and responding to consumer interests. There is much truth in this. However, I would counter that development work in the most difficult environments introduces aspects of cultural and environmental assessment that pale in comparison to those in which most business entities engage.

Given the good arguments that can be put forward on both sides of this debate, this is an area in which better empirical information would be helpful. Yet measuring cultural sensitivity across different types of development models is very difficult, so I have little confidence that such empirical work will be influential. Rather, I am simply inclined to advocate for the need to incorporate cultural sensitivity into planning efforts associated with all of the models considered here. As should be obvious, the more that cultural mores and practices differ from those of social change agents, the more important carefully crafted interactions to understand community needs, interests, and capabilities become.

Questionable Scaling, Targeting Effectiveness, and Geographic Reach

Although in the previous section I presented scaling as a strength of market-based models, this positive attribute largely exists at the conceptual level. The extent to which scaling of market-based initiatives actually occurs is much less clear, and there are several concerns in this respect. For one thing, many small-scale change agents do not have the resources to scale up successful initiatives, which has led some to suggest that approaches such as social entrepreneurship are much better for creating than for scaling initiatives (Light, 2008). Even if scaling is desired, many change efforts lack the infrastructure or authority to nimbly move successful initiatives from one site to another.

There are related concerns about the geographic reach and targeting effectiveness of market-based change initiatives. From a geographic perspective, market-based change agents may or may not have the desire or capability to extend their efforts geographically, and generally are under no pressure to do so. Targeting effectiveness extends beyond geography to issues such as the relative saturation of an innovation within a geographic area. In this sense, market-based change agents again generally have no particular advantages in providing extensive benefit coverage to a particular area and, as noted in a previous section, often have financial disincentives for doing so.

These geographic and targeting effectiveness difficulties stem partially from the lack of authority and mandate for voluntary efforts to cover broader populations. As a result, voluntary efforts of all types often experience limitations in the planning capacities and incentives required to successfully scale initiatives. It is in these areas that governments have distinct advantages. I will turn next to discussing these more explicitly and to considering how these strengths may be drawn upon to improve the reach of voluntary market-based initiatives.

THE ROLE OF GOVERNMENTS IN MARKET-BASED SOCIAL CHANGE

The limitations described in the previous section are common to decentralized voluntary systems that lack central authority. If one believes that there is a need to focus at least some level of benefit provision on substantive areas that societies agree are most needed and that have the greatest possibility of positive returns, voluntary systems always will be inadequate. The geographic reach and targeting effectiveness of voluntary systems furthermore will be variable and underdeveloped. It is in these respects that governments are uniquely suited to provide leadership in social development. Only governments have the authority and resources necessary to aggregate societal preferences related to social issues, and then to translate these into programming with consistent reach and targeting considerations. Having said this, the desired role of governments as contributors to the implementation of the market-based models considered here remains complex and controversial. I therefore will begin with a few overview observations regarding perceptions of governmental roles before proceeding to some more specific possibilities for government engagement and intersection.

A first general point is that, for many proponents of these models, governments are treated either as nonplayers or as enemies to be avoided. This should not be surprising, given that many market-based advocates come from business backgrounds and are distrustful of governmental planning expertise, bureaucratically oriented decision making, and free-market restrictions and regulations. Governments often are uniformly regarded as inefficient and noninnovative. The most conservative critics therefore primarily are interested in surveilling and in influencing governments to minimize regulatory obstacles to nongovernmental change initiatives. They likewise may advocate limiting governmental roles in the social sectors more generally. The common mantra is for government simply to "get out of the way" of a more innovative private or nonprofit sector. It is noteworthy that such views most often emanate from selected proponents of social entrepreneurship, PSD, and nonadvocacy oriented versions of CSR; they are less likely to be associated with fair trade or advocacy-based CSR proponents.

At the opposite end of a continuum regarding the desirability of government involvement are those who view most nongovernmental change efforts as ineffective substitutes for broader governmental roles (Karnani, 2010). These critics generally assess market-based change models within a framework that criticizes the downsizing of traditional welfare states and the associated rise of neoliberal policies. They therefore view urging governmental involvement in market-based alternatives as not worth the effort, or even as counterproductive in the sense that it may lead change agents to focus too much energy on approaches with marginal pay-offs. Some critics of neoliberalism further argue that the goodwill and marginal positive changes that limited government involvement in such efforts generates deflects attention from more fundamental issues, including a deeper and more systemic analysis of government performance in the delivery of social welfare benefits. This of course is not a new argument or one unique to government involvement in support of nongovernmental or market-based change efforts. It rather is consistent with a long line of political argumentation that questions incremental or residual approaches to welfare state benefit delivery, in contrast with more systemic government approaches for creating structures and benefit systems to assure that disadvantaged members of society receive some basic package of provisions (Gilbert & Terrell, 2010).

Neither of the criticisms of government involvement described here enjoys anything approaching consensual empirical support. I join the critics of neoliberalism in my concern about the superficiality of government involvement in many of these change efforts, and likewise believe that market-based development proponents completely understate the level of positively directed or influenced governmental development initiatives. However, I worry that a lack of governmental involvement in voluntary market-based initiatives may undercut or limit the development of promising innovations. I also doubt the presumed counterfactual—that lack of government involvement in such voluntary efforts necessarily will lead to a growth in dissatisfaction resulting in more fundamental government provision.

Resolution of this issue is at any rate beyond the scope of this book. However, it is notable that there has been growing governmental funding support for social entrepreneurship, especially in the United Kingdom but also to a lesser extent in the United States (Nicholls, 2010). I consequently will focus the remainder of this section on describing more pragmatic tensions between government officials and market-based program initiators and, in turn, on exploring ways in which governments may be supportive of nongovernmental change strategies. Some of these ideas regarding possible governmental support pertain to all or most of the change efforts described in previous chapters, although others are more relevant to a particular approach.

Tensions Between Governmental Officials and Market-Based Program Developers

The distrust that market-based change agents often have for governments already has been noted. However, it should be added that government officials similarly may be distrustful of or skeptical about market-based change agents. In particular, these change agents typically propose taking calculated risks in seeking innovative social responses, and such risk taking may be problematic in the context of governmental political and accountability demands. Although governments may be seeking innovative and effective responses to social problems, they generally must do so in political environments that place limits on their freedom of operation. This often creates tensions between an interest in innovation and the need for accountability (DeLeon and Denhardt, 2000). On the one hand, the desire for innovation suggests a need to allow contractors as much flexibility as possible to encourage the risk taking and experimentation critical to innovation. However, such freedom also can lead to careless or inappropriate use of public funds unless the actions of social entrepreneurs are circumscribed in important ways. Just as market-based change agents take risks as they seek to develop innovative program initiatives, governmental officials incur risks of their own if they are not cautious in the initiatives they support.

Despite these natural tendencies for distrust between government officials and market-based change agents, it seems that useful linkages between these actors are possible and can result in otherwise unobtainable social benefits. For example, the close association between governments and nonprofit agencies in the United States is well-known to academics but poorly understood by the public. That is, governments and nonprofits are engaged in a symbiotic relationship in which nonprofits provide large amounts of service through government contracts or grants (Lynn, 2002; Salamon, 2003; Smith, 2009). Such contracting is necessary for governments because of public resistance to the hiring of public employees, as well as a desire by many government agencies to maintain greater programming flexibility (Kramer, 1994; Lynn, 2002).

In addition, in a time of rapid change and difficult fiscal constraints, governments are under constant pressure to innovate. This arguably has led to a significant increase in government efforts to develop procedures and policies to facilitate involvement in social innovations, including the development of offices in some governments expressly for this purpose (Schwab, 2013). The Schwab Foundation for Social Entrepreneurship (2013), for example, recently has released a report that argues for improved governmental policy models for stimulating social innovations, and which provides useful case examples in this direction from many governments.

The question, then, is not whether useful linkages potentially can be established between governments and market-based voluntary initiatives, but rather what rules of engagement are necessary to allow mutually beneficial relationships. The following sections describe more specific avenues through which beneficial developmental interactions between governments and market-based change agents can be encouraged.

Seeding Social Innovations

Most consonant with the emphasis on small-scale social development emphasized throughout this book, governments can play important roles in supporting innovative seed projects responsive to issues of public interest. Especially with respect to problem areas with poorly developed service technologies, governments can use the contracting mechanisms mentioned earlier to stimulate innovative program responses. For example, in funding research and demonstration projects, governments can define broad problem areas and can encourage new ideas to test solutions. Although this already occurs in the funding for many demonstration projects, the challenge in encouraging innovation is not being overly prescriptive in defining the program approaches that are fundable.

Even if granting flexibility, government officials generally are in the position of needing considerable documentation and reporting on program efforts to demonstrate the specific purposes for which public funds were expended. Yet, the more that monitoring or other restrictions are seen as limiting flexibility in creating programming, the less interested innovative change agents will be in contracting with the government. This suggests the need for government officials to avoid overly burdensome reporting requirements, and in particular to limit such requirements to those essential to assuring public accountability and organizational learning.

Fostering Scaling of Innovations

Governments also can interact with market-based developers by helping to scale up program ideas that already have been shown to be effective on a smaller level. In this context, change agents may have created and tested social innovations related to subject areas in which the government seeks to provide services. The government may then serve to extend such innovations by purchasing service technology or by supporting wider replications. The case study of Victoria Khosa described in Chapter 4 provides an interesting example of the possibilities of this process. As described in Bornstein (2007), Khosa started a service that used former prostitutes and other community members to provide home care to acquired immune deficiency syndrome (AIDS) victims in Africa. The service was an innovative attempt to provide employment alternatives while simultaneously helping those in dire need of care. Khosa developed extensive training in support of her service model, and in time developed an entire home-care curriculum for those working with AIDS victims. As the government increasingly engaged in this service domain due to the AIDS epidemic, government officials needed a consistent program approach and related training materials. Rather than developing the curriculum through public means, they turned to Khosa's model and began using it across the country. This led to an extension in the reach of Khosa's programming ideas far beyond what she would have been able to accomplish without the influx of government resources.

This example should suggest the rich possibilities that may arise if governments can combine the approaches of first stimulating seed projects, and then using their resources to bring successful projects to scale. That is, the process can begin with governments making funds available to change agents to experiment with program ideas in a substantive area of government interest. Then, by monitoring and assessing results of the seed projects, government officials can determine those that appear most promising. Governmental decisions subsequently can be made to scale the more effective seed projects through the injection of resources to allow geographic expansion. This approach has many similarities to a distinction made by Light (2008) with respect to organizations more generally. He asserts that the nimbleness and creativity often associated with small-scale entrepreneurship appear especially well-suited to initiating and testing ideas. Then, larger and more developed organizational structures and related resources may be needed to bring successful innovations to scale.

Adoption of Innovations within Government Operations

Governments increasingly have come under pressure to modify their own methods of operation, due to concerns with overly bureaucratic and inefficient procedures and related cost problems (Osborne & Gaebler, 1992; Kettl, 1998). The resulting encouragement of administrative and service delivery innovations often includes many of the aspects of program development on which market-based change agents have created useful innovations. For example, interest in using technology in new ways to improve governmentally sponsored service delivery is common as are an increasing array of fees and other revenue strategies to partially offset inadequate tax revenues (West, 2004).

Development of various mechanisms for "paying for performance" likewise has introduced market features into a wide range of government funded social programs. As opposed to traditional contracting based on program effort or activity completion, performance-based contracts pay service providers for successful program completions or outcomes, much as businesses generally are rewarded only if they produce acceptable products. For example, employment and training agencies may have payments tied to whether or not participants obtain jobs, or the reimbursements offered to educational contractors may depend on how many participants graduate.

Government as "Rules of the Game" Setter and Regulator

Governments typically are viewed as most critically impacting the well-being of disadvantaged groups by establishing policies and programs for allocating social benefits. This includes the development of welfare state programs such as income and retirement supports, medical care, child care, and other services. However, governments also affect outcomes for people and for institutions through broader rules and regulations that control or incentivize wide-ranging spheres of activity. There are two primary senses in which such government regulatory activities are important. First, and most fundamentally, governments profoundly affect the prospects of all societal members through the broad rules they promulgate regarding how commerce is conducted, what rights workers and capital holders have, how environmental issues are treated, what constitutes property rights, and so forth (Lindblom, 2001; Stiglitz, 2007). These "rules of the game" substantially determine the social and economic contexts in which change agents operate, and powerfully affect choices they make regarding how best to focus their efforts.

Many of these broader governmental roles are especially important with respect to the market-based approaches discussed in this book. In particular, the laws governments establish to regulate corporate and business activities affect the need to engage corporations in change efforts, as well as the options most suitable for doing so. For example, in the absence of strong governmental laws protecting the rights of corporate workers, advocates may be more likely to select CSR or fair trade strategies as necessary vehicles for forwarding worker rights. The rules that governments establish regarding the transparency of corporate activities similarly affect the feasibility of various strategies for engaging corporations and their consumers in change efforts. In addition, the developmental prospects of initially small-scale change strategies such as social entrepreneurship, fair trade, and private social development are affected by the extent that governmentally created market systems favor larger corporate production in relation to smaller businesses and entrepreneurs.

Governments affect these social change models in a second and narrower sense through the rules they establish to more specifically regulate activities related to particular change efforts. Through the development of policies on issues such as licensing requirements, tax treatment, and other rules pertaining to organizational operations, governments may either make experimentation with voluntary service establishment easy or difficult. The manner in which governmental bureaucracies perform their functions related to these policies likewise can have powerful effects on the ease of establishing and operating new ventures. Relatively "friendly" and well-functioning bureaucracies, for example, serve to lower the cost of entry into new ventures and to lessen ongoing transaction costs. In contrast, restrictive policies and cumbersome regulatory implementation can combine to discourage start-up ventures.

THE NEW HORIZONS OF SOCIAL PROVISION: MORE GENERAL LESSONS FOR CHANGE AGENTS

Whether or not change agents choose to engage in any of the market-based approaches described in this book, some model strengths and lessons are valuable in framing nearly any social change strategy designed to benefit disadvantaged groups. In particular, if the impact of initiatives is to be maximized in emerging global contexts, it is particularly important for change agents to carefully think through and build skills around five aspects of change emphasized in many market-based approaches. These include innovation, technology, the business of change, culture and empowerment, and socially responsible consumption. These attributes parallel model strengths discussed earlier in the chapter, but are reframed slightly here to highlight their importance in broader change development and in framing teaching and learning strategies for change agents. I believe that strategies for building these skill sets offer important opportunities for teachers and practitioners, and can benefit substantially from partnerships between those with advanced technical or business skills and those with social service backgrounds.

Innovation

It probably is passé to reiterate that we are living in a rapidly changing world; and there seems to be little dispute that the pace of change will continue to accelerate. The implications of this environment for social change efforts and the well-being of disadvantaged groups nonetheless are profound. Change agents will be under continual pressure to adapt to broader societal trends and events if they are to be successful, which will require a spirit of ongoing innovation uncommon in most organizations.

Like other individual and organizational attributes, an orientation toward innovation can be nourished, and I believe several directions are especially useful in this respect. First, change agents need to train themselves and those with whom they work to think about social problems and related solutions in new ways, as opposed to only considering common approaches and incremental adjustments. This is very difficult for most of us to do for a host of reasons, and so generally requires conscious attempts to stimulate; the challenge is to break away from routine thought patterns so that a broader array of solutions is contemplated. This can partially be accomplished by training and by forcing ourselves to think beyond what initially seem like the most obvious or superior solutions to social issues.

Innovation, especially in rapidly changing environments, also benefits from a high level of environmental surveillance. It is critical for change agents to be connected to as many information circuits as possible, so that they keep closely in touch with emerging challenges and opportunities. In an age of information explosion, this is very difficult to do because information conduits are everywhere. Change agents nonetheless need to develop a solid understanding of those information outlets that are most likely to contribute new ideas, and then to engage in aggressive and ongoing surveillance of them.

Thinking innovatively and monitoring relevant environments benefit from extending professional and social networks beyond people with whom we are most closely aligned, because associating only with similar thinkers constrains our range of ideas and limits the diversity of information we obtain. Yet, we generally are most comfortable in interacting with those with whom we share common experiences, expertise, and values. Breaking away from this natural tendency thus requires foresight and conscious effort. Change agents in particular need to think through the types of backgrounds that potentially are most valuable in terms of the problems in which they engage, and then to pursue interactions along these lines.

Technology

Effectively providing benefits to disadvantaged groups always has involved the use of various technologies. However, consistent with the image of human service organizations as "people-processing" systems that rely primarily on constructive human interactions between staff and clients (Hasenfeld, 2009), technology generally has taken a back seat to properly structuring these relationships, hiring staff with appropriate people-processing skills, and providing related training to them. The role of technology often has been relegated to more mundane functions such as processing payrolls, documenting services delivered, and completing various reporting functions. This perspective has been reinforced in most social work and human services-related professional programs, which to the extent they have emphasized technology usually do so by narrowly focusing on management information systems or on general administrative contexts. It is no wonder that human services students often have avoided or yawned their way through these topics, with the occasional faculty technology geek essentially spitting into the disciplinary winds.

Some may view this characterization as stereotypical and outdated, and I hope that is the case. I would nonetheless argue that changes with respect to technology preparation and use patterns in human services-related academic programs and organizations are not occurring rapidly enough. As suggested earlier and illustrated by examples throughout this book, emerging technologies are creating tremendous opportunities for serving the world's most disadvantaged people. It therefore is critical for change agents to thoroughly assess technological possibilities as they build change initiatives, and to establish linkages with more technologically inclined individuals who can assist them in this respect.

Well-meaning human services professionals have long complained about the invasion of masters of business administration (MBAs) and other business-trained individuals into the ranks of human services agencies. Such individuals typically are viewed as lacking the human interaction training and experience that are so fundamental to service provision. However, their emergence at least partially derives from the fact that they bring skill sets deficient among those trained in the social sciences or related professional programs, and the more cutting edge use of technology is among these.

If human services-trained change agents are to play leadership roles in coming generations of change initiatives so needed in our societies, it is incumbent on them and the academics who educate them to thoroughly rethink how best to inculcate learning about technology, as well as to develop strategies that allow change agents to more easily stay abreast of new technology innovations. This consideration cannot be viewed simply in the context of management and administration, as it so often is. It rather must permeate our ways of thinking about all aspects of service delivery—from assessments of clients in one-on-one interactions, to the selection of appropriate services, to the linkages between interrelated change agents. The new technology now stands at the forefront of social change, and failing to understand and make creative uses of it will seriously impede efforts to help the most disadvantaged.

The Business of Change

A related but broader point relates to what I refer to as "the business of change," of which effective technology use is only a small part. By the business of change, I mean all of the planning and management operational features associated with the delivery of benefits. These are the often mundane tasks required to make a program or project work smoothly and efficiently on a day-to-day basis, as well as the functions required in interacting with and maintaining the support of all relevant stakeholders.

Many human services professionals cringe when presented with seemingly incessant attention to efficiency when considering of social service delivery. This is a justifiable reaction to the reality that efficiency language often masks more fundamental inattention to and related lack of resources for basic human needs, as characterized by the incessant admonition to "do more with less." However true, this reaction is self-defeating, because failing to manage efficiently ultimately undercuts the delivery of benefits to the most disadvantaged. Although the need to advocate for sufficient resources must be ongoing, the lack thereof should not be used as an excuse to minimize sound management.

Change agents interested in social development therefore need to develop skills related to basic program operational functions, including but not limited to needs assessment, planning, fundraising, marketing and recruitment, and fiscal and programmatic management. As with technology development, performance in these areas can benefit substantially through collaborations and other linkages with persons having specialized expertise. Nonetheless, at least basic levels of understanding are needed if change agents are to enter into effective partnerships, so that broad parameters regarding possibilities are known and appropriate collaborations are sought.

I consequently believe that social work, public policy, nonprofit development, and other programs oriented toward training students for social development work need to carefully think through the business and technical training provided to their students. Training of this nature in many programs has been weak and has not kept pace with the rapidly changing information required for intelligent functioning along the business and technical dimensions essential to the operation of even small-scale social programs. Human services educated change agents sometimes shy away from training in these aspects of social program development, either because they find the content unappealing or else are intimidated by some of the more challenging technical aspects. It is the responsibility of human services faculty members interested in program development to foster student talents in these respects, through the creation of relevant content in their own disciplines and by encouraging the incorporation of selected business, information technology, and related classes into their curricula.

Culture and Empowerment

Being culturally sensitive and being concerned with empowering clients as part of service interventions are fundamental aspects of social work and many other community development orientations, so it may seem odd to focus upon them as a useful contribution from market-based models. Yet, there is an interesting overlap between human services considerations that focus on sensitivity to client needs on the one hand and market approaches emphasizing the needs, capabilities, and tastes of customers on the other.

There are two related but distinct reasons why cultural sensitivity and client empowerment should be emphasized in development. First, a developmental intervention is unlikely to be even modestly successful unless attention to culture has been adequately considered. Customer needs, wants, capabilities, and stylistic preferences all may affect receptivity to interventions, so needs assessments that are not sensitively conducted with direct input from targeted beneficiaries most likely will be deficient. These shortcomings may not only diminish program impact, but in the worst cases may totally undermine the potential success of a program—much like poor market research by businesses can result in the development of products with insufficient consumer demand.

Second, a focus on how to best empower clients or customers is critical to the longer-term impact of programs. Thinking through model behavioral logic from an empowerment perspective should force change agents to carefully consider what they ultimately expect beneficiaries to do differently based on an intervention, as opposed to merely indicating what the intervention will provide. That is, with a few exceptions, it is difficult to envision programs that simply continue to provide goods and services to people as maximizing social good unless some developmental trajectory can be envisioned, and empowerment provides an excellent lens for considering this dimension of program development.

Similarly, demonstrating how interventions empower recipients is critical to the longer-term sustainability of social programs. Stakeholders who provide financial and other support for programs are unlikely to continue to do so unless they can be convinced that the social intervention is helping targeted beneficiaries move forward in some important respect. In addition, an interesting aspect of some interventions is that those who initially receive assistance improve their own circumstances and subsequently give back to the program, creating a virtuous and sustainable cycle.

This discussion has focused on change agents considering empowerment as they think through and then describe the impact of social interventions. It should be noted, however, that those most serious about empowerment emphasize the importance of beneficiary involvement in assessing needs and devising solutions. This is useful in three respects. First, it begins a process of beneficiaries doing something positive to further their own interests, as opposed to merely receiving a benefit. Second, it can be influential in establishing the credibility of change agents, in that beneficiaries will be more likely to view them as respectful and interested in mutual collaborations. Finally, insufficient interaction with beneficiaries during developmental stages has the potential to seriously undercut interventions, in that change agents do not adequately understand the issues facing beneficiaries and the context in which these issues are embedded.

Polak's (2009) discussion of this latter phenomenon in developing programs for the homeless and for poor rural farmers provides excellent guidance in this respect. In summarizing his approach of interacting extensively with beneficiaries before developing intervention strategies, he recounts how he benefited from interactions with a particular homeless person: "What my afternoon with Joe confirmed for me is that coming up with practical solutions for homelessness requires going to the places where homeless people live, learning from them what their lives are like, why they do what they do, and what opportunities they take advantage of now and hope to take advantage of in the future" (p. 8). Polak adds, "I think the furniture of our professional training—of the middle-class contexts in which most people from Europe, North America, and prosperous Asia are raised—contributes to our inability to see and do the obvious about poverty" (p. 9–10).

Conducting the up-front needs assessments and planning efforts needed to fulfill the aforementioned objectives in diverse and often difficult environments can be very challenging for change agents, given factors such as language barriers, cultural discomfort, safety concerns, and other issues. However, these processes can be shortchanged only at great risk to effective programming, so developing an awareness of and skills related to sensitive cultural assessments and inclusive program creation should be of great importance to any change agent.

Those with well-developed social interaction skills can play leadership roles in this respect. In particular, individuals engaged in teaching about various dimensions of social interaction and community development can contribute to educating those in business and technical schools, so that their educational preparation increasingly includes social components. This already has begun to occur in some business schools, through the incorporation of classes on business ethics, social entrepreneurship, and related socially oriented courses. This consequently is an area in which human services-related professional programs should and often do provide leadership, and change agents from business backgrounds would do well to cross over into these programs for more serious training of this nature.

Socially Responsible Consumption

Human services-oriented change agents traditionally have focused on developing approaches for directly influencing the behavior of potential beneficiaries, and then have sought financial support from governmental officials or well-endowed individuals to operationalize related social programs. This approach has fostered the development of many fine programs, and continues to be important. However, it also often has relieved pressure on important societal actors to think about how their actions affect the well-being of those disadvantaged groups with which they are not closely connected.

The role of markets in providing socially desired outcomes is a longstanding related concern. The extent to which markets are viewed as desirable social mechanisms usually derives from their perceived capacity to make partners better-off in an exchange, which is seen as resulting when each pursues their own narrow self-interest. This conception is limited in that it ignores side issues known as externalities, and also does not lend itself to many social issues that are not primarily exchange oriented.[2] Yet, designing markets to provide mutually rewarding exchanges has been a growing phenomenon across countries for many years, and even market skeptics concede that individual and collective benefits can result from carefully constructed exchanges. The main questions pertaining to markets thus no longer revolve around their general viability, but rather concern how best to use markets for constructive social purposes and how to best respond to their inevitable limitations.

One of the most fascinating aspects of the market-based approaches is that they bring additional stakeholders into clearer focus in considering social well-being. I have referred to such groups as intermediaries, and I believe that they have grown increasingly important as the world has become more globalized and as governmental powers have attenuated. Perhaps the roles played by corporate entities and consumers are the most far-reaching in this respect, and the construction of linkages between these two intermediary groups is at the heart of much of the work described in this book. The challenge for change agents is to understand these intermediaries well, and to be creative in developing strategies for better engaging them to promote collective well-being.

Scholars also have more broadly brought increasing attention to the importance of consumptive practices, and this is a movement that merits careful consideration by human services professionals interested in social justice issues. What is interesting about some market approaches is that they move beyond narrow economic conceptions of self-interest. In particular, fair trade and externally driven CSR proponents rely on consumers as their most important intermediaries in driving social change. But they do not appeal to consumers solely along the lines of narrow economic self-interest, as is the case with most conceptions of market behavior. Rather, they appeal to consumers to consider the broader social good as they make purchasing decisions. They may do so by considering what is "fair" for those who produce the goods and services they purchase, or by accounting for broader social issues related to their consumption, such as environmental impacts. In either case, consumers are being asked to think of more than their own economic interests as they make purchasing decisions, and it is in this respect that market-based approaches are novel and potentially most important.

I earlier referred to such socially oriented consumption as providing "psychic" benefits to consumers, in the sense that they feel better as the result of more altruistic or collectively oriented consumption. Archer and Fritsch (2010) have considered such behavior more broadly in terms of how it reaches beyond traditional economic theory self-interest conceptions, and instead incorporates social norms into decision making. Micheletti (2003) has referred to such consumers as "political consumers," and others have explored the ethics of consumption and have offered varying prescriptions for what this entails (Harrison, Newholm, & Shaw, 2010; Micheletti, Follesdal, & Stolle 2006).

Some have criticized such notions as being unsustainable, because they are so dependent on the vagaries of relatively well-off consumers. The general fear is that, even if well-intentioned, consumers always will be weighing such ethical considerations against their more narrow and tangible economic self-interests (Leclair, 2002). Especially when economic circumstances become more fragile, the concern is that price will win out as the most convincing decision-making factor. In this sense, the consumer senti-ment driving much of the fair trade and CSR movements may be viewed as a luxury good that is subservient to the more general well-being of middle- and upper-class consumers.

One need look no further than the success of Walmart ("Low prices. Everyday. On everything.") and other large price-focused retailers to under-stand the powerful sway that prices have on consumer decision making; price-based competition in loosely regulated global economic markets will continue to assure the availability of relatively inexpensive goods in most developed markets. This reality suggests the depth of commitment among consumers needed to sustain and grow market-based social change models; it requires ongoing education and persuasion regarding the collective val-ues furthered through socially responsible consumption.

Calls for consumers to be less narrowly materialistic in their purchas-ing patterns are nothing new, and have included diverse critiques regard-ing the destructiveness of materialism on broader societies (Kasser, 2002; Ryan & Dziurawiec, 2001; Leff, 1995). However, recent global attention to issues such as environmental degradation seem to have created new poten-tial to engage consumers in serious consideration of the social impacts of consumption, and hence may indicate a new opening for market-based change agents oriented toward more responsible consumption. In fact, the market-based models discussed here fit well within the new attention to sustainability that is becoming increasingly prominent in many fields. Sustainability has many definitions, which often focuses more on the man-agement of depletable resources and the minimization of environmental damages. However, sustainability advocates likewise may consider fairness in returns to producers. There are important intersections in these sustain-ability considerations with both human capital development and political stability. From the human capital perspective, providing fairer returns to workers can be argued to increase motivation and commitment over time, leading to a more stable and productive workforce. From the political per-spective, more just returns to producers may increase the political stability of regimes, in that more satisfied workers may be important as the social glue that helps hold societies together.

These ideas may seem utopian and of course are subject to empiri-cal scrutiny. But it nonetheless seems that the new focus on sustainable production and consumption is a serious one given wide-ranging global threats, so change agents should work to establish both human and environmental dimensions in these domains. Educating consumers about the meaning of their purchases in a broader social context then is an ongoing and significant challenge, especially given the constant barrage of appealing "shop price" messages with which consumers are inundated. Nonetheless, the shrinking of the world through globalization, as well as the new technological innovations that allow unprecedented communications across space and audiences, suggest that the possibilities in this realm are great.

Thoughtful social change agents should carefully consider the implications of political and ethical consumption. Many of us for too long have blamed corporations and the well-off for creating social problems, even though we simultaneously engage in consumption patterns that fuel the outcomes about which we complain. A hard-headed assessment of consumption should concern not just which items we buy from particular producers, such as fair trade versus mass-developed corporate products, although such considerations are important to social development. It more fundamentally requires us to review how much we consume and the broader impact of that consumption. This is an individual journey that is unlikely to be monitored by anyone but ourselves, and yet it is fundamental to progress on social development, sustainability, and social justice.

SUMMING UP: MARKET-BASED INITIATIVES
IN BROADER PERSPECTIVE

Nearly 40 years ago, Lindblom (1977) in his classic work *Politics and Markets* assessed the mutual contributions of markets and governmental structures in delivering societal benefits. He and contemporaries (see, for example, Schultze, 1977) did much to articulate the potential of market-based incentives and disincentives in delivering collective benefits, while simultaneously recognizing the limitations of markets as vehicles of social change. At that time, there was considerable skepticism in the social sciences about the utility of markets in providing benefits for the disadvantaged, and the work of these scholars helped influence diverse change agents to consider market-based approaches as viable options for social change.

Much has changed since that time. The march of globalization and neoliberal political policies has pushed loosely regulated markets to the forefront of social provision. In fact, the dependence on markets in social provision has become so well established that, coupled with increasing cynicism about governmental performance, the central challenge now is not to lose sight of the unique capabilities of governments in more heavily privatized systems.

As previously mentioned, the shortcoming of many market-based social advocates is that they fail to recognize these distinctive contributions, and instead denigrate government efforts with a broad stroke. These tendencies are at best naïve and reflect a fundamental misunderstanding about the uniquely positive attributes of governmental entities and the limitations of unregulated markets. At worst, they represent more self-serving attempts by the well-off to undercut efforts to redistribute resources to the disadvantaged.

The task for change agents now is to build on what has been learned about the strengths and weaknesses of both governments and markets in various aspects of social provision. In this concluding section, I will highlight what I see as the most important issues in this respect; I also will offer a closing assessment of the most fundamental strengths and weaknesses of market-based approaches in the broader context of working for positive social change for the disadvantaged in the developing world.

The preceding discussion of strengths and weaknesses suggests the complexity of issues in play when considering the advisability of various market-based approaches, and I leave my examination of the potential contributions of these models to social development with mixed emotions. From the standpoint of one trained in the social sciences and social work, and then practicing in the governmental sector and social work academic fields, I believe that the perspectives and practices emphasized in these models can significantly enrich social development discussions. In fact, in a time of dramatic needs and ongoing conflicts over resource deployments, social change agents who fail to carefully consider potential applications of business models and practices may have difficulty establishing sustainable initiatives. I would further suggest that not drawing lessons from these approaches is irresponsible, because change agents who are deficient in skills stressed in these models are likely to forego useful knowledge for impacting the groups they wish to serve. Nowhere is this more evident than in the novel applications of new technologies in service development and delivery, as the rapid and creative deployment of cell phones in the developing world nicely illustrates.

There are many reasons why stronger linkages between human services-trained change agents and persons with business or technical backgrounds have tended to be the exception rather than the rule. On the one hand, those trained in the social sciences and related professions often perceive those from the business world to be exploitive, especially of the poor populations they profess to help. They also may be worried about cleanwashing or greenwashing ploys by business agents. In addition, they at times appear to be intimidated by the superior technical skills that business-trained individuals bring to program development efforts, and may view them as overly narrow in their perspectives.

On the other hand, business professionals and academics often look on those in human services related professional programs as being "soft" and ineffective, and they may give short shrift to issues such as culture and capacity-building that are heavily emphasized in social science models. These differences in perspectives and expertise are common to many emerging interdisciplinary collaborations, and require careful nurturing of relationships by change agents to assure that all collaborators understand the specific contributions of their colleagues. Assuming that change agents foster such understanding, however, I believe that the difficulties noted here can be overcome.

Other aspects of the discussions surrounding these models are more troubling. In particular, the notion that relying more heavily on the goodwill and expertise of corporate officials and social entrepreneurs will lead to substantial improvements in global well-being typically reflects a naïve and uninformed knowledge of social problems and the difficulty of solving them. Yet this is exactly the tone, and sometimes is the more explicit admonition, expressed in the writings of many market-based change proponents.

Such attitudes often are accompanied by denigrations of the efforts of other social change agents. They begin with an oversimplified and shallow historical context that sets up a straw man of "everything else has failed"—so now new business approaches can step in and solve the problems of the developing world. An accompanying distrust of government social provision, as well as a disdain for the nonprofit sector, are common corollaries. With respect to government, the notion is that substantial progress could be made if only governments were less regulatory and bureaucratic, and if they stayed away from "big government" solutions to social problems.

Nonprofits are viewed more kindly by many market-based advocates, but at times there is an undertone of perceived general incompetence regarding how they approach social issues and implement responses. These rather stereotypical characterizations not only are inaccurate, but are deeply offensive to those in government, the nonprofit sector, and to others who have struggled for years against difficult odds to improve the well-being of the disadvantaged around the world. Unfortunately, they serve as additional obstacles that must be overcome to encourage those from the social sciences and related professional programs to seriously consider market-based approaches.

Just as with conservative economic philosophy more generally, the overarching attitude is that social progress will occur if we can just get government out of the way and allow those with more finely honed business skills to take charge of social provision. The problem is that these are the same people and institutions whose single-minded pursuit of self-interest is among the greatest contributors to many of the problems they are purporting to solve. For example, one need look no further than the current global warming disaster or the recent corporate financial scandals engulfing the world to be very skeptical of the promise of internally directed corporate social responsibility as a change approach. These large-scale corporate problems are accompanied by a daily barrage of more fine-grained corporate malpractice or greed illustrations that increasingly are well-covered in the media. For example, on the day I am drafting these thoughts, I am confronted with three front page *New York Times* articles reporting that GlaxoSmithKline has agreed to a record settlement of $3 billion in fines related to misrepresentation of its products (Thomas & Schmidt, 2012), that JPMorgan Chase financial advisors disregarded client needs in favor of home institution sales (Craig & Silver-Greenberg, 2012), and that the aggressive practices of companies administering probation services for local governments are leading to huge fees and jail time for poor people as they accumulate debt for minor infractions (Bronner, 2012). Although I recognize these are only slivers among the great multitude of corporate endeavors around the world, they certainly do not inspire confidence about corporate performance in addressing social problems.

Perhaps even more disconcerting in much of the market-based writing is an implication that those who have become rich in market systems know what is best for society and, in particular, that they can best guide social development. A positive aspect of fair trade, social entrepreneurship, and PSD approaches is their congruence with many community development and social work principles regarding indigenous community involvement and empowerment in decision making. It is here that I believe community-based change agents have the most to gain from market-based approaches—through careful attention to the needs of consumers or "customers" coupled with a heightened pragmatic sense of how best to implement many facets of goods and service provision.

Unfortunately, this basic and important contribution of these approaches often is lost in many presentations, where the focus instead is on the heroic qualities of those leading the change efforts. This is especially true of many media accounts praising these initiatives, but it also is emphasized in much of the social entrepreneurship literature regarding the personal qualities of social entrepreneurs, as well as in the somewhat fawning descriptions of the world's richest who have turned their attention to social causes. Although I join many in welcoming this attention to social issues, I fear that the response to it by many carries much of the hero-worshipping and celebratory features that represent the worst features of American culture.

Perhaps nowhere are these concerns crystallized as well as in the book, *Philanthrocapitalism: How Giving Can Save the World* (Bishop & Green, 2009). This book has much to offer in terms of describing positive market-based aspects of philanthropy, and I have few doubts the authors believe the approaches they describe will substantially improve well-being for those with the greatest disadvantages. However, with a concentration on the efforts of well-off individuals, and chapter titles such as "Virtue's Middlemen" (with Bill Clinton as chief protagonist), "Enter the Celanthropist" (celebrity givers), and "Billanthropy" (Bill Gates philanthropic giving), one is consumed with an overriding air of how grateful society should be that these titans are redefining social provision.

Such portrayals paint the rich working as heroic individuals, or in consort with their wealthy allies, to tackle the problems of development, bringing the same drive and expertise that they already have exercised in conquering the business world. But fundamental issues such as democratic participation in change, the importance of indigenous decision making, and sensitivity to local cultures in change are given little emphasis, unless they happen to be attended to by a particular philanthrocapitalist. The following two passages from the book are illustrative in this respect.

> In 2001, David Rockefeller (a grandson of the Rockefeller Foundation founder and a mentor of Bill Gates) and his daughter, Peggy Dulany, launched one such organization: the hugely influential Global Philanthropists Circle, of which Dulany has become de facto chief mentor. Described by *Business Week* as "the most elite club in the world," it brings together many of the most respected individuals and families from every part of the globe who are committed to using their time, influence, and resources to address some of the world's most significant problems. In 2007, its members represented 68 wealthy families from 22 countries. In 2003, a junior version of the Circle was created, the Next Generation Group, to encourage younger people from their teens to early thirties to be involved in philanthropy" (Bishop & Green, p. 227).

> In America, the Wealth and Giving Forum, founded in 2003, is an exclusive, invitation-only club where the rich can meet in private "to reflect with their peers on how best to allocate their wealth" (Bishop & Green, p. 228).

In affectionately praising this new spirit of social engagement among the rich, Bishop and Green suggest that philanthropic networks have changed for the better, and have become a more generous and effective "club." But this still is a rich club marked by exclusivity in membership and decision making, and so lacks many of the participatory elements valued in many change approaches. Furthermore, to the extent that market-based approaches highlight the accomplishments of well-off individuals and institutions, they may turn attention away from more fundamental concerns with our economic systems and the manner in which they allocate economic rewards to citizens. The well-publicized efforts of the rich become feel-good stories not only about the benefactors, but more generally about societal good nature in responding to social issues. Yet these efforts represent only a drop in the bucket of need with respect to the economic and social problems facing the world's poor.

This deflection of attention issue, and the related one of top-down charitable decision making, are serious ones. As Michael Edwards (2008) has provocatively asked, should we be praising Carlos Slim and other multibillionaires for their charitable efforts, or rather be raising more fundamental questions about economic systems that produce such unequal outcomes? I would argue the latter, because it is only through governmental decision making regarding broader rules of the game and associated outcomes that a sense of reasonable fairness in society can be created. It also is only through democratic participation, and a sense of inclusiveness in voluntary developmental endeavors, that a sense of meaningful citizen involvement can be generated so that collective benefits are viewed as developmentally created and shared and not monarchically or patriarchically given.

In his blistering critiques of philanthrocapitalism, Edwards (2008, 2010) raises another major concern about market-based approaches. He contends that the nature of markets is to reduce all transactions to dollars and cents, and in the course of doing so to minimize other features of social relationships. Yet, other values have been at the heart of much of what has been accomplished in social provision, especially in the voluntary relationships characteristics of the nonprofit sector. Edwards fears that a focus on markets, efficiencies, and bottom lines will seriously distort many of these effective communitarian values and consequently undercut many of the good things that have been done through such mechanisms.

I share Edwards's concerns about many of the limitations of philanthrocapitalism, and encourage anyone interested in market-based social provision to review his books. However, I think that some of his criticisms about market limitations miss the mark a bit. In particular, as has been well-articulated by prominent economists and political scientists, markets are tools that can be used effectively for many purposes (see, for example, Schultz, 1977; Lindblom, 1977, 2001). If properly constructed, they can allow a great deal of flexibility and individual choice while still resulting in collective benefit provision. The trick seems to be to engage markets after more fundamental values about collective goals and desired outcomes are established through participatory oriented discussions among diverse stakeholders. Then, constructing systems that provide the best opportunities to move productively toward these outcomes can be developed, and various market mechanisms can be important tools in this direction.

The difficulties noted in the discussions here may seem intractable to some, but I remain convinced that much good can come from a careful examination and sensitive application of market-based principles in social change efforts. The more positive note to which I referred earlier is born of the common desire of change agents to seek new solutions to assist the poorest of our citizens; I believe this desire resonates powerfully both in the market-based literature and in community development literature that long has populated the social sciences. This commonality of intentions, coupled with an increasing focus on interdisciplinarity in problem solving and in advancing communications capabilities, holds the promise of greatly enriching social development initiatives and strategies. My hope is that colleagues from all disciplines will be aggressive and open-minded in seeking the best strategies from different fields in incorporating their own innovative solutions and in teaching new students about approaches to social development. If this occurs in a context that correspondingly engages the world's poor as intelligent consumers and planners of their own destinies, and that also appropriately engages the nonprofit and governmental sectors, truly transformational developmental possibilities can emerge.

INTRODUCTION TO MARKET-ORIENTED SOCIAL
DEVELOPMENT APPROACHES

1.   Elements and examples of these approaches also have at times been discussed under the term "philanthrocapitalism," which itself is loosely defined but generally refers to more strategic, businesslike, and investor driven philanthropic giving strategies by the well-off (Bishop & Green, 2009; Jenkins, 2011). This term is too broad to be analytically or conceptually meaningful, and so I will avoid it here except in referring to the work of those who use it. In addition, although the approaches described here often involve philanthropic support from the well-off, they extend much further and involve a wide array of individuals and organizations that do not bring extensive personal wealth to their change efforts.

2.   Among other market-based social change approaches that have received growing attention are impact investing (Bugg-Levine, & Emerson, 2011), venture philanthropy (Frumkin, 2003), and social impact bonds (Liebman, 2011). Although literature and practice experience have emerged around these approaches, they are in my opinion less well-developed and have a much less extensive experiential base than the approaches to be assessed.

3.   It is noteworthy that by these standards very few people in developed countries live in poverty, which reinforces my aim to discuss the change approaches presented here primarily with respect to their promise in developing countries. Nonetheless, relative poverty considerations within developed countries remain important in social policy and program development. In addition, some of the approaches to be discussed, especially social entrepreneurship and corporate social responsibility, at times focus on more diverse target groups or on social concerns that extend beyond poverty issues. Therefore, although I will emphasize developing world poverty related interventions, at times I will refer to services for other disadvantaged

groups that appear to be especially innovative or particularly illustrative of a change approach.

4. I will mention at various points in the text "social sciences" or "social sciences training," by which I mean traditional social science disciplines such as political science, sociology, psychology, anthropology, and so on. I also will refer to "related professional programs" or training that typically intersects closely with the social sciences, such as social work, behavioral counseling, human and family development, community development, public policy, and other applied programs. Although training in such programs varies, it often relies heavily on concepts from the social sciences; my general attempt is to contrast this with business-oriented training.

DEVELOPING SOCIAL CHANGE MODELS

1. I will use the terms "model" and "approach" interchangeably throughout the book. By either, I mean to convey an organized set of activities and related logic designed to bring about change in a specified target group.

2. Some may object to my definitional focus on one group of actors helping another, because it may seem to underestimate the importance of groups of people instigating change on their own behalf. For example, in self-help oriented change efforts, the initiators and leaders are also generally the primary intended beneficiaries. In addition, many participatory approaches emphasize change agents working closely with potential beneficiaries in defining and implementing the change. I view participatory change ideas as very important, and I incorporate them in the more generalized approach to be articulated. Nonetheless, even highly indigenous development approaches often rely quite heavily on outside instigators in their initial stages. In these instances, those targeted for change may in turn become change agents as part of the change implementation process.

3. There may be some confusion between my definitions of "model" and "approach" on the one hand, and "initiative" and "effort" on the other. The distinction pertains primarily to breadth of analytic focus. The former terms are conceptual constructs aimed at broad categorization, while the latter are more concrete examples within such categories. For example, the corporate social responsibility approaches discussed in Chapter 3 define general strategies for attempting to change corporate behavior. In comparison, a boycott of a particular corporation is seen as an initiative or effort that exemplifies such a broader change approach.

4. There actually are slight differences in meaning between these terms as commonly used. In particular, the term beneficiaries may be seen as somewhat broader in that it can include all people who receive a benefit—whether or not that benefit was intended for them. A target group rather implies a set of intended beneficiaries. Although recognizing these differences, to aid simplicity and variety of presentation, I will use the terms interchangeably throughout, with an emphasis on considering those for whom benefits are intended.

5. There are many other approaches that focus more on organizational development or political mobilization. However, I would argue that these approaches typically have the ultimate goal of improving circumstances for some defined set of people. The goal of political mobilization, for example, typically is to allow disenfranchised groups in society to more effectively garner benefits or otherwise improve their well-being through the political process; I would thus view these largely as political capital building approaches, as will be discussed later in this chapter.

6. I will use the terms life circumstances and well-being interchangeably and in a general sense throughout the book. Given my focus on poor persons, I most often will be referring to better basic life circumstances such as improved employment, wages, health, or literacy. The section later in this chapter on "what benefits are delivered" provides a flavor of the range of how change efforts may affect such life circumstances, but I do want to make clear that I use such terms in a general and non-technical manner.

7. This is akin to a very similar problem emerging in many social service fields regarding how best to respond to multiproblem families, which likewise has encouraged attention to new intervention strategies. As recognition has grown, a related thrust in academic and practice oriented settings has been to advocate for the creation of multidisciplinary teams in conducting research and providing services. A central tenet of such approaches is to link persons with differing backgrounds, expertise, and perspectives in a manner that creates new thinking about problems and related intervention strategies (see, for example, Bornstein, 2007).

8. I should note a variation of focus in model descriptions that at times is confusing. That is, although it is widely agreed that the point of providing benefits ultimately is to affect *outcomes* for beneficiaries, many model descriptions focus more upon the processes through which benefits are delivered and in turn on the *outputs* of these processes. For example, the benefits provided through prenatal care programs are specific health-related products or services for

expectant mothers, and in descriptive terms, proponents may focus on describing the particular processes and action steps required to deliver these benefits. They likewise may emphasize the quantity of these benefits that are delivered or the characteristics of those who receive benefits. Yet, the effectiveness of such programs ultimately depends not just on the success of benefit delivery but on the accuracy of the underlying causal logic—that provision of such benefits to expectant mothers in turn leads to better health and/or cognitive developmental outcomes for children.

This point is well understood in various academic and program development fields, and is the focus of much program evaluation and applied research that attempts to distinguish between program outputs and outcomes (Kettner, Maroney, & Martin, 2013). I mention it here because this book is much more about change model explication than outcome evaluation, and hence in describing various models, I generally will focus more heavily on the processes change agents employ to produce and deliver various benefits. The extent to which such benefits in turn lead to intended outcomes for targeted beneficiaries and for broader societies is a more difficult evaluation issue that requires ongoing empirical assessment. Nonetheless, I believe it is essential to establish the causal logic through which delivered benefits should be expected to affect outcomes, and so I will attempt to articulate such implied causal logic when it is not done so explicitly by model proponents.

9. Although logic models should be sufficiently specific to allow one to clearly classify intended change processes that fall within their purview, it should be noted that many different operational tactics may be consistent with implementation of a particular logic model. For example, proponents of externally driven corporate social responsibility (CSR) believe that corporations only will change behavior in socially desirable ways if pressured by outside advocates; therefore, the logic model proposed by such persons emphasizes bringing external pressure to bear on corporate officials. Yet, there are many specific operational tactics that are consistent with doing so, such as boycotts, lobbying, and socially conscious investing strategies. I will refer to these more specific operational devices implemented in the context of a general change strategy as "tactics." These typically fall under the auspices of more detailed implementation plans. It is in this sense that the behavioral model sometimes overlaps with "the politics of change" aspect to be discussed in a subsequent section. The behavioral model may serve as an umbrella of sorts that defines a broad approach, with several more specific tactics possible in bringing it to

operational fruition. Change agents then are left to consider and choose from such tactics based on their philosophical inclinations, coupled with a reading of the socio-political environment in which the change approach is to be implemented.

10. There is a fine line here in some cases between bona fide capabilities needed for a program to have a chance of succeeding, and what is known as "creaming." The idea of creaming is that program managers consciously select beneficiaries who have the greatest chance of succeeding, but here I am referring to capabilities that at least give beneficiaries a reasonable chance of success.

11. The terms primary, secondary, and tertiary prevention often are used in the health-care field in thinking about possible intervention points. According to Gordon (1983:107), these terms are defined as follows: "primary—practiced prior to the biologic origin of disease; secondary—practiced after the disease can be recognized, but before it has caused suffering and disability; and tertiary—practiced after suffering or disability have been experienced, in order to prevent further deterioration." The definition has the limitation of not corresponding closely to what we think of as "prevention" in non-health-care fields, which usually implies programs in which problems have yet to affect individuals. Gordon (1983:109) consequently proposed the following alternative to flesh out differences in prevention programming: "we propose to define prevention as measures adopted by or practiced on persons not currently feeling the effects of a disease, intended to decrease the risk that that disease will afflict them in the future. Prevention is classified into three levels on the basis of the population for whom the measure is advisable on cost-benefit analysis. Universal measures are recommended for essentially everyone. Selective measures are advisable for population subgroups distinguished by age, sex, occupation, or other evident characteristics, but who, on individual examination, are perfectly well. Indicated measures are those that should be applied only in the presence of a demonstrable condition that identifies the individual as being at higher than average risk for the future development of a disease."

12. I recognize that whether or not to include paid transactions in describing interactions between change agents and various actors is a gray area. I choose not to do so because I feel the more important struggle in this respect is raising sufficient resources to allow such paid transactions to occur. That is, although selecting the best paid providers remains an important challenge even for those change agents who acquire resources, I assume that doing so falls more under the "business of change" functions discussed in the following section. In most

situations, I assume that skilled change agents can make reasonable decisions about the deployment of resources for various operational purposes once these resources are obtained.

13. I should note that the term community engagement has been used in different ways by many others in considering change processes, and that there is no commonly accepted standard definition. Important applications of this idea are now prominent in community based participatory research strategies, as well as in a movement to engage students in community work. For example, the Committee on Community Engagement of the Centers for Disease Control Prevention (1997) has defined community engagement related to research as "the process of working collaboratively with and through groups of people affiliated by geographic proximity, special interest, or similar situations to address issues affecting the well-being of those people" (p. 9). In addition, the notion of collaborating with diverse sets of citizen groups has been prominent in some forms of community organization work, and in attempts by governments to involve citizen groups in policy or program decision-making or implementation (see, for example, Head, 2007). Although not always the case, definitions such as these commonly imply a process of cooperation and consensus building among different groups of community stakeholders.

14. A buycott is basically the opposite of a boycott. It involves organized efforts to persuade consumers to purchase goods or services from particular companies, in order to reward selected positive behaviors by these companies (Friedman, 1996).

15. Books focusing on these more technical aspects of program development are common in social work, public administration, and business administration. Some examples include Kettner, Maroney, and Martin, 2013; Calley, 2011; and Dimock, 2004.

16. This issue has received considerable attention in treatments of advocacy and political agenda setting. For example, Kingdon (2002) has articulated a process of "softening up" key decision-makers and the public regarding specific issues, which is seen as an initial step before substantial changes related to that issue are likely to occur.

CORPORATE SOCIAL RESPONSIBILITY

1. Southern New Hampshire University, for example, offers an entire online MBA in corporate social responsibility. Examples of certificate or executive education programs include the Alberta School of Business Executive Education Corporate Social Responsibility Program, Pepperdine University Certificate in Strategic Corporate Responsibility, Queen's School of Business Certificate in Corporate Social Responsibility, and University of California Berkeley Extension course on corporate social responsibility reporting. Details of these programs and courses may be found on the Web sites of these programs.

SOCIAL ENTREPRENEURSHIP

1. I should note that many devotees of social entrepreneurship will disagree with me on this point, because they view personality and leadership traits as fundamental. For example, Bill Drayton, one of the most influential leaders in the development of applied SE through his creation and stewardship of the Ashoka foundation, emphasizes personality characteristics in describing social entrepreneurs (Ashoka, 2012; see also Bornstein, 2007, and Light, 2008, for interesting discussions of personality and leadership traits considered to be important in SE).
2. The information that follows on the Grameen Bank development is derived from Yunus (2007). There are many other accounts of Yunus and Grameen Bank. Among them is an interesting video short included in the PBS *New Heroes* series.
3. The information that follows on Victoria Khosa is derived from Bornstein (2007).
4. The materials for the case example are drawn from information on the Kiva Web site (www.kiva.org) and from a profile of Kiva in Welch (2008).

PRIVATE SUSTAINABLE DEVELOPMENT

1. Descriptions of Prahalad's ideas in this section all are derived from Prahalad (2005).
2. The description that follows on Hindustan Level Ltd. is derived from Prahalad (2005).

3. Such development could be considered either as a BOP or ITC strategy. If, as increasingly is the case, information technology is viewed as a basic good that cuts across productive and consumptive domains, it seems more useful to consider it as a BOP strategy. In addition, the simple mass distribution of information technology devices, as opposed to more careful interactions to tailor information technology devices to local needs, does not fit well with ITC philosophies. For these reasons, I present the following information technology example as illustrative of BOP, but I also think specific information technology applications will enjoy increasing importance as part of ITC strategies. For example, many emerging programs are demonstrating the creative use of Internet and mobile technologies to improve local producer knowledge of market prices for goods, as well as to eliminate the need for some intermediaries in market transactions (Abraham, 2006; Eggleston, Jensen, & Zeckhauser, 2002).

4. The information on KickStart is from the KickStart Web site (www.kickstart.org).

FAIR TRADE

1. The description of Ten Thousand Villages is derived from the following sources: Ten Thousand Villages (2012, 2013).

2. In 2012, there were about 45 Ten Thousand Villages stores in Canada, with total Canadian sales of more than $14 million. Although also affiliated with the Mennonite Church, the Canadian initiative is incorporated separately and operates independently of Ten Thousand Villages in the United States.

3. The description of GoodWeave International is derived from the following sources: GoodWeave International (2013); GoodWeave USA (2012); and Welch (2008).

4. The description of Cafédirect is derived from the following sources: Davies, Doherty, & Know (2010); and Cafédirect (2011, 2012).

MARKET-BASED SOCIAL CHANGE MODELS: REFLECTIONS ON STRENGTHS, LIMITATIONS, AND DIRECTIONS FOR SOCIAL CHANGE ADVOCATES

1. There are several interesting dimensions to such debates. For example, for any given amount of money, one can extend benefits to higher numbers of people by focusing on those with lower levels of need. In addition, if an individual's level of need or dysfunction is extremely high, even high benefit dosage levels

may be ineffective in bringing about the desired change. Even if change is possible with high dosage levels, program developers are left to contemplate whether it is preferable to serve higher numbers of beneficiaries with lesser needs or to serve smaller numbers of beneficiaries with higher needs. This represents a difficult trade-off between equity and adequacy and also has important implications in terms of community spillover benefits that may result from these choices.

2. Externalities refer to costs or benefits of an exchange relationship that accrue to persons not involved in the exchange; thus, they fall outside of the narrowly construed relationship. The cost of air pollution to those not involved in industrial production is a commonly offered example of an externality with negative ramifications. In contrast, positive externalities also sometimes occur, such as when a person educated in one community with local taxpayer funding moves to another locality.

Abraham, R. (2007). Mobile phones and economic development: Evidence from the fishing industry in India. *Information Technologies & International Development 4*(1), 5–17.

Adjei, J., Arun, T., & Hossain, F. (2009). Asset building and poverty reduction in Ghana: The case of microfinance. *Savings and Development, 33*(3), 265–291.

Ahmed, F. (2012). Nobel laureate faces fresh trouble over his banking tenure. Retrieved from www.cnn.com/2012/08/02/world/asia/bangladesh-nobel-laureate

Alvord, S. H., Brown, L. D., & Letts, C. W. (2004). Social entrepreneurship and societal transformation. *The Journal of Applied Behavioral Science, 40*(3), 260–282.

Andersen, K. (2011, January 2). From the Arab spring to Athens, from occupy Wall Street to Moscow. *Time 178*(25),pp. 53–89.

Anderson, G. (2009). *The future of public employee retirement systems*. Oxford: Oxford University Press.

Anderson, S. G., Zhan, M., & Scott, J. (2007). Improving the understanding of low-income families about banking and predatory financial practices. *Families in Society, 88*(3), 443–452.

Archer, C., & Fritsch, S. (2010). Global fair trade: Humanizing globalization and reintroducing the normative to international political economy. *Review of International Political Economy, 17*(1), 103–128.

Arora, S., & Romijn, H. (2011). The empty rhetoric of poverty reduction at the base of the pyramid. *Organization, 19*(4), 481–505.

Association for Social Advancement (ASA) (2012). *Grants free, cost efficient, sustainable and innovative microfinance*. Retrieved from http://asa.org.bd/?page_id=18

Babb, S., & Buira, A. (2004, March). Mission creep, mission push and discretion in sociological perspective: The case of IMF conditionality. Paper presented at the XVIII G24 Technical Group Meeting, Geneva. Retrieved from www.g24.org/TGM/012gva04.pdf

Bacon, C. (2005). Confronting the coffee crisis: Can fair trade, organic, and specialty coffees reduce small-scale farmer vulnerability in northern Nicaragua? *World Development*, 33(3), 497–511.

Bakan, J. (2004). *The corporation: The pathological pursuit of profit and power.* New York: Free Press.

Baker, S. D., & Comer, D. R. (2012). "Business ethics everywhere": An experiential exercise to develop students' ability to identify and respond to ethical issues in business. *Journal of Management Education, 36*(1), 95–125.

Balabanis, G. (2012), Surrogate boycotts against multinational corporations: Consumers' choice of boycott targets. *British Journal of Management.* Online publication. doi: 10.1111/j.1467–8551.2012.00822.x

Bandhan Financial Services (2011). We are looking at a pan India coverage. *Hope Horizon 2*(5), 10–13. Retrieved from www.bandhanmf.com/report/Hope_Horizon_March_2011.pdf

Barboza, D., & Bradsher, K. (2012, September 24). Riot at Foxconn factory underscores rift in China. *New York Times.* Retrieved from www.nytimes.com/2012/09/25/business/global/foxconn-riot-underscores-labor-rift-in-china.html?_r=1&

Barnes, C., Keogh, E., & Nemarundwe, N. (2001). *Microfinance program clients and impact: An assessment of Zambuko Trust, Zimbabwe.* Washington, D.C.: Assessing the Impact of Microenterprise Services (AIMS).

Becchetti, L., & Costantino, M. (2008). The effects of fair trade on affiliated producers: An impact analysis on Kenyan farmers. *World Development, 36*(5), 823–842.

Becker, G. S. (1994). *Human capital: A theoretical and empirical analysis, with special reference to education.* Chicago: University of Chicago Press.

Bendell, J. (2004). *Barricades and boardrooms: A contemporary history of the corporate accountability movement.* Geneva: United Nations Research Institute for Social Development.

Bendell, J., & Kearins, K. (2005). The political bottom line: The emerging dimension to corporate responsibility for sustainable development. *Business Strategy and the Environment, 14*(6), 372–383.

Bennett, W. L. (2003). New media power. In N. Couldry, & J. Curran (Eds.), *Contesting media power: Alternative media in a networked world* (pp. 42–70). Lanham, Md.: Rowman & Littlefield.

Berry, W. D., Fording, R. C., & Hanson, R. L. (2003). Reassessing the "race to the bottom" in state welfare policy. *Journal of Politics*, 65(2), 327–349.

Bhatt, N., & Tang, S. Y. (2001). Delivering microfinance in developing countries: Controversies and policy perspectives. *Policy Studies Journal, 29*(2), 319–333.

Bhawe, N., Gupta, V., & Jain, D. (2006, June). The entrepreneurship of the good samaritan: A development framework to understand social entrepreneurship using insights from qualitative study. Paper presented at Babson Research Conference, Madrid.

Bishop, M., & Green, M. (2009). *Philanthrocapitalism: How giving can save the world.* New York: Bloomsbury Press.

Blomström, M., & Kokko, A. (1998). Multinational corporations and spillovers. *Journal of Economic Surveys, 12*(3), 247–277.

Bornstein, D. (2007). *How to change the world: Social entrepreneurs and the power of new ideas.* Oxford: Oxford University Press.

Bourdieu, P. (1986). The forms of capital. In J. Richardson (Ed.). *Handbook of theory and research for the sociology of education* (pp. 241–258). New York: Greenwood.

Bowen, H. R. (1953). *Social responsibilities of the businessman.* New York: Harper & Row.

Brisson, D. S., & Usher, C. L. (2005). Bonding social capital in low-income neighborhoods. *Family Relations, 54*, 644–653.

Brock, D. (2008). Social entrepreneurship teaching resources handbook. Retrieved from www.community-wealth.org/sites/clone.community-wealth.org/files/downloads/tool-ashoka-teaching-resources.pdf

Brock, D., Steiner, S., & Kim M. (2008). Social entrepreneurship education. Is it achieving the desired aims? *Proceedings of USASBE National Conference,* 1133–1148.

Bronner, E. (2012, July 3). Poor land in jail as companies add huge fees for probation. *New York Times,* pp. A1, A15.

Bronstein, L. R. (2003). A model for interdisciplinary collaboration. *Social Work, 48*(3), 297–306.

Brown, D. K., Deardorff, A., & Stern, R. (2004). The effects of multinational production on wages and working conditions in developing countries. In R. Baldwin and L. Winters (Eds.), *Challenges to globalization: Analyzing the economics* (pp. 279–330). Chicago: University of Chicago Press.

Brown, D. L., & Moore, H. M. (2001). Accountability, strategy, and international nongovernmental organizations. *Nonprofit and Voluntary Sector Quarterly, 30*(3), 569–587.

Bugg-Levine, A., & Emerson, J. (2011). Impact investing: Transforming how we make money while making a difference. *Innovations, 6*(3), 9–18.

Cafédirect (2011). Living up to our gold standard in challenging times: Annual report 2010. Retrieved from http://cafedirect.co.uk/wp-content/uploads/downloads/2012/03/Cafedirect-Annual-Report-2010-with-accounts-Final.pdf

Cafédirect (2012, July). Media statement: New CEO joins Cafédirect. Retrieved from http://cafedirect.co.uk/wp-content/uploads/downloads/2012/07/Cafe-direct-announces-new-CEO.pdf

Calley, N. G. (2011). *Program development in the 21st century: An evidence-based approach to design, implementation, and evaluation.* Los Angeles: Sage Publications.

Carey, M. (2008). Everything must go? The privatization of state social work. *British Journal of Social Work, 38*(5), 918.

Carroll, A. B. (1979). A three-dimensional conceptual model of corporate social performance. *Academy of Management Review, 4,* 497–505.

Carroll, A. B., & Shabana, K. M. (2010). The business case for corporate social responsibility: A review of concepts, research and practice. *International Journal of Management Reviews, 12*(1), 85–105.

Castles, F. G. (2004). *The future of the welfare state: Crisis myths and crisis realities.* Oxford: Oxford University Press.

CDC/ATSDR Committee on Community Engagement (1997). Prevention Principles of Community Engagement (1st ed.). Atlanta: Centers for Disease Control.

Center for Innovation, Creativity, and Entrepreneurship (2013). Villanova University. Retrieved from www.villanovaice.com

Chatterji, A. K., Levine, D. I., & Toffel, M. W. (2009). How well do social ratings actually measure corporate social responsibility? *Journal of Economics & Management Strategy, 18*(1), 125–169.

Chen, S., & Ravallion, M. (2004). *How have the world's poor fared since the early 1980s?* World Bank Policy Research Working Paper 3341. *World Bank Research Observer, 19*(2), 141–169. Retrieved from http://wbro.oxfordjournals.org/content/19/2/141.abstract

Cheney, G., Roper, J., & May, S. (2007). Overview. In S. May, G. Cheney, & J. Roper (Eds.), *The debate over corporate social responsibility* (pp. 3–12). New York: Oxford University Press.

China Daily (2009, August 27). Li Ka-shing among Fortune's top 14 philanthropists. Retrieved from www.chinadaily.com.cn/china/2009-08/27/content_8623856.htm

Christensen, L. J., Peirce, E., Hartman, L. P., Hoffman, W. M., & Carrier, J. (2007). Ethics, CSR, and sustainability education in the financial times top 50 global business schools: Baseline data and future research directions. *Journal of Business Ethics, 73*(4), 347–368.

Chua, A. (2003). *World on fire: How exporting free market democracy breeds ethnic hatred and global instability*. New York: Doubleday.

Clarke, S. E. (2001). The prospects for local democratic governance: The governance roles of nonprofit organizations. *Review of Policy Research, 18*(4), 129–145.

Clayton, R., & Pontusson, J. (1998). Welfare-state retrenchment revisited: Entitlement cuts, public sector restructuring, and inegalitarian trends in advanced capitalist societies. *World* Politics, *51*(1), 67–89.

Cnaan, R., & Rothman, J. (2008). Capacity development and the building of community. In J. Rothman, L. J. Erlich, & J. Tropman (Eds.), *Strategies of community intervention* (pp. 243–262). Peosta, Iowa: Eddie Bowers Publishing.

Cohen, M., & Barnes, C. (1996). *Assets and the impact of microenterprise finance programs*. AIMS Project. Washington DC: Management Systems International.

Coleman, J. S. (1988). Social capital in the creation of human capital. *The American Journal of Sociology, 94*(1), S95–S120.

Cooper, R. G., & Kleinschmidt, E. J. (1993). Screening new products for potential winners. *Long Range Planning, 26*(6), 74–81.

Corbett, E. L., Marston, B., Churchyard, G. J., & De Cock, K. M. (2006). Tuberculosis in sub-Saharan Africa: Opportunities, challenges, and change in the era of antiretroviral treatment. *Lancet, 367*(9517), 926–937.

Cornelius, N., Wallace, J., & Tassabehji, R. (2007). An analysis of corporate social responsibility, corporate identity and ethics teaching in business schools. *Journal of Business Ethics, 76*(1), 117–135.

Cortés, M., & Rafter, K. M. (Eds.). (2007). *Nonprofits and technology: Emerging research for usable knowledge*. Chicago: Lyceum Books.

Craig, S., & Silver-Greenberg, J. (2012, July 3). Conflict seen in sales tactic at JPMorgan: Bank is said to favor own products. *New York Times*, pp. A1, B4.

Crutchfield, L. R., & Grant, H. M. L. (2008). *Forces for good: The six practices of high-impact nonprofits*. San Francisco: Jossey-Bass.

Cull, R., Demirgüç-Kunt, A., & Morduch, J. (2009). Microfinance meets the market. *The Journal of Economic Perspectives, 23*(1), 167–192.

Cummins, A. (2004). The Marine Stewardship Council: A multi-stakeholder approach to sustainable fishing. *Corporate Social Responsibility and Environmental Management, 11*(2), 85–94.

Dahlsrud, A. (2008). How corporate social responsibility is defined: An analysis of 37 definitions. *Corporate Social Responsibility and Environmental Management, 15*(1), 1–13.

Datar, S. R., Epstein, M. J., & Yuthas, K. (2008). In microfinance, clients must come first. *Stanford Social Innovation Review,* (Winter), 38–45.

Darby, M. R. (1982). The price of oil and world inflation and recession. *The American Economic Review, 72*(4), 738–751.

Davies, I. A., Doherty, B., & Know, S. (2010). The rise and stall of a fair trade pioneer: The Cafédirect story. *Journal of Business Ethics, 92*, 127–147.

Dees, J. G. (1998). Enterprising nonprofits. *Harvard Business Review, 76*, 54–69.

Dees, J. G. (2007). Taking social entrepreneurship seriously. *Society, 44*(3), 24–31.

Dees, J. G., Emerson, J., & Economy, P. (2001). *Enterprising nonprofits: A toolkit for social entrepreneurs.* New York: John Wiley & Sons Inc.

Dees, J. G., Emerson, J., & Economy, P. (2002). *Strategic tools for social entrepreneurs: Enhancing the performance of your enterprising nonprofit.* New York: John Wiley & Sons Inc.

DeLeon, L., & Denhardt, R. B. (2000). The political theory of reinvention. *Public Administration Review, 60*(2), 89–97.

Deloitte Center for Financial Services (2011). *The next decade in global wealth among millionaire households.* New York: Deloitte Development LLC.

De Pelsmacker, P., Driesen, L., & Rayp, G. (2005). Do consumers care about ethics? Willingness to pay for fair-trade coffee. *Journal of Consumer Affairs, 39*(2), 363–385.

Deshpanda, R. (2001). *Increasing access and benefits for women: Practices and innovations among microfinance institutions—survey results.* New York: United Nations Capital Development Fund.

Devinney, T. M. (2009). Is the socially responsible corporation a myth? The good, the bad, and the ugly of corporate social responsibility. *The Academy of Management Perspectives, 23*(2), 44–56.

DeWinter, R. (2001). The anti-sweatshop movement: Constructing corporate moral agency in the global apparel industry. *Ethics & International Affairs, 15*(2), 99–115.

DiMaggio, P. J., Weiss, J. A., & Clotfelter, C. T. (2002). Data to support scholarship on nonprofit organizations: An introduction. *American Behavioral Scientist, 45*(10), 1474–1492.

Dimock, H. (2004). *Outcome-based program development and evaluation.* Concord, Ontario: Captus Press.

Disney, R. (2007). Population ageing and the size of the welfare state: Is there a puzzle to explain? *European Journal of Political Economy, 23*(2), 542–553.

Doherty, B., & Tranchell, S. (2006, September). *"Radical mainstreaming" of fair trade: The case of the Day Chocolate Company*. Paper presented at the 6th Annual Corporate Responsibility Research Conference, School of Earth and Environment, University of Leeds.

Drayton, B. (2003). *Ashoka's theory of change*. Retrieved from: http://ssrn.com/abstract=980092.

Du, S., Bhattacharya, C. B., & Sen, S. (2007). Reaping relational rewards from corporate social responsibility: The role of competitive positioning. *International Journal of Research in Marketing, 24*(3), 224–241.

Eagleton-Pierce, M. (2001). The Internet and the Seattle WTO protests. *Peace Review, 13*(3), 331–337.

Eamon, M. (2004). Digital divide in computer access and use between poor and non-poor youth. *Journal of Sociology & Social Welfare, 3(2)*, 91–112.

Easterly, W. (2006). *The white man's burden: Why the west's efforts to aid the rest have done so much ill and so little good*. New York: Penguin Press.

Edgcomb, E., Doub, M., Rosenthal, W., Flint, C., Niebling, M., Losby, J., . . . & Williams, K. (2002). *Improving microenterprise training and technical assistance: Findings for program managers*. Washington, DC: Aspen Institute.

Edwards, M. (2008). *Just another emperor? The myths and realities of philanthrocapitalism*. New York: Demos.

Edwards, M. (2010). *Small change: Why business won't save the world*. San Francisco: Berrett-Koehler Publishers.

Eggleston, K., Jensen, R., & Zeckhauser, R. (2002). Information and communication technologies, markets, and economic development. In G. S. Kirkman, P. K. Cornelius, J. D. Sachs, & K. Schwab (Eds.), *The Global Information Technology Report 2001–2002: Readiness for the networked world*. New York: Oxford University Press.

Elkington, J. (1998). Partnerships from cannibals with forks: The triple bottom line of 21st-century business. *Environmental Quality Management, 8*(1), 37–51.

Elkington, J., & Hartigan, P. (2008). *The power of unreasonable people: How social entrepreneurs create markets that change the world*. Boston: Harvard Business.

Emerson, J., & Twerksy, F. (1996). New social entrepreneurs: The success, challenge and lessons of non-profit enterprise creation. *Journal of Business Venturing, 18*, 105–123.

Epstein, M. J. (2008). *Making sustainability work: Best practices in managing and measuring corporate social, environmental, and economic impacts*. San Francisco: Berrett-Koehler Publishers.

Escobar, A. (1997). Anthropology and development. *International Social Science Journal, 49*(154), 497–515.

Esping-Anderson, G. (1990). *The three worlds of welfare capitalism*. Princeton: Princeton University Press.

European Fair Trade Association (2001). *Fair trade in Europe 2001*. Retrieved from www.european-fair-trade-association.org/efta/Doc/FT-E-2001.pdf

Evans, P. (1995). *Embedded autonomy: States and industrial transformation*. Princeton, N.J.: Princeton University Press.

Fairtrade International (FLO) (2012). *For producers, with producers* (Annual Report 2011/2012). Retrieved from www.fairtrade.net/fileadmin/user_upload/content/2009/resources/2011-12_AnnualReport_web_version_small_Fairtrade International.pdf

Fair World Project (2011). New premium, minimum price and trade standards in coffee. Retrieved from http://fairworldproject.org/in-the-news/flo-new-premium-minimum-price-and-trade-standards-in-coffee/

Farmer, P. (2005). *Pathologies of power: Health, human rights, and the new war on the poor*. Berkeley, CA: University of California Press.

Fisher, E. (2009). Introduction: The policy trajectory of fair trade. *Journal of International Development, 21*(7), 985–1003.

Fleishman, J. L. (2009). *The foundation: How private wealth is changing the world*. New York: Public Affairs.

Forman, S., & Stoddard, A. (2002). International assistance. In L. M. Salamon (Ed.), *The state of nonprofit America* (pp. 240–274). Washington D.C.: Brookings Institution Press.

Fortun, K. (2009). *Advocacy after Bhopal: Environmentalism, disaster, new global orders*. Chicago: University of Chicago Press.

Fox, J., & Gershman, J. (2000). The World Bank and social capital: Lessons from ten rural development projects in the Philippines and Mexico. *Policy Sciences, 33*, 399–419.

Frandano, A., Karamchandani, A., & Kubzansky, P. (2009). *Emerging markets, emerging models: Market-based solutions to the challenges of global poverty*. Retrieved from http://community-wealth.org/sites/clone.community-wealth.org/files/downloads/report-karamchandani-et-al.pdf

Frechtling, J. A. (2007). *Logic modeling methods in program evaluation*. San Francisco: Jossey-Bass.

Freestone, O. M., & McGoldrick, P. J. (2008). Motivations of the ethical consumer. *Journal of Business Ethics, 79*(4), 445–467.

Freire, P. (2000). *Pedagogy of the oppressed*. London: Continuum International Publishing Group.

Fridell, G. (2004). The fair trade network in historical perspective. *Canadian Journal of Development Studies/Revue Canadienne d'Études Du Développement, 25*(3), 411–428.

Friedman, M. (1970, September 13). The social responsibility of business is to increase its profits. *New York Times Magazine*, pp. 32–33.

Friedman, M. (2006). Using consumer boycotts to stimulate corporate policy changes: Marketplace, media, and moral considerations. In M. Micheletti, A. Follesdal, and D. Stolle (Eds.), *Politics, products, and markets: Exploring political consumerism* (pp.45–62). New Brunswick, N.J.: Transaction Publishers.

Friedman, T. L. (2000). *The lexus and the olive tree*. New York: Anchor Books.

Friedman, T. L. (2007). *The world is flat: A brief history of the twenty-first century*. New York: Farrar, Straus and Giroux.

Frumkin, P. (2003). Inside venture philanthropy. *Society, 40*(4), 7–15.

Gakidou, E., Cowling, K., Lozano, R., & Murray, C. (2010). Increased educational attainment and its effect on child mortality in 175 countries between 1970 and 2009: A systematic analysis. *The Lancet, 376*(9745), 959–974.

Garikipati, S. (2008). The impact of lending to women on household vulnerability and women's empowerment: Evidence from India. *World Development, 36*(12), 2620–2642.

Giacalone, R. A., & Thompson, K. R. (2006). Business ethics and social responsibility education: Shifting the worldview. *The Academy of Management Learning and Education ARCHIVE, 5*(3), 266–277.

Gilbert, N. (2001). *Targeting social benefits: International perspectives and trends*. New Brunswick, N.J.: Transaction Publishers.

Gilbert, N. (2002). Transformation of the welfare state: The silent surrender of public responsibility. New York: Oxford University Press.

Gilbert, N., & Terrell, P. (2010). *Dimensions of social welfare policy*. Boston: Allyn & Bacon.

Gjølberg, M. (2009). Measuring the immeasurable? Constructing an index of CSR practices and CSR performance in 20 countries. *Scandinavian Journal of Management, 25*(1), 10–22.

Goetz, A. M., & Gupta, R. S. (1996). Who takes the credit? Gender, power, and control over loan use in rural credit programs in Bangladesh. *World Development, 24*(1), 45–63.

Goetz, S. J., & Rupasingha, A. (2006). Wal-Mart and social capital. *American Journal of Agricultural Economics, 88*(5), 1304–1310.

Gogoi, P. (2006, November 29). What's with Walmart's sales woes? Business Week. Retrieved from: http://www.businessweek.com/stories/2006-11-29/whats-with-wal-marts-sales-woes-businessweek-business-news-stock-market-and-financial-advice

Gonzalez-Vega, C., Schreiner, M., Meyer, R. L., Rodriguez-Meza, J., & Navajas, S. (1997). BancoSol: The challenge of growth for microfinance organizations. In H. Schneider (Ed.), *Microfinance for the poor* (pp. 129–170). New York: Office for Economic Cooperation and Development.

GoodWeave (2013). Retrieved from www.goodweave.org

GoodWeave USA (2012). *2011 annual report: A journey to the end of child labor.* Retrieved from www.goodweave.org/index.php?pid=9422

Gordon, R. S., Jr. (1983). An operational classification of disease prevention. *Public Health Reports, 98*(2), 107–109.

Grameen Bank (2003). Bank for the poor. 2003–07, Issue 283.

Grameen Bank (2013). Bank for the poor. 2013–07, Issue 407.

Grameen Bank (2014). *Grameen Bank monthly update in Taka.* Retrieved from www.grameen.com/index.php?option=com_content&task=view&id=452&Itemid=526

Green, C. J., Kirkpatrick, C. H., & Murinde, V. (2006). Finance for small enterprise growth and poverty reduction in developing countries. *Journal of International Development, 18*(7), 1017–1030.

Greenberg, J., & Knight, G. (2004). Framing sweatshops: Nike, global production, and the American news media. *Communications & Critical/Cultural Studies, 1*(2), 151–175.

Guo, C. (2007). When government becomes the principal philanthropist: The effects of public funding on patterns of nonprofit governance. *Public Administration Review, 67*(3), 458–473.

Gupta, G. R., Parkhurst, J. O., Ogden, J. A., Aggleton, P., & Mahal, A. (2008). Structural approaches to HIV prevention. *The Lancet, 372*(9640), 764–775.

Hacker, J. S. (2004). Privatizing risk without privatizing the welfare state: The hidden politics of social policy retrenchment in the United States. *The American Political Science Review, 98*(2), 243–260.

Hafner-Burton, E. M., & Tsutsui, K. (2005). Human rights in a globalizing world: The paradox of empty promises. *American Journal of Sociology, 110*(5), 1373–1411.

Haight, C. (2011). The problem with fair trade coffee. *Stanford Social Innovation Review, 3*, 74–79.

Haltiwanger, J., Jarmin, R., & Krizan, C. J. (2010). Mom-and-pop meet big-box: Complements or substitutes? *Journal of Urban Economics, 67*(1), 116–134.

Hamad, R., & Fernald, L. C. (2010). Microcredit participation and nutrition outcomes among women in Peru. *Journal of Epidemiology and Community Health, 66*(6). Retrieved from: www.freedomfromhunger.org/sites/default/files/Microcredit_Participation_Nutrition_Outcomes_Peru.pdf

Harrison, A., and Scorse, J. (2010). Multinationals and anti-sweatshop activism. *The American Economic Review, 100*(1), 247–247.

Harrison, R., Newholm, T., & Shaw, D. (2010). *The ethical consumer*. Los Angeles: Sage Publications

Hart, S. (2005). *Capitalism at the crossroads: The unlimited business opportunities in solving the world's most difficult problems*. Upper Saddle River, N.J.: Wharton School Publishing.

Hart, S. L., & Christensen, C. M. (2002). The great leap. *Sloan Management Review, 44*(1), 51–56.

Harvie, C. (2005). The contribution of micro-enterprises to regional economic recovery and poverty alleviation in East Asia. In C. Harvie & B. C. Lee (Eds.), *Sustaining growth and performance in East Asia: The role of small and medium sized enterprises, studies of small and medium sized enterprises in East Asia* (pp. 72–98). UK: Edward Elgar Publishing.

Hasenfeld, Y. (Ed.) (2009). *Human services as complex organizations*. Newbury Park, Calif.: Sage Publications.

Hayes, M .G. (2006). On the efficiency of fair trade. *Review of Social Economy, 64*(4), 447–468.

Head, B. W. (2007). Community engagement: Participation on whose terms? *Australian Journal of Political Science, 42*(3), 441–454.

Henderson, D. (2008). Fair trade is counterproductive and unfair. *Economic Affairs, 28*(3), 62–64.

Hess, D., & Warren, D. E. (2008). The meaning and meaningfulness of corporate social initiatives. *Business and Society Review, 113*(2), 163–197.

Holahan C. & Trebilcock B. (2011, May 17). *What to Buy at Walmart*. Retrieved from www.cbsnews.com/8301-505144_162-51372457/what-to-buy-at-walmart

Holland, T. P., & Ritvo, R. A. (2008). *Nonprofit organizations: Principles and practices*. New York: Columbia University Press.

Hoque, M. Z. (2004). Stagnated growth of microenterprises and flawed role of credit NGOs: Evidence from Bangladesh. *Humanomics, 20*(1), 32–39.

Hulme, D., & Mosley, P. (1996). *Finance against poverty* (Vol. 2). New York: Routledge.

Innovation, Creativity, and Entrepreneurship: Program History (2013). Wake Forest University. Retrieved from http://entrepreneurship.wfu.edu/about-us/program-history-model

Jaffee, D. (2009). *Brewing for justice: Fair trade coffee, sustainability, and survival.* Berkeley: University of California Press.

Jenkins, G. (2011). Who's afraid of philanthrocapitalism? *Case Western Reserve Law Review, 61*(3), 753.

Jenkins, R. (2005). Globalization, corporate social responsibility and poverty. *International Affairs, 81*(3), 525–540.

Kang, J., Anderson, S., and Finnegan, D. (2012). The evaluation practices of U.S. international non-governmental organisations. *Development in Practice, 22*(3), 317–333.

Karnani, A. (2010, April 23). The case against corporate social responsibility. *Wall Street Journal.* Retrieved from http://online.wsj.com/news/articles/SB10001424052748703338004575230112664504890

Karnani, A. (2012). Markets of the poor: Opportunities and limits. *International Journal of Rural Management, 8*(1–2), 7–17.

Kasser, T. (2002). *The high price of materialism.* Cambridge: MIT Press.

Kauffman Foundation. (2008). *Entrepreneurship in American higher education.* A report from the Kauffman Panel on Entrepreneurship Curriculum in Higher Education. Retrieved from www.kauffman.org/~/media/kauffman_org/research%20reports%20and%20covers/2008/07/entrep_high_ed_report.pdf

Keck, M. E., & Sikkink, K. (1998). *Activists beyond borders: Advocacy networks in international politics.* Ithica, N.Y.: Cornell University Press.

Kendall, B. E., Gill, R., & Cheney, G. (2007). Consumer activism and corporate social responsibility: How strong a connection? In S. May, G. Cheney, & J. Roper (Eds.), *The debate over corporate social responsibility* (pp. 241–264). New York: Oxford University Press.

Keohane, R. O., & Nye, J. S., Jr. (2000). Globalization: What's new? What's not? (And so what?). *Foreign Policy,* 118, 104–119.

Kessel, F., Rosenfield, P., & Anderson, N. (2008). *Expanding the boundaries of health and social science: Case studies in interdisciplinary innovation.* Oxford: Oxford University Press.

Kettl, D. F. (1998). *Reinventing government: A fifth-year report card.* Washington, D.C.: The Brookings Institution.

Kettner, P. M., Maroney, R. M., & Martin, L. L. (2013). *Designing and managing programs: An effectiveness-based approach.* Los Angeles: Sage.

KickStart. (2013). Retrieved from: www.kickstart.org.

Kingdon, J. W. (2002). *Agendas, alternatives, and public policies* (Longman Classics Edition). London: Longman Publishing Group.

Knight, G. (2007). Activism, risk, and communicational politics. In S. May, G. Cheney, & J. Roper (Eds.), *The debate over corporate social responsibility* (pp. 305–318). New York: Oxford University Press.

Knorringa, P. (2010, November). *A balancing act: Private actors in development processes.* Inaugural lecture delivered at the International Institute of Social Studies, Erasmus University of Rotterdam, Rotterdam.

Kohli, A. (2005). *State directed development: Political power and industrialization in the global periphery.* Cambridge: Cambridge University Press.

Korpi, W. (1985). Economic growth and the welfare state: Leaky bucket or irrigation system? *European Sociological Review, 1*(2), 97–118.

Korten, D. C. (2001). *When corporations rule the world.* San Francisco: Kumarian Press.

Kramer, R. M. (1994). Voluntary agencies and the contract culture: "Dream or nightmare?" *Social Service Review, 68*(1)33–60.

Krier, J. (2006). *Fair trade in Europe 2005.* Brussels: Fair Trade Advocacy Office.

Kumlin, S. (2007). Overloaded or undermined? European welfare states in the face of performance dissatisfaction. In S. Svallfors (Ed). *The political sociology of the welfare state: Institutions, social cleavages, and orientations* (pp. 80–116). Stanford, CA: Stanford University Press.

Kuriyan, R., Ray, I., & Toyama, K. (2008). Information and communication technologies for development: The bottom of the pyramid model in practice. *The Information Society, 24*(2), 93–104.

Lal, D. (2006). *Reviving the invisible hand: The case for classical liberalism in the twenty-first century.* Princeton, N.J.: Princeton University Press.

Laufer, W. S. (2003). Social accountability and corporate greenwashing. *Journal of Business Ethics, 43*(3), 253–261.

Leach, F., Abdulla, S., Appleton, H., El-Bushra, J., Cardenas, N., Kebede, K., ... & Sitaram, S. (2000). *The impact of training on women's micro-enterprise development* (Department for International Development Education Research Report No. 40). London: Department for International Development.

Leach, F., & Sitaram, S. (2002). Microfinance and women's empowerment: A lesson from India. *Development in Practice, 12*(5), 575–588.

Leclair, M. S. (2002). Fighting the tide: Alternative trade organizations in the era of global free trade. *World Development, 30*(6), 949–958.

Leff, E. (1995). *Green production: Toward an environmental rationality.* New York: Guilford Press.

Lenski, G. E. (1966). *Power and privilege: A theory of social stratification.* Chapel Hill, NC: University of North Carolina Press.

Liebman, J. B. (2011). Social impact bonds: A promising new financing model to accelerate social innovation and improve government performance. Center for American Progress. Retrieved from: www.americanprogress.org/issues/open-government/report/2011/02/09/9050/social-impact-bonds.

Light, P. C. (2008). *The search for social entrepreneurship.* Washington, D.C.: Brookings Institution Press.

Lindblom, C. (1977). *Politics and markets: The world's political-economic systems.* New York: Basic Books.

Lindblom, C. (2001). *The market system: What it is, how it works, and what to make of it.* New Haven, CT: Yale University Press.

Lindgreen, A., Swaen, V., & Johnston, W. J. (2009). Corporate social responsibility: An empirical investigation of U.S. organizations. *Journal of Business Ethics, 85*, 303–323.

Lister, R. (2002). A politics of recognition and respect: Involving people with experience of poverty in decision making that affects their lives. *Social Policy and Society, 1*(1), 37–46.

Littlefield, E., Morduch, J., & Hashemi, S. (2003). *Is microfinance an effective strategy to reach the Millennium Development Goals?* Washington D.C.: Consultative Group to Assist the Poor.

Llewellyn, D. J., & Wilson, K. M. (2003). The controversial role of personality traits in entrepreneurial psychology. *Education & Training, 45*(6), 341–345.

Lynn, L. E., Jr. (2002). Social services and the state: The public appropriation of private charity. *Social Service Review, 76*(1), 58–82.

MacGillivray, A. (2000). *The fair share: The growing market share of green and ethical products.* London: New Economics Foundation.

Mahajan, V. (2005). From microcredit to livelihood finance. *Economic and Political Weekly, 40*(41), 4416–4419.

Mair, J., & Marti, I. (2006). Social entrepreneurship research: A source of explanation, prediction, and delight. *Journal of World Business, 41*(1), 36–44.

Mandelbaum, M. (1982). Vietnam: The television war. *Daedalus, 111*(4), 157–169.

Manik, J. A., & Yardley, J. (2012, December 17). Bangladesh finds gross negligence in factory fire. *New York Times.* Retrieved from http://www.nytimes.com/2012/12/18/world/asia/bangladesh-factory-fire-caused-by-gross-negligence.html?_r=0

Margolis, J. D., Elfenbein, H. A., & Walsh, J. P. (2009, March 1). Does it pay to be good . . . and does it matter? A meta-analysis of the relationship between corporate social and financial performance. Retrieved from http://papers.ssrn.com/sol3/papers.cfm?abstract_id=1866371

Marrewijk, M. (2003). Concepts and definitions of CSR and corporate sustainability: Between agency and communion. *Journal of Business Ethics, 44*(2), 95–105.

Martin, R. L., & Osberg, S. (2007). Social entrepreneurship: The case for definition. *Stanford Social Innovation Review, 5*(2), 28–39.

May, S. K., Cheney, G., & Roper, J. (Eds.) (2007). *The debate over corporate social responsibility.* Oxford: Oxford University Press.

McCleary, R. M., & Barro, R. J. (2008). Private voluntary organizations engaged in international assistance, 1939–2004. *Nonprofit and Voluntary Sector Quarterly, 37*(3), 512.

McIntosh, C., Villaran, G., & Wydick, B. (2011). Microfinance and home improvement: Using retrospective panel data to measure program effects on fundamental events. *World Development 39*(6), 922–937.

McIntosh, M. (2007). Progressing from corporate social responsibility to brand integrity. In S. May, G. Cheney, & J. Roper (Eds.), *The debate over corporate social responsibility* (pp. 45–56). New York: Oxford University Press.

McMillan, J. (2007) Why corporate social responsibility; Why now? How? In S. May, G. Cheney, & J. Roper (Eds.), *The debate over corporate social responsibility* (pp. 15–29). New York: Oxford University Press.

McWilliams, A., & Siegel, D. (2001). Corporate social responsibility: A theory of the firm perspective. *The Academy of Management Review, 26*(1), 117–127.

Mead, L. M. (1986). *Beyond entitlement: The social obligations of citizenship.* New York: Free Press.

Micheletti, M. (2003). *Political virtue and shopping: Individuals, consumerism, and collective action.* New York: Palgrave.

Micheletti, M., Follesdal, A., & Stolle, D. (Eds.) (2006*). Politics, products, and markets: Exploring political consumerism past and present.* New Brunswick, N.J.: Transaction Publishers.

Midgley, J. (1997). *Social welfare in global context.* Thousand Oaks, CA: Sage Publications.

Mkandawire, T. (2005). *Targeting and universalism in poverty reduction* (Social Policy and Development Programme Paper No. 23). Geneva: United Nations Research Institute for Social Development.

Moore, G. (2004). The fair trade movement: Parameters, issues and future research. *Journal of Business Ethics, 53*(1), 73–86.

Moran, M. (2000). Understanding the welfare state: The case of health care. *British Journal of Politics and International Relations, 2*(2), 135–160.

Mossberger, K., Tolbert, C. J., & Stansbury, M. (2003). *Virtual inequality: Beyond the digital divide.* Washington, D.C.: Georgetown University Press.

Murero, M. & Rice, R. E. (2006). *The Internet and health care: Theory, research and practice.* London: Lawrence Erlbaum Associates.

Murray, C. (1984). *Losing ground: American social policy, 1950–1980.* New York: Basic Books.

Murray, D. & Reynolds, L. (2000). Alternative trade in bananas: Obstacles and opportunities to progressive social change in the global economy. *Agriculture and Human Values, 17,* 65–74.

Newton, K., & Norris, P. (2000). Confidence in public institutions. In S. J. Pharr & R. D. Putnam (Eds.), *Disaffected democracies: What's troubling the trilateral countries* (pp. 52–73). Princeton, N.J.: Princeton University Press.

Nga, J. K. H., & Shamuganathan, G. (2010). The influence of personality traits and demographic factors on social entrepreneurship start up intentions. *Journal of Business Ethics, 95*(2), 259–282.

Nicholls, A. (2010). The legitimacy of social entrepreneurship: Reflexive isomorphism in a pre-paradigmatic field. *Entrepreneurship Theory and Practice, 34*(4) 611–633.

Nicholls, A., & Opal, C. (2008). *Fair trade: Market-driven ethical consumption.* Los Angeles: Sage Publications.

Nicholson, C. Y., & DeMoss, M. (2009). Teaching ethics and social responsibility: An evaluation of undergraduate business education at the discipline level. *Journal of Education for Business, 84*(4), 213–218.

Nisbet, M. C., & Aufderheide, P. (2009). Documentary film: Towards a research agenda on forms, functions, and impacts. *Mass Communication and Society, 12*(4), 450–456.

O'Connor, C. (2013, May 14). New app lets you boycott Koch Brothers, Monsanto and more by scanning your shopping cart, *Forbes.* Retrieved from www.forbes.com/sites/clareoconnor/2013/05/14/new-app-lets-you-boycott-koch-brothers-monsanto-and-more-by-scanning-your-shopping-cart

Ongkrutraksa, W. Y. (2007). Green marketing and advertising. In S. May, G. Cheney, & J. Roper (Eds.), *The debate over corporate social responsibility* (pp. 365–378). New York: Oxford University Press.

Organization for Economic Co-operation and Development (2011). *An overview of growing income inequalities in OECD countries: Main findings.* Retrieved from www.oecd.org/els/soc/49499779.pdf

Osborne, D., & Gaebler, T. (1992). *Reinventing government: How the entrepreneurial spirit is transforming government.* Reading, MA: Addison-Wesley.

Papic, M., & Noonan, S. (2011, February 3). Social media as a tool for protest. *Stratfor Global Intelligence.* Retrieved from http://www.stratfor.com/weekly/20110202-social-media-tool-protest?utm_source=SWeekly&utm_medium=email&putm_campaign=110203&utm_content=readmore&elq=8a864881cc2546359a7360759abocfb3

Pareto, A. M., & McLean, M. (2010). Indigenous development and the cultural captivity of entrepreneurship. Retrieved from http://ssrn.com/abstract=1612476

Pavolini, E., & Ranci, C. (2008). Restructuring the welfare state: Reforms in long-term care in western European countries. *Journal of European Social Policy, 18*(3), 246.

Peterson, P. G. (1999). Gray dawn: The global aging crisis. *Foreign Affairs, 78*(1), 42–55.

Pierson, P. (1996). The new politics of the welfare state. *World Politics, 48*(2), 143–179.

Pivato, S., Misani, N., & Tencati, A. (2008). The impact of corporate social responsibility on consumer trust: The case of organic food. *Business Ethics: A European Review, 17*(1), 3–12.

Plambeck, E.L., & Denend, L. (2008). The greening of Walmart. *Stanford Social Innovation Review*, Spring, 53–59.

Polak, P. (2009). *Out of poverty: What works when traditional approaches fail.* San Francisco: Barrett-Koehler Publishers.

Prahalad, C. (2005). *The fortune at the bottom of the pyramid: Eradicating poverty through profits.* Upper Saddle River, N.J.: Wharton School Publishing.

Pretty, J. N., Noble, A. D., Bossio, D., Dixon, J., Hine, R. E., De Vries, F. P., & Morison, J. I. L. (2006). Resource-conserving agriculture increases yields in developing countries. *Environmental Science & Technology, 40*(4), 1114–1119.

Psacharopoulos, G., & Patrinos, H. A. (2004). Returns to investment in education: A further update. *Educational Economics, 12* (2), 111–134.

Public Broadcasting System. (Producer). (2005). *The New Heroes* [DVD]. Available from Oregon Public Broadcasting, South Burlington, Vermont.

Putnam, R. D. (2000). *Bowling alone: The collapse and revival of American community*. New York: Simon & Schuster.

Rahman, A. (1999). Micro-credit initiatives for equitable and sustainable development: Who pays? *World Development, 27*(1), 67–82.

Raynolds, L. T. (2008). Mainstreaming fair trade coffee: From partnership to traceability. *World Development, 37*(6), 1083–1093.

Razin, A., Sadka, E., & Swagel, P. (2002). The aging population and the size of the welfare state. *The Journal of Political Economy, 110*(4), 900–918.

Reich, R. B. (1998). The new meaning of corporate social responsibility. *California Management Review, 40*(2), 8–17.

Reimann, K. D. (2006). A view from the top: International politics, norms and the worldwide growth of NGOs. *International Studies Quarterly, 50*(1), 45–68.

Renard, M. (2003). Fair trade: Quality, market and conventions. *Journal of Rural Studies, 19*(1), 87–96.

Renard, M. (2005). Quality certification, regulation and power in fair trade. *Journal of Rural Studies, 21*(4), 419–431.

Ritter, B. A. (2006). Can business ethics be trained? A study of the ethical decision-making process in business students. *Journal of Business Ethics, 68*(2), 153–164.

Ronchi, L. (2002). *The impact of fair trade on producers and their organizations: A case study with Cococafe in Costa Rica* (PRUS working paper No. 11). Brighton, UK: University of Sussex.

Roodman, D. (2010, February 10). Grameen Bank, which pioneered loans for the poor, has hit repayment snag. Center for Global Development. Retrieved from www.cgdev.org/blog/grameen-bank-which-pioneered-loans-poor-has-hit-repayment-snag.

Rudra, N. (2002). Globalization and the decline of the welfare state in less-developed countries. *International Organization, 56*(2), 411–445.

Ruiz, F. (2009). *International non-governmental organizations (INGOs): A different process of internationalization.* Retrieved from www.ead.fea.usp.br/semead/12semead/resultado/trabalhospdf/88.pdf

Ryan, L., & Dziurawiec, S. (2001). Materialism and its relationship to life satisfaction. *Social Indicators Research, 55*(2), 185–197.

Sachs, J. (2005). *The end of poverty: Economic possibilities for our time*. New York: Penguin Books.

Sachs, J. (2008). *Common wealth: Economics for a crowded planet*. New York: Penguin Books.

Salamon, L. M. (1987). Of market failure, voluntary failure, and third-party government: Toward a theory of government-nonprofit relations in the modern welfare state. *Nonprofit and Voluntary Sector Quarterly, 16*(1–2), 29–49.

Salamon, L. M. (1992). *America's nonprofit sector*. Washington, D.C.: Foundation Center.

Salamon, L. M. (1994). The rise of the nonprofit sector. *Foreign* Affairs, 73(4), 109–122.

Salamon, L. M. (2003). The resilient sector: The state of nonprofit America. *Social Service Review, 78(1), 172.*

Salamon, L. M., Sokolowski, S. W., & List, R. (2003). *Global civil society: An overview.* Center for Civil Society Studies, Institute for Policy Studies. Baltimore: The John Hopkins University.

Salamon, Sokolowski and Associates (2010). *Global Civil Society,* 3rd ed. Sterling, Va.: Kumarian Press.

Schramm, C. (2010). All entrepreneurship is social. *Stanford Social Innovation Review (Spring),* 21–22.

Schreiner, M. (1999). Self-employment, microenterprise, and the poorest Americans. *Social Service Review, 73*(4), 496–523.

Schreiner, M., & Woller, G. (2003). Microenterprise development programs in the United States and in the developing world. *World Development, 31*(9), 1567–1580.

Schultze, C. L. (1977). *The public use of private interest*. Washington, D.C.: Brookings Institution Press.

Schumpeter, J. A. (1942). *Socialism, capitalism and democracy*. New York: Harper & Row.

Schuster, T., & Holtbrugge, D. (2011). Market entry of multinational companies in markets at the bottom of the pyramid: A learning perspective. *International Business Review, 21*(5), 817.

Schwab Foundation for Social Entrepreneurship (2013). *Breaking the binary: Policy guide to scaling social innovation.* Retrieved from: www.weforum.org/pdf/schwabfound/PolicyGuide_to_ScalingSocial%20Innovation.pdf.

Schwab, H. (2013, April 24). A guide to scaling social innovation. *Stanford Social Innovation Review.* Retrieved from www.ssireview.org/blog/entry/a_guide_to_scaling_social_innovation

Schwartz, P., & Gibb, B. (1999). *When good companies do bad things: Responsibility and risk in an age of globalization.* New York: John Wiley & Sons.

Sebstad, J., Neill, C., Barnes, C., & Chen, G. (1995). *Assessing the impacts of microenterprise interventions: A framework for analysis* (USAID Managing for Results Working Paper No. 70). Washington, D.C.: USAID's Center for Development Information and Evaluation.

Selsky, J. W., & Parker, B. (2005). Cross-sector partnerships to address social issues: Challenges to theory and practice. *Journal of Management, 31*(6), 849–873.

Sen, A. (1999). *Development as freedom.* New York: Anchor Books.

Senauer, B., & Sur, M. (2001). Ending global hunger in the 21st century: Projections of the number of food insecure people. *Review of Agricultural Economics, 23*(1), 68–81.

Servon, L. J. (2008). *Bridging the digital divide: Technology, community and public policy.* Hoboken, NJ: Wiley Online Publishing.

Shaw, J. (2004). Microenterprise occupation and poverty reduction in microfinance programs: Evidence from Sri Lanka. *World Development, 32*(7), 1247–1264.

Shaw, W. H. (1996). Business ethics today: A survey. *Journal of Business Ethics, 15*(5), 489–500.

Sherman, S. (2012, September 10). The brawl over fair trade coffee. *The Nation.* Retrieved from www.thenation.com/article/169515/brawl-over-fair-trade-coffee

Sherraden, M. (1991). *Assets and the poor: A new American welfare policy.* New York: M. E. Sharpe.

Shirky, C. (2010). *Cognitive surplus: How technology makes consumers into collaborators.* New York: Penguin Books.

Sidwell, M. (2008). *Unfair trade.* London: Adam Smith Institute.

Siegel, D. S., & Vitaliano, D. F. (2007). An empirical analysis of the strategic use of corporate social responsibility. *Journal of Economics & Management Strategy, 16*(3), 773–792.

Silver, N. (2013, January 17). What is driving growth in government spending? *New York Times,* p. A16.

Smith, A. M. (2008) The fair trade cup is "two-thirds full" not "two-thirds empty": A response to the Adam Smith Report and an alternative way to think about measuring the content of the fair trade cup. BRASS Comment and Analysis Paper. Cardiff, UK: Cardiff University.

Smith, A. M. (2009). Evaluating the criticisms of fair trade. *Economic Affairs, 29*(4), 29–36.

Sodhi, M. S., & Tang, C. S. (2011). Social enterprises as supply-chain enablers for the poor. Socio-Economic Planning Sciences, 45, 146–153.

Soros, G. (2008, January 22). The worst market crisis in 60 years. *The Financial Times.* Retrieved from www.ft.com/intl/cms/s/0/24f73610-c91e-11dc-9807-000077b07658.html

Stiglitz, J. (1998). Distinguished lecture on economics in government: The private uses of public interests: Incentives and institutions. *The Journal of Economic Perspectives, 12*(2), 3–22.

Stiglitz, J. E. (2007). *Making globalization work.* New York: W. W. Norton.

Stohl, M., Stohl, C., & Townsley, M. C. (2007). A new generation of global corporate social responsibility. In S. May, G. Cheney, & J. Roper (Eds.), *The debate over corporate social responsibility* (pp. 30–44). New York: Oxford University Press.

Stratford, M. (2012, July 30). Senate report paints damning portrait of for-profit higher education. *The Chronicle of Higher Education.* Retrieved from http://chronicle.com/article/A-Damning-Portrait-of/133253

Subrahmanyan, S., & Gomez-Arias, J. T. (2008). Integrated approach to understanding consumer behavior at bottom of pyramid. *Journal of Consumer Marketing, 25*(7), 402–412.

Swibel, M. (2007, December 20). The world's top microfinance institutions. *Forbes.* Retrieved from www.forbes.com/2007/12/20/top-microfinance-philanthropy-biz-cz_ms_1220intro.html

Tallontire, A. (2000). Partnerships in fair trade: Reflections from a case study of Cafédirect. *Development in Practice, 10*(2), 166–177.

Taylor, R. (2002). Interpreting global civil society. *Voluntas: International Journal of Voluntary and Nonprofit Organizations. 13*(4), 339–341.

Tedeschi, G. (2008). Overcoming selection bias in microcredit impact assessments: A case study in Peru. *Journal of Development Studies, 44*(4), 504–518.

Ten Thousand Villages (2012). *Creating opportunities: Annual report.* Retrieved from www.tenthousandvillages.com/downloads/Annual%20Report%202012.pdf

Ten Thousand Villages (2013). Retrieved from: www.tenthousandvillages.com

Thomas, K., & Schmidt, M. S. (2012, July 3). Drug firm guilty in criminal case: Glaxo to pay $3 billion for actions on drugs. *New York Times*, pp. A1, B6.

Tout, K., Starr, R., Soli, M., Moodie, S., Kirby, G., Boller, K., . . . & Martinez-Beck, I. (2010). *The child care quality rating system (QRS) assessment: Compendium of quality rating systems and evaluations.* Washington, D.C.: Child Trends DataBank.

United Nations Conference on Trade and Development (2007). *World investment report 2007: Transnational corporations, extractive industries and development.* New York: United Nations Publications.

United Nations Conference on Trade and Development (2008). *Trade and development report 2008.* New York: United Nations Publications.

United Nations Educational Scientific and Cultural Organization (UNESCO) Institute for Statistics (2013). International literacy data 2013. Retrieved from www.uis.unesco.org/literacy/Pages/data-release-map-2013.aspx

UPS Foundation (2012). The logistics of caring. Retrieved from: http://responsibility.ups.com/community/Static%20Files/sustainability/SIR%20FINAL%20small1.pdf

U.S. Census Bureau. (2010). *Income, poverty, and health insurance coverage in the United States: 2009*. Washington, D.C.: U.S. Government Printing Office.

Van De Donk, W., Loader, B. D., Nixon, P. G., & Rucht, D. (Eds.). (2004). *Cyberprotest: New media, citizens and social movements*. New York: Routledge.

Viswanathan, M., Sridharan, S., & Ritchie, R. (2010). Understanding consumption and entrepreneurship in subsistence marketplaces. *Journal of Business Research,63*(6), 570–581.

Vogel, D. (2004).Tracing the American roots of the political consumerism movement. In M. Micheletti, A. Follesdal, & D. Stolle (Eds.) *Politics, products, and markets: Exploring political consumerism past and present* (pp. 83–100). New Brunswick, N.J.: Transaction Publishers.

Vogel, D. (2006). *The market for virtue: The potential and limits of corporate social responsibility*. Washington, D.C: Brookings Institution Press.

Walmart (2008). Wal-Mart launches exclusive Sam's Choice line of organic, rainforest alliance and fair trade certified coffees. Retrieved from http://news.walmart.com/news-archive/2008/03/31/wal-mart-launches-exclusive-sams-choice-line-of-organic-rainforest-alliance-fair-trade-certified-coffees

Walmart (2011). *Global responsibility report*. Retrieved from www.walmartstores.com/sites/ResponsibilityReport/2011/environment_products_Feature.aspx

Wan, G., & Zhang, X. (2012). Rising inequality in China. *Journal of Comparative Economics, 34*(4), 651–653.

Wang, H. (2005). Asian transnational corporations and labor rights: Vietnamese trade unions in Taiwan-invested companies. *Journal of Business Ethics, 56*(1), 43–53.

Waples, E. P., Antes, A. L., Murphy, S. T., Connelly, S., & Mumford, M. D. (2009). A meta-analytic investigation of business ethics instruction. *Journal of Business Ethics, 87*(1), 133–151.

Ward, T., and Phillips, B. (2009). *Seafood ecolabelling: Principles and practice*. Ames, Iowa: Wiley-Blackwell.

Warschauer, M. (2003). Demystifying the digital divide. *Scientific American, 289*(2), 42–47.

Weaver, G. R., Treviño, L. K., & Cochran, P. L. (1999). Corporate ethics programs as control systems: Influences of executive commitment and environmental factors. *The Academy of Management Journal, 42*(1), 41–57.

Weerawardena, J., & Mort, G. S. (2006). Investigating social entrepreneurship: A multidimensional model. *Journal of World Business, 41*(1), 21–35.

Weidner, K. L., Rosa, J. A., & Viswanathan, M. (2010). Marketing to subsistence consumers: Lessons from practice. *Journal of Business Research, 63*(6), 559–569.

Wei-Skillern, J., Austin, J. E., Leonard, H., & Stevenson, H. (2007). *Entrepreneurship in the social sector.* Thousand Oaks, CA : Sage Publications.

Welch, W. H. (2008). *The tactics of hope: How social entrepreneurs are changing our world.* San Rafael, CA: Earth Aware.

Welford, R. (2002). Globalization, corporate social responsibility and human rights. *Corporate Social Responsibility and Environmental Management, 9*(1), 1–7.

Werhane, P. H. (2007). Corporate social responsibility/corporate moral responsibility: Is there a difference and the difference it makes. In S. May, G. Cheney, & J. Roper (Eds.), *The debate over corporate social responsibility* (pp. 459–474). New York: Oxford University Press.

West, D. M. (2004). E-Government and the transformation of service delivery and citizen attitudes. *Public Administration Review, 64*(1), 15–27.

Wilensky, H. L. (1974). *The welfare state and equality: Structural and ideological roots of public expenditures* (Vol. 140). Berkeley: University of California Press.

Wilkinson, J. (2007). Fair trade: Dynamics and dilemmas of a market oriented global social movement. *Journal of Consumer Policy, 30*(3), 219–239.

Winzelberg, G. S. (2003). The quest for nursing home quality: Learning history's lessons. *Archives of Internal Medicine, 163*(21), 2552.

W. K. Kellogg Foundation. (2001). Logic model development guide: Using logic models to bring together planning, evaluation, and action. Battle Creek, MI: W. K. Kellogg Foundation.

Wolff, E. N. (2007). *Recent trends in household wealth in the United States: Rising debt and the middle-class squeeze* (Levy Economics Institute Working Paper No. 502). Retrieved from www.levyinstitute.org/pubs/wp_502.pdf

Wood, D. J. (2010). Measuring corporate social performance: A review. *International Journal of Management Reviews, 12*(1), 50–84.

World Bank (2013a). Poverty overview. Retrieved from www.worldbank.org/en/topic/poverty/overview

World Bank (2013b). Remarkable declines in global poverty, but major challenges remain. Retrieved from http://www.worldbank.org/en/news/press-release/2013/04/17/remarkable-declines-in-global-poverty-but-major-challenges-remain

World Hunger Educational Service (2013). 2013 world hunger and poverty facts and statistics. Retrieved from www.worldhunger.org/articles/Learn/world%20hunger%20facts%202002.htm

World Trade Organization (2013). Trade liberalisation statistics. Retrieved from www.gatt.org/trastat_e.html

Wulfson, M. (2001). The ethics of corporate social responsibility and philanthropic ventures. *Journal of Business Ethics, 29*(1), 135–145.

Yunus, M. (1999). The Grameen Bank. *Scientific American, 281*(5), 114–119.

Yunus, M. (2007). *Creating a world without poverty: Social business and the future of capitalism.* New York: Public Affairs.

Zadek, S. (2007). The path to corporate responsibility. *Corporate Ethics and Corporate Governance, 82*(December), 159–172.

Zhang, S., Anderson, S. G., & Zhan, M. (2011). Differentiated impact of bridging and bonding social capital on economic well-being: An individual level perspective. *Journal of Sociology & Social Welfare, 38*(1), 119–142.

Zhu, T., Singh V., & Dukes A. (2005). Local competition and impact of entry by a dominant retailer. Unpublished paper, Carnegie Mellon University.

Zosa-Feranil, I., Green, C. P., & Cucuzza, L. (2009). *Engaging the poor on family planning as a poverty reduction strategy.* Washington, D.C.: Futures Group, Health Policy Initiative, Task Order 1.